Addicted To Tragedy

By Michael Friedlander Misetich

Most of the names of people living have been changed in this memoir to protect their privacy. To honor those that have died, real names were used.

Smoking Boots Publishing

P.O. Box 624
Los Angeles, CA 90035

michael@addictedtotragedy.com

First Printing November 2015

10987654321

Addicted To Tragedy: Pop culture / memoir / addiction / skateboarding / surfing / punk rock / family / death / murder/ comedy / life

Cover artwork by Conor Colvin Hunter
Picture layout by Darren Ayres

Contents

Prologue

1.   Pacific Palisades California

2.   Arson, Orgasms & Petty Theft

3.   Mom, Michele, Swiss Family Nutbag, CES, The British Are Coming

4.   Music, Skate Or Die, Friends, & The Big White Buddha

5.   1984   The Most Fun Year Of My Life

5-B.   Hitting The Clubs

6.   Outsiders, Acid, & Grease

7.   Pali High, Parties, Davis, Catalina, & Attempted Manslaughter

8.   12th Grade, Senior year. This is going to be the best year of my life!!

Act II

9.   Survival Skills When You Are On Your Own, Sensational Murder

10.   The Death Of Fame, The Fame Of Death

11.   PLB

12.   Crazy Horse, Crazy H, Crazy

13.   The University Of California At Santa Cruz

14.   "Its fun to play at the Y-MCA!" Limp Dick

15.   My Valentine, Crackomedy

16.   Coach Mike, My Bank, A Suicide Success Story

17.   Sobriety, Julie, & 9-11

18.   Children Are Our Future, The Death Of Personal Responsibility

19.   Businessman, AA Kidnapping Of A Hollywood Mogul, Internet Dating; Rape Me, & A Gothic Hoedown

20.   _____
    (Insert meaningful last chapter title here)

21.   Last One I Swear

This book is dedicated to the memory of my big sister
Michele Marie Misetich Friedlander

Mother's day 1987. We celebrated, if you can call it that, at grandmas house. Jesus Christ! My poor mom. We were going through the motions when we heard tires skidding. I was up and walking out the door by the time we heard the impacts. Grammas house being just off Sunset, it was a quick six house walk to the boulevard. I must have gotten there within 30 seconds of the accident. There were 5 people in a car just south of the traffic light. 5 people, none moving. One person was smashed half way between the front and back seat in between the car door and the front seat. There was about a 3 inch space that her body was stuffed through. She had to be crushed, she had to be dead.

I walked on through the other cars in the accident as if I was window shopping for flip flops for my next beach day. I felt nothing. Literally nothing. There was no soul crushing sadness that I had been carrying with me for months, I wasn't worried about my mother trying to make it through her first mothers day since the accident, I didn't feel anything about the possibly dead body I just walked past...I felt nothing. I just sort of floated through the carnage like a ghost.

My favorite smell has always been the smell of a spring rain on hot asphalt. It's a super distinct smell that always brings back memories of my childhood. That mothers day, along with the smell of water on the asphalt, you could also smell gas, oil, antifreeze and blood all mixing together. I did not know it at the time but freshly bent metal actually has a smell to it as well. Once I placed all those scents in my mind, I realized that for the first time in months I actually felt at peace.

5

There was another smashed car off to my right that had people moving slowly around in it, trying to open their doors. I could tell they were probably going to be ok. They ended up in the driveway of a girl that used to baby-sit me. What was her name?? I think it was Jane?? Or Janet??...something like that. Up the hill a little was a car flipped upside down. I heard screaming so I walked around the car and saw a kid maybe a year younger than me lying half way out of the car with blood gushing out of his head onto the pavement. His head was pointing up the hill so the blood had to pass his face as it made a little river pouring back under the car. I didn't know him.

The yelling was coming from the young driver of the car who was still strapped in his seat upside down trying to get someone to help him out of the car. He was obviously scared the car was going to blow up but the only other person besides me that could have helped him was this Indian guy that must have seen the accident because he was leaning down and yelling at the kid for driving like an idiot. I actually laughed a little because he had such a thick accent and it sounded sort of funny to me at the time.

As I stood up I noticed people arriving to check out the carnage. I just walked past them back to grandmas. A part of me knew that whoever was going to live was going to live no matter what I did. Most of me was just tripping on the fact that I felt peaceful for the first time since that day earlier in my senior year of high school that changed everything.

Later on I heard that only one person died in that accident. Was it the no seatbelt wearing head wound kid hanging out the window? Was it the lady crushed into a space that she couldn't fit in? Did I miss somebody?? My money was on the squished chick. Truthfully when I heard it was only one... I don't know why, but... it made me a little bit mad.

Prologue:

In 1976, Michael Medved and David Wallechinsky wrote a book called *What Really happened to the Class of 65?* . The book was in response to a 1965 Time Magazine article about "today's" teenagers. The teenagers they chose to look at were from the lush Los Angeles suburb of Pacific Palisades California. Back in those days, there were ordinary middle class people that lived right along side of the rich and famous. They all shared this little gem of a town nestled in the hills between Santa Monica and Malibu. With a new prototypical state of the art high school just built in Temescal Canyon, there were high hopes for the young adults that would be graduating from the newly opened Pacific Palisades High School.

Twelve years after the book, came my graduating class, the class of 1988. We had some magazine articles, newspaper articles, and a piece on the news show 20/20 about us as well, though they were in a slightly different vein. This is not a story specific to the class of 1988, but a lot of the key players graduated, or should have graduated that year.

The following is a true story about the wonder, joy, and misery of growing up in Pacific Palisades California in the 1970's and 80's.

Chapter 1

Pacific Palisades
California

I was born November 5th 1970 at St. Johns Hospital in Sunny Santa Monica, Southern California. A friend of mine Milton Goller was born there the same day. I always gave him shit because his family had a lot of money and we had just enough to get by. I told him we were switched at birth but we could call it even if he gave me half of his allowance. That one never panned out.

I was almost Puerto Rican… Well I was almost born in Puerto Rico and that's where I was conceived. My mom was living with my dad who was also working there. My mom had gone home to see her mother and got a phone call from a friend that had told her that my dad was banging other chicks. So my mom left my dad and just stayed at her mom's house in the Palisades. My dad had to call the hospital to find out if I was a boy or a girl. He found out through a doctor that my mom had named me Michael (after her younger half brother Mike). She also gave me her real brothers first name Brock to me as my middle. Mike was actually the one who gave Brock the pills he killed himself with. After that he crawled into a bottle and never came out. So I am named after a drunk (who might or might not be dead, I'm not sure) and a guy who killed himself. Still a pretty cool name though. Michael Brock.

I was the 2nd child of my mom and dad. Eleven months before I was born, Evelyn and Marcus Misetich welcomed Michele Marie into the world. Michele would end up doing a great deal of the parenting in my life. She was the one constant that I could count on growing up in somewhat of a broken home.

My mom remarried when I was a baby and we moved into a house on Miami Way, near the El Medio bluffs in Pacific Palisades California. The bluffs or "palisades" were where the neighborhood just dropped off a couple hundred feet to the Pacific Coast Highway and then Pacific Ocean below. Back then the Palisades was much more middle class then the exclusive neighborhood that it is today. There was even a poor side of town. The Bishop estates, as some of the oldies called them were also known as the alphabet streets; all named after Methodist Bishops, smaller plots of land with smaller houses than most of the Palisades. There was also the "rich" part of town; which was the Huntington Palisades. You could tell you were in the Huntington because the houses got huge and there were no telephone poles anywhere in sight (they put all that shit underground). The Highlands wasn't even really on the map. Being 3 miles up a long road towards the end of town, it might as well have been another planet back then. My mother grew up by the Swarthmore bluffs across Temescal Canyon from Miami way. Both of those parts of town were pretty much the same. A couple blocks to the bluffs that overlook the beautiful Pacific Ocean, truly a picturesque town.

The man my mother married was a man named Richard Friedlander. Richard began dating my mom when she was separated from my dad. He knew she had kids so I'm not sure how the courtship process went. Was he super romantic and did he sweep her off her feet? Or was my mom just too scared to be raising kids alone that she would put up with someone that wasn't really the "sweeping you off your feet" type a guy.

When I was very young I had a recurring nightmare that I can't fully remember. I do know that it stopped by the time I was about 10. The dream started out softly and would end super loud and scary. It was just Richard and me in the dream and I was terrified. Something happened. Something when I was a baby. It could have been that I fell out of my crib when he was in the room or something innocent like that. It also could have been something else.

What I do know is that I was paddled like a lot of kids when I was young. Then my mom didn't like that happening so she stopped the physical stuff. Which is not as great as it sounds. This was because Richard for some reason decided to be an absolute Jedi level asshole to my sister and me. He even had the dick cop/stepdad mustache that unfortunately has come back into style.

As we grew up, my mom actually got him to get involved in my life and put on appearances. The only problem was the whole time he was just a dick. Funny thing was that was what he liked to be called. So, that is how I will refer to him for the rest of this story. It was truly astounding to everybody in my neighborhood who would come by our house, what a dick Dick was.

Here was Dick being involved in our lives. Michele and I both played AYSO. Soccer… "Everyone plays!!" Every parent that could, would be out on that field. Dick

was no exception. Coach??? No… Assistant coach????
No…. The lady that brought the oranges for halftime???
No….Dick's idea of being involved??? He was the referee.
How far removed from your "child" are you when you
decide to be the referee?? Everyone hates the refs! I think
he just did it for the control over people and the exercise. It
couldn't have been for us because he eventually became
head ref and did it many years after we were not playing
any more.

As a kid I was always curious how things worked.
That meant taking shit apart and seeing how it ticked but I
was unfortunately not very good at putting anything back
together again. To take something apart… you need tools,
being a little boy I had no tools so I had to borrow Dicks.
Now I'll be the first to admit I didn't have the greatest
focus in the world. In fact the school recommended I be put
on medication to calm me the fuck down. And this was
back in the 70's, when there were maybe 3 kids in the
whole school that were medicated for attention deficit
disorder (before they threw the hyperactivity in ADHD).
Not the insane number of kids today that they pump full of
pharmaceuticals so they don't have to deal with them.
You can imagine it was tough for me to put
everything back exactly as I found it. So I would get it.
Dick would storm into wherever I was and start to yell at
me. He even made me open the door while I was taking a
shit just so he could yell at me because I put the
screwdrivers where the wrenches went. "Sorry dad" 'Sorry
is not good enough! I want you down there putting every
tool back exactly where it belongs and you are not to use
them again without my permission!' "Ok dad." Then he
paused, looking at me sitting on the toilet, shaking his head
like I was the most disgusting thing he had ever seen in his
life. Then just walk away.. Leaving the door open and me
sitting there with toilet paper in my hand. "Can I wipe my

ass first??" Yeah, I wished I were that strong. I just put my head down, finished up then went out and put the tools back to the best of my ability. He would no doubt check my work, see that I didn't have each wrench back in the exact same spot and just shake his head in disgust at me every time he saw me for the rest of the day.

It wasn't always when I was in as compromising a position as that, but the end result was always the same. I apologized and Dick just shook his head at what a fuck up I was. There was never one single time during my entire childhood when my apology was accepted. Not once did I hear an.. "Its ok son...." or "Now you know how to do it right son." It was always "Michael Brock Friedlander, you get over here right now!!!!" Then ending with at best a "don't do it again!", the usual shaking of the head in disgust, or on special occasions, some speech about how I can't do anything right.

To add a little more to the 'fuck me' category, I had to call Dick dad, but he never called me son. To be fair to him that father son thing was something about my mom wanting to have us look like a normal family.

In her defense, in the late 60's early 70's, it was not socially acceptable to be a single mother or to have kids with two last names. That's why my mom and Dick put Michele and me into school under Dicks last name. It was such an accepted practice that it didn't matter that our legal last name was Misetich. They even got us social security cards with Dicks name on them. (Thank God I switched it back before September 11, 2001. That's something that's almost impossible to do now.)

Around the house, Michele and I had weekly chores to do like most kids. It's a good thing to show a child some sense of responsibility at an early age. The earliest I remember doing them was at about 7 years old. We did things like weeding, cutting the grass, sweeping the front and back yard.... the usual. Dick would always make sure to check our work and if it wasn't up to his par he would say, "Are you finished??" while giving us that same stink eye. That would crush me as a little boy. But Michele, as a not much older little girl wouldn't take his shit and just ask him, 'Is there something else we need to do?'

We shared a bathroom so we took turns cleaning it every other week. Those were the days that the bottom cabinet that most families now will put a child proof latch on was easy to open so we had access to the Ajax, hull cleaner (Drano) and bleach.

If we managed to get some chores done when Dick wasn't home and he didn't like what he saw when he got back he would whistle for us to come home and tell us about it. (if we couldn't hear the whistle it was always much worse) I would show up back at the house, maybe with a friend in tow and he would start yelling about how crappy a job we did.... "You need to do your chores right. There are still weeds all over the side of the house, leaves in the front yard, and I haven't even been in the back yard yet!!" Every time I wanted to bring someone over to play they had the same question.... "Is your dad going to be home???" A good day for me would be walking in with a friend and saying 'Hi dad.' And him saying nothing back from his lazy boy

Jessica Lee

My mother and Dick had a baby 5 years after I was born and her name was Jessica Lee. She and I have become closer since we have grown up, but things didn't begin very well. Let me start by saying, Dicks dick-ness didn't have the same effect on Michele as it did on me. I don't know if it was because a boy needs a strong male role model or that she was just way stronger than I was. So Michele loved Jessica... and I hated her. In my eyes, Dick spoiled her shitless. That was his kid so she could do no wrong. I guess I should be thankful that things weren't worse than they were. I've seen those nature shows. Momma bear shows up with cubs…. new male bear kills/eats said cubs… new male bear has cubs with momma bear. So I guess I should be happy he didn't kill me and eat me (or to be real, I'm thankful he wasn't a violent drunk, he didn't beat me or molest me).

Things that I used to do that were punishable by yelling and giving that "you are a piece of shit" look that Dick had perfected were not even met with a stern word to Jessica. "She's young and doesn't know any better." Would be his response. She could literally take something that I was using and run away with it. I would chase her down and take it back, then she would start crying and daddy would come to her rescue. "Why did you make Jessica cry? You can see you are much bigger and older than her! You need to try harder to get along with your sister." 'But dad she took something from me and'….. "You need to try a little harder or you need to stay in your room!" She would smile as Dick was laying into me. Knowing that there was nothing I could do to her.

So Dick was nice to Jessica, took her side in any, and I mean any situation. Bottom line, I had serious resentment towards her. Again, Michele, who was probably shit on by Dick more than me, had no problem with her. Loved her just like she loved me.

My and Michele's birth father was in our lives a little more when we were super young. He was like a cross between Baloo the bear from the jungle book, John Wayne and Santa Claus. He was 6'5", had a deep voice, was super nice and loved us very much. Once I hit about 5 years old Michele and I only saw him around one time a year. He worked big construction jobs overseas and would take us to Busch Gardens or something like that whenever he was in

15

town. He would buy one of those endless beers they used to sell as we cruised around the park. Either Michele or I would sit on his lap and steer the car most of the way home. This is when I was about 6 years old. Then he would be gone for another year or maybe even two.

Because Dick was such a dick, I looked at my daddy Marcus (that's what Michele and I used to call him) like he was a super hero. Every time we saw him he would shower us with love and finish the visit with a trip to Toy's R Us. I had a knack for quickly finding a present that was within one dollar of the limit he gave us. Besides the yearly visit, he we would also get a phone calls from the jungle or dessert once every 3 or 4 months just to say hi…. and this was back when it took almost 5 or 6 seconds for your voice to travel that far. You had to start a sentence and commit to it or you would just be talking over each other the entire time.

I knew from an early age that my dad wouldn't let Dick adopt me and that he paid all of his child support. Not always on time because it sometimes takes a while to get a letter out of the frozen tundra or some sort of monkey mail from an uninhabited island off the coast of Irian Jaya (New Guinea). All these things made me look at my dad like he was the most amazing man in the world. I told him when I was a bout 8 years old that as soon as I could I would change my name back to his and two weeks after I turned 18 I did.

The reality of the situation was that our father could have gotten a job in the states and been more a part of our lives. It would have been less money but he could have done it. He could have been there for all of Michele's and my milestones. He could have been the positive male role model that I so desperately needed, but he wasn't. I don't think he could handle someone else raising his kids so he got as far away from us as possible. I knew he loved us for sure, but I don't think he could handle it. The hardest part for me now, was that he knew that Dick was an asshole. He knew it and he left me there with him. It is possible that the situation was a little more complicated than that but it still doesn't change how being away from him ultimately made me feel.

By all outward appearances, we were the normal all American family. 2 parents, 3 children, a dog and a cat. We would come together every night at the dining room table for our Norman Rockwell picturesque moment. On our table we would have good old fashioned cold war American processed cuisine. Mac and cheese with hotdogs cut up in it, hamburger helper, sloppy Joes, some sort of casserole if it was leftovers, and something special like pork chops on Sunday.

Most families would take the dinner hour as an opportunity to talk about how everyone's day was and check in with each other. Not so much for us. I was my usual whipped puppy self from pissing Dick off earlier in the day, Jessica as usual could do no wrong and Michele couldn't be more ambivalent to it all. She was just happy.

Dick sat there, maybe asked Jessica about her day, had his two beers, finished his meal, and then walked off to his layzboy. The stress of trying to make Dick be nice to her two eldest children had my mom grinding her teeth at night to the point that she had to put a guard in her mouth to keep them from breaking.

Chapter 2

Arson, Orgasms, & Petty Theft

I had a hard time getting along with people in Elementary school. I remember feeling angry a lot, but people who knew me then say I was pretty much out of control. Outside of our house I would do the opposite of anything anyone in authority said. Being out from under Dicks thumb, at school I pretty much just exploded everyday.

That made it difficult for me to make friends. I was too much of a spaz and I lacked basic social skills that most kids had. I also didn't have any confidence in myself so that didn't make it any easier. I never really felt like I was a part of the school. I felt like it was the whole school, and then me. It actually felt about right when the kids in my class nicknamed me scumbag. I couldn't help flinging myself into the dirt like I had just taken a bullet to the head and I wasn't a real big fan of soap, so couple that dirty little boy with a social retard and that's what you get… A boy named scum

I was in serious need of the life lessons that help a boy go out into the world. I needed a strong father figure to help me develop those social skills that nurture you and help you to grow. I at least needed someone to say, "have a good day".. or "have a day"… I got Dick.

Schools had money in the 70's because we had a full time nurse and even a councilor to talk to me and try and find out why I had such trouble making friends. Why couldn't I be good in the classroom?? Were there any problems at home??? Yeah, my stepdad is a fucking asshole! (We all have a fall guy right??) How was I supposed to figure out this 'being a man' stuff, even if it was a little man, when my only consistent male role model made me feel like I was a worthless piece of shit.

My whole home life consisted of me walking on my tiptoes trying not to get yelled at. Actually, most days would start like that, then after a while I would hit a tripwire and the yelling commenced. My mom would intervene and my parents would go to their room and have 'a talk'. The talk consisted of loud arguing for the rest of the night. So I would spend all that time with my big sister Michele in her room until it was time for bed.

I got some guidance from a group of teenagers much older than I was that played football outside my house. Wrestling with them when I was little and they were in high school was where I learned all I ever needed to know about fighting. Daddy Marcus, my real dad had a short lived career as a professional boxer, but seeing him only one time a year made his training program leave more than a little to be desired. Plus the fact that he said he used to rent out advertising space on the bottom of his shoes (IE- he got knocked out a lot). I did have a few kids that I would play with that were just a bit younger than me. My short-lived career as an arsonist started with those guys when I was 9 years old.

"FIRE!!!!"

The El Medio bluffs two blocks from my house were covered with the dry chaparral that is indigenous to the hills around Southern California. In the 1970's, you could also find cigarette butts, condoms and dirty magazines mixed in with the native flora and fauna. On this particular day, I was picking up old cigarette butts and smoking them with 2 younger boys, Tom Kline 8 and Matt Pronger 7. At some point, one of us (uhh, that was probably me) had the brilliant idea to light little patches of dried grass on fire and then stomp them out. Small fire… 6 feet stomping… the idea was sound.

Out of nowhere a remote control plane swooped down past our heads and we turned and watched it fly out of sight. When we turned back the wind had set the whole hillside on fire. We started to run to the top of the bluffs but I had to make sure that we didn't get into trouble so I grabbed Tom and Matt and said, "It wasn't us! It was a guy with long brown hair and a blue Dodger hat and he ran down the hill!" We all agreed and ran back up to the top of the bluff.

There stood the guy with the remote control plane who was trying to bring his little Red Barron in for a landing while watching the flames roar towards the homes at the end of the bluff. Instead of being blamed, we were heroes that day. Knocking on doors, warning people to start hosing off their roofs and making sure all pets where accounted for. Once the fire department showed up we felt our jobs had been done and we all went our separate ways.

I must say the rush was intense. All that commotion just for us! All that power in the palms of my hands! Controlling the future of all of these people..... with that simple.. beautiful.... flame... Yeah, I can't even continue. I was choking back tears thinking about all the homeless, and barbequed squirrels out there because of me. I made it back to my house and was half freaking out and half thinking I had just pulled off the crime of the century. Then I heard a knock at the door. I looked out the window... Fire truck.

Shit!! Pronger Cracked. Goddamnit!! Never trust a 7 year old when you pick your arson team. See apparently his parents actually looked at him and cared how he and his friends were doing. His mom (sweetest woman ever.. not just because she would buy us beer later on, just because she was) took one look at him and said "What really happened?" That boy sang like a canary. 'It was Mikes fault! He brought the matches he lit the grass on fire, it was all him!'

Now, I'm not disputing the truth of these statements but.... come on. So I had an arson record for a few years after that. Besides finding a sandstone cave and using it to burn model tanks and airplanes and whatever toy I had become bored with (including all of my star wars figures.... Damnit!), fire didn't really play a role in my life after that.

Marquez Elementary

Marquez Elementary School was a beautiful little school that was pushed up next to a canyon where I would ride my BMX bike. My first year was kindergarten and my first teacher was Mrs. Hill. We drove her insane and she quit halfway through the year. You might think I am embellishing here, but my mother volunteered teaching art at the school and she will tell you the same thing. She might say, "She just wasn't cut out for teaching young children." But I'll tell you what, she was a teacher for 20 years, and then me and this crew of little knuckleheads threw her over the edge. One of the current counselors at Palisades High School was in my class and she will tell you the same.

So Miss Hill was out, then we got a new teacher. Mrs. Ota. She went on to become principle of Marquez and was actually there not too long ago. I got to talk to her and believe it or not, she remembered me! We were apparently her first class as a teacher. I told her that all I could remember about her class was a red chair. She laughed and told me that was the chair I had to sit on in the corner every day when I was bad.

I like to think I battle hardened Mrs. Ota and made her into the teacher and principal she became. Not the case with all my teachers. Take my 2nd grade teacher Mrs. Kannan. Mrs. Kannan didn't like my disruptive ways or my defiant attitude. So one day I was sent to the principal's office for hitting a girl. When I walked back into the classroom Mrs. Kannan announced that "Michael just got back from the principals office for hitting a girl" and on cue, the whole class pointed and laughed at me.

So I am left to believe, some sort of speech was given, about how it is not ok to hit, and I was the example. So much for any school therapist doing anything positive for me at school. I ran into Mrs. Kannan a few years back. I recalled for her the details of hitting the girl and then being laughed at by the class as a result of her using me as an example. Her response, "That doesn't sound like me" and walked away. Two words Mrs. K … Fuck, and the next one is, You!

Around this time a supreme court judge ruled that the LAUSD was running a segregated school system and the city was ordered to begin to redistribute students by race to obtain more racial balance in the schools. That meant taking my lily-white ass from Marquez in the Pacific Palisades, to Coliseum Street School in the south central neighborhood dubbed the Jungle. The Jungle started off as a lush green nice neighborhood that had since become one of the more dangerous gang infested neighborhoods in South Central L.A. The phenomena that resulted from this district wide action was dubbed "white flight."

Almost Every kid I knew was taken out of public school and put into private. Not me and Michele. My mom thought it would be a good idea for us to go to school for a semester in a neighborhood that wasn't as nice as our own (I also don't think she really had much of a choice). We lived in the Palisades but we didn't have any extra money for things like private school. We didn't have a gardener or a maid, like some of the kids I knew. Fabric softener was a luxury (half sheet per load), no cable, no super fancy toys; I was always one or two big fads behind every kid in my neighborhood.

Once I got my first Jim Muir Dragon design Dog Town skateboard at 8 years old, thankfully I had found what would be my outlet for the rest of my life. Other kids started getting tricked out BMX bikes then mini bikes and off road motorcycles and I just said "Fuck it." and skated to the bluffs with the other "poor" kids to find old cigarette butts to smoke.

So Michele and I were bussed to the Jungle. She may have been on the bus with me but I was basically by myself. The first day I walked off the bus a black girl who ended up being in my class named Chantal walked up to me and said "whassup white boy" and smacked me across the face. Welcome to Coliseum Street School!

Our new teacher was Mr. Nithian. I pretty quickly found out why the kids called him filthy Nithian. When most normal teachers were writing their name on the board and introducing themselves to the class, this guy was laying down a curse-riddled tirade about how nobody better fuck around in his fucking class or there would be major fucking consequences. Ok, remember, sheltered kid from the Palisades here. I thought the sky was going to fall on my head. I thought a SWAT team was going to bust through the windows into the classroom and carry him out in a straight jacket. But I looked at the kids around me and they didn't seem like it was a big deal.

I did end up with a few friends that helped guide me through my time in the Jungle. A couple of them were best friends and visually quite funny; one very tall and very black, the other very short and very white, (but he was black) almost as white as me. The tall black one was David Biggs and the short white one was Robert Fairfax. I knew these two guys for some years after and consider them a couple of my first real school friends.

One thing I couldn't figure out, was how this kid on the yard was selling candy for the same price as the liquor store? I saw him across the street from the school one day and I watched him go into the liquor store. His friend went in after him and started talking to the clerk. While the clerk was distracted, the kid who sold the candy started filling his socks up with everything he could grab. I couldn't believe my eyes. It was so simple. Just be sneaky, and you can just take stuff that you want! I know this is shitty to say, but going to school in the ghetto taught me that stealing things is an acceptable thing to do.

I didn't have the relationship with my parents like Pronger did. Maybe if I had, I would have told Dick what I saw and he would have taught me a life lesson about taking things that aren't yours. Instead this was the beginning of my second short-lived career, a petty thief. (Another California Supreme Court ruling would eventually overturn mandatory bussing. That was the only year I spent in the Jungle.)

Now that I knew about stealing, I began to cut my chops so to speak. My time at the California state penal colony of Coliseum Street Elementary School was up so I was sent back to the Palisades. As soon as I got back I started stealing from Pronto Market on my way to Marquez Elementary. Mom and Dick both worked so I walked the mile and a half to Marquez for the rest of 4th grade.

I had gotten pretty brazen by the time I walked into Pronto with a thin backpack and large jacket on over it. I took off the jacket filled up the backpack with soda and candy and put the jacket back over the top. I had done it so many times without getting caught I didn't even notice the guy coming out from behind the register when I was walking to the door. I was busted….sort of. I got a ride home and the guy talked to my mom and told her what I had done. I was so scared that I was going to get it from Dick when he got home but was surprised when all I got was the usual disappointed shake of the head, silent treatment and walking away. It actually made me feel kind of cheated. I deserved to be yelled at. I deserved to be berated. What the hell just happened?!

It was around this time that I got a paper route. This expanded my career as a criminal from storefronts to cars and mailboxes. This is back when kids rode their bikes around and delivered papers to their little section of the neighborhood. There was one thing sketchy about the paper routes in the Palisades… Herb. The papers would be delivered to us at a few different stops in town. You and the 4 or 5 paper boys for your area would get the papers, sit, fold and rubber band them, then put them into your bags. Throw the bags onto the handlebars of your bike and you were off on your route.

Herb was the guy that dropped off the papers. He would often sit and talk with us for a while. Tell us stories about how when he and his friends were our age, they would go skinny dipping down by the ole fishing hole. He told us one story every other week about how one time they were all sitting on the bank and didn't realized they were sitting in poison oak. "Oh boy how my balls swelled up!"

Herb looked like a classic pederast. He had the silver mustache, silver tooth and silver hair that hung just above his shoulders. Gold watch gold rings and a golden lady leg necklace to round it all out. You could tell on sight that something was definitely off about him and not just that he could talk to us kids about inappropriate shit for hours. I know ole Herb got one or two of us to check out the cool magazines in the shelled bed of his El Camino. I'm just not sure who it was.

Marijuana would eventually become an easy escape for me. I had already tried it a couple times, mostly on Boy Scout camping trips (thank you Anthony Tittelli). One car I broke into had about a quarter of an ounce of bud in it, so I grabbed it and called my friend CK (one of the other social retards from Miss Hills class) to come over. He happened by the car I broke into and a guy and a girl were there freaking out. They asked him where he was going because apparently I had been spotted. Thankfully I had stashed some of the weed before hiding the big bag so when the hippy stoners came by my house looking for their weed, I was able to give them the very much-shortened bag. Of course they bitched a whole lot but I knew they couldn't exactly call the cops on me.

The good thing was that whole situation kind of scared me into not wanting to steal shit anymore. It also made me think about the people I was taking from and how upset they must get. I still didn't give a shit about stealing from stores, but having that experience making people feel that upset, made me feel at first scared, then shitty. That pretty much ended my career as a petty thief.

As you can probably tell, that little voice that tells you "You probably shouldn't do that," never really developed in me. I guess I am lucky that I'm a pretty sensitive guy. That kept me from being a complete piece of shit when I grew older. That and following my sister Michele's example. I never consciously tried to be good; it was more that I couldn't handle being uncomfortable, which happened when I was a shitty person. I didn't so much have a value system to speak of, because that shit is taught, but I didn't like people being mad or upset with me…except of course Dick was something of a constant.

Any life lessons I got from him went as smooth as his Birds and the Bees speech. Sometimes my prepubescent curiosity would lead me to hang onto one or two of the dirty magazines that could be found down at the bluffs. On this particular occasion I found an extremely dirty magazine that featured a naked girl being gang-banged by like 10 guys. I didn't understand why I wanted to take it so bad but I brought it home and hid it in my clubhouse.

The next time I went out there I opened up the door and was greeted by Dick holding up the magazine open to that very page. He pointed to the girl who had at least 3 cocks in her and said, "What if that was your mother?" Dropping the magazine and walking out of my clubhouse. I was 10 years old.

Now I'm no criminal profiler, but I'm pretty sure that's how you end up with a guy that has a rape bunker under his house. Anything else to do with girls that I didn't figure out for myself was taught to me by kids I knew. My friend Brad told me what a period was when Michele did a handstand in her bathing suit in front of us then ran away when I asked her if she shit herself. I asked Chuck what old bag ladies used for tampons and everybody laughed at me. He sarcastically said "Its ok, not everybody knows about menopause." He later pulled me aside and told me what it was.

Most things I just figured out on my own. The year before my second grade nightmare teacher Mrs. Kannan, I was in Mrs. Demarie's first grade class. Believe it or not, that was where I had my first orgasm. Not like I got a hard on and started jacking it in the corner, but I was working the slide projector and the side of it was rubbing against my little thingy until…. Bam! I was volunteering for projector duty for the rest of the year. I actually thought that I had found a stomach cramp cure. All the shit we would eat as kids would put me on the toilet every once in a while with a tummy ache. I would just wiggle my legs back and forth until it felt really good and my tummy ache would be gone. It wasn't until I was about 11 and something came out that I realized I was whacking myself off for the past 5 years.

If you beat a child's ass when they fuck up, then give them love when they don't, I would think you get a pretty well adjusted kid. If you give them nothing but negative reinforcement their entire lives, at some point they are going to be starving for either love, a beating or any other kind of interaction from an adult. Anything besides shaking your head and just walking off. When we found out that Herb had molested some of the kids he delivered papers to, I couldn't understand the feelings that I had. I was so starved for attention, that on some level, I was bummed it wasn't me.

Chapter 3

Mom, Michele, Swiss Family Nutbag, CES, The British Are Coming

      I haven't said very much about my mom. My mom is and always has been an amazing, beautiful and strong person. She had been through a lot early in her life. The book I mentioned earlier, *What Really Happened to the Class of 65?* (Medved, Wallechinsky) had a chapter in it about her younger brother Brock entitled, "Brock Chester, the Dreamboat." Besides his looks, he excelled in track, football (all western league end for two years in a row), and he was captain of the baseball team. He was part of the first graduating Palisades High School class, the class of '65. Brock went on to Santa Monica City College for a while, and then he got into acting. He had an agent at William Morris that took a personal interest in his career getting him a supporting role in the TV series *Bracken's World* (stared Leslie Nielsen and a young Tom Selleck among others and sending him to acting classes to make sure he was ready for auditions. Then, one day, Uncle Brock went on a camping trip by himself like he would do when he needed time to think. He wrote a 7 page suicide note, took a bunch of pills then drank a bottle wine and died. He was 24 years old.

I can't know how all of that played out. What I do know is that he had a physically and mentally abusive stepfather (that was way worse than Dick) who told him what a piece of shit he was every single day. Also that his on again off again girlfriend had just broken up with him. He couldn't handle it. My mothers abuse was worse. She tried to go to her mother about it but gramma didn't want to hear about it. So she learned how to block shit out at a very young age. I guess Brock was too sensitive. He must have taken all of that shit too his heart.

I think family history is important, but I'm not going to write my moms story here. I will tell you how she was with me. My mother loved me. She loved Michele and me so much that she sacrificed herself so we could have a chance to grow up in the Pacific Palisades. She loved us so much that she stayed with an angry bitter man that argued and fought with her just about every second of every day.

Mom's survival technique of blocking things out came off as strength, but the result was she wasn't all the way there when we were kids. She pretended everything was fine to cope like she did when she was a child. A good example of this is my mother could not keep any houseplants alive. This was because during the times of uneasy truce, or in-between battles with Dick, she would manically water the plants. She would effectively drown them in one to two weeks max. I imagined the plants being all happy they have a new home. Then they get walked through the front door onto death row. Seeing all its fellow plants waiting for their turn to die. When I got older Just to fuck with her I bought her a cactus on mothers day. The next time she went to water the plants, she just locked up in front of it. I caught her eye and she and I actually had a good laugh.

Describing my sister Michele is something that is difficult to do, partially because my view of her changed over the years as I grew up. She was always very eccentric and full of energy, to the point of actually embarrassing me at times when I was young. I mean who is this freak singing at the top of her lungs or pretending she was a British royal or an undiscovered 5th brother of the Bee Gees? Oh yeah, that's my sister Michele.

In my world at home, it was keep your head down, avoid eye contact and no one will fuck with you. She always did the exact opposite. She just rode wild in everything she did. Singing in the halls at school, dancing her way into the house, being an overall whirlwind of positive energy.

Even when she was young she had a definite look. She had strawberry blonde hair, light freckles and she kind of stuck her butt out when she walked. She also had shitty eyesight so she was always squinting too. Head forward butt out, loud and crazy. So she was this full on sensory overload. She eventually grew into what our friend Rob would describe as a punk rock *I Love Lucy*. Always the center of attention, total ham, loving everybody and just as wild and crazy as she wanted to be.

Most people who stand up too quick and get a head rush, will sit back down and gather their bearings before trying to get up again. I remember one time she was in front of her make up table getting ready for a show and she stood up real quick and yelled out the question.. "Ready to rock out???" Then said "Oh shit!" and fell face first into the table and onto the floor. She would do the same thing every time that happened. No matter where she was. Room full of people… friends house for dinner… I would always laugh at her when she told me how it had happened this time. "We finished eating, I was all excited to go out, I jumped up then apparently put my arms up and fell into the table then onto the floor with my skirt over my head in front of Kristina's parents." There was nothing subtle about this girl.

She was also super cool to everyone. I had a friend remember when Michele and I were in Jr. Life guards with her. She recounted this story.

"The first day of Jr. Lifeguards, 1983, and I'm getting a lecture from the head guard in front of everyone about wearing a non-regulation blue pinstriped one-piece bathing suit from the trendy Canyon Beachwear shop, instead of the official ugly navy speedo from Big Five. I was feeling embarrassed and off to a bad start-being one of the youngest kids in my division and already in trouble-when all of a sudden an older, cool girl with a halo of red curls that sparkled in the sun sat down across from me, apparently listening very intently to the lecture I was getting. She looked like a punk rock mermaid, and I was instantly drawn to her, as was everyone else. She had a kind of magnetism that made you want to stare at her, which she caught me doing a couple of times.

Then all of a sudden, right at the end of the dress code lecture, she stood up and took off her sweatshirt to reveal the same pinstriped suit that I was wearing. The head guard took a double take and then included Michele in the reprimand. She nodded convincingly as the guard told of the perils of not wearing the same bathing suit as everyone else, and as my smile of gratitude grew bigger and bigger she looked over at me and winked. WINKED AT ME!!!! It was so surprising and cool. And with that wink I felt like everything was going to be ok, and that I belonged- if not in Jr. Lifeguards, then in a wayyyy cooler club that Michele was a part of."

I always felt like it was Michele and me versus everyone else. Even though she loved Jessica, I still always felt like it was us that were the team. Michele was my full blood sister. Jessica got the best treatment by far, and then it was me and Michele. Dick treated me like shit or ignored me, Michele just got ignored.

There were very few times that I felt like I got justice when it came to Jessica. One was when she was about 5, I was about 10 and Michele was about 12. We had some kind of dinner with candles lit and we all wanted to blow out a candle. Jessica blew out the first two candles so there was only one left. Michele and I got ready to blow it out together when Jessica started crying. Dick said "We are going to let Jessica Blow them all out tonight." I got all pissed off and Michele was like 'whatever.' Jessica started smiling with her head back and eyes closed, shaking her head back and forth because she was so happy she got her way again.

Dick put the candle, which was much bigger than the other candles, right in front of Jessica for her to blow out. She took a huge breath…. And blew as hard as she could. All of the hot wax in the candle immediately blew back up into Jessica's face. She immediately started screaming and I started laughing hysterically. Michele did her best to cover her face so her little sister wouldn't see her laughing at her but it was no use. Dick was quick to yell at us to shut our mouths and go to our rooms. We both made it back to Michele's room before she broke up laughing. It was too perfect. Not even Dick could put a damper on that one.

The only time I saw Michele actually freak the fuck out on Jessica was a couple years later. Michele was having a pool party at gramma's and papa's. She was making invitations by cutting each letter for each invitation out of magazines. She was also cutting out images to go along with the theme of the party she was having. Jessica was teasing me and a friend of mine, trying to get us to chase her. We would, and then she would get to Michele's door and threaten to tell her we had hit her. Michele had her 20 invitations covering most of the floor in her bedroom and was getting out the glue to put them all together when Jessica, being chased by me, flung open the door and ran right through the invites scattering them all over the place.

I had never seen a look of true fear on Jessica's face before that day, but I saw it as Michele yelled at her and smacked her across the face. It was one of the funniest yet scariest things I have ever seen. Jessica walked up and down the street crying for the next 2 hours with Michele trying to calm her down till mom got home.

The point is that these stories stuck out in my head and I remember them well because these were things that never happened. Michele was never angry or yelling or mean to anyone (well, accept for me after going through her drawers or being a pesky little brother).

She also stood up to Dick. Because her eyes were not very good, occasionally her pupils would look dilated. I remember one time in high school he was yelling at her accusing her of being on drugs. She took him head on. She got on her toes, to his eye level and yelled right back at him. "I don't know what you are talking about Richard! I have done nothing wrong Richard! Leave me alone Richard!" She took on the beast and didn't give an inch. Eye to eye, her actions were saying; You hold NO power over me! I was in awe of her that day… and to me, calling him Richard was way better than calling him Dick!

Michele also stood up to our real father for me a couple of years before that. Daddy Marcus found a pot pipe in my jacket and I told him it was a friends. That's what I was used to doing, lying because it was the only thing I knew to do. I couldn't admit to it where I was from. If I admitted it in my world I would get a serious brow beating, no life lesson, grounded and even with an apology, no hope for redemption. Michele caught him getting ready to unload on me for it and Michele stopped him. I don't know what she said but whatever it was it made him drop it completely. A few times since then he has brought it up. Like he couldn't believe he was so soundly put in his place by a 16 year old girl.

We would often sit on the couch in the den, watching TV with our backs to the armrests feet pressed flat together using the pressure to easily lift up our legs. We also had a blast playing together in the back yard. We had cardboard blocks that we used to throw around the clubhouse in back of the garage like we were in a twister that brought us to a new land (a la *Wizard Of Oz*). Then we walked around the back yard like we had landed in the *Land Of The Lost* We would even sing the theme song together. "Marshall Will and Holly, on a routine expedition, met the greatest earthquake.. ever known…." We had dress up clothes that were moms old hand me downs. Daddy Marcus probably wouldn't have approved of some of that shit but some stuff you had to do when you've got a big sister. We would play dress up and make train cars out of crates with our stuffed animals in them from my bedroom door to hers.

When Mom and Dick were fighting, Michele's room was the place to be. She had records like the Beatles, Supertramp and Cat Stevens and cool posters on the walls.

Most importantly her room was as far away from mom and
Dicks as you could get and still be inside the house. We
mainly listed to music and sang songs and stuff like that.
When the yelling got loud enough, we would talk about
what an idiot Dick was. But I don't ever remember her
being malicious about it. I wanted to hit him in the face
with a baseball bat; she just shook her head at how sad it
was that a person that lived in our house could be such an
asshole. She was the one thing that, even when I was very
young, made me feel like everything was going to be ok.

Jessica would eventually get my room. Michele's
time with me would go from sitting in her room listening to
those records while Dick and mom fought, to sitting in my
new room upstairs on the flower ledge smoking cigarettes
and talking about music and life.
I can't paint the perfect picture here either. I was
still her little brother, still a little shit, still a pain in the ass.
Case in point… Here is a little something that I found a
long time ago.

Today I am pissed at dad. Mike was in
my room going through my drawer so I
punched him in the nutz. A little noise and
"Go to your room both of you!" A bunch
of bull shit.

Enjoy.
Michele Friedlander April 26, 1980

We stayed close and as we got older, we had fun
messing with each other. Take for instance the hotdog
show. There was a place called the hotdog show in town
that obviously sold hot dogs. They also had a train that ran
around the restaurant that all the kids loved. That has

nothing to do with this story. I knew Michele eyes weren't great and saw she didn't have on her glasses. I went to the fridge and unzipped my pants. I stuck a hot dog through the opening in my pants and turned to her and said, "Hey look!" She screamed and ran out of the room. She was so mad at me. I showed her the hotdog, which actually made her even angrier. Awesome, just awesome

Outside of the house and at school I would hear from every different group of kids how nice she was to them. Outcasts she had a smile for. Nerds she felt a kinship with. Popular kids were just other kids.

I recently spoke with Cherry, the current play production teacher at Pali High School. She recalled a time when she was discouraged by teachers and not sure if she wanted to act any more. She was unhappy with how she looked and thinking that she really might not want to do this with her life.

The hierarchy of the class back then was that the seniors (Michele and her friends) got the parts in the plays. Cherry, an underclassmen, was upset but was pushing on with a small part she managed to get in the fall play. Right before she was going to go on Michele came up to her and told her how beautiful she thought she was and how she owned the stage when she was out there and that the world was hers if she wanted it. She and Michele had that connection from then on. She also said she never doubted what she wanted to do with her life again and will never forget that moment. After a successful Broadway career she now helps the high school drama kids much in the same way as Michele helped her.

Michele was the girl that would throw you a party and hand make you a birthday present. If it wasn't your birthday she might just stop you to tell you how cool she thought you were and why. One of her older friends spent a semester in London England and she took a tape recorder around a raging party of all of their friends and spent almost a half an hour getting everybody to say hi to Johnny and titled it "Letters To London" and sent it off for him to enjoy.

Without actually meeting Michele it is very hard to describe her. There are not really any people you can compare her to.

As for my extended family I got to see most of them during my weekly escape that was family night dinner. We had dinner every Wednesday night at grandmas and papas, about 6 blocks away from us off of Bienveneda Avenue in the Palisades. It was the one time of week I think I felt normal; Dick had to be nice, heated swimming more than half the year, gramma cooked good food, candy jar, cool uncles and ants, cool cousins…. 2 Christmases, 2 birthdays… all the things to make a child happy. Being my sanctuary I saw it as a perfect place. It wasn't until many years later that I got a grip on what the reality of that situation was. I hated my home life so much that my crazy extended family I was a part of didn't even register.

My grandmother had divorced my grandfather when my mom was a small child. So my mom came from the same type of family as I did. It was her and her brother then came a stepdad and 2 half siblings. As I said, her stepfather was way worse than mine. He was an evil man but he had some Hollywood credits so gramma was just fine with him. Thankfully he died before I was born. She remarried a wonderful man that I would know as papa for my first 20 years on this planet until he died. His name was Sheldon Stark.

Shelly was for all intents and purposed my grandpa. I loved him and looked forward to seeing him every week. He was a writer that started in radio and was one of the founding members of the Writers Guild. So all you Hollywood writers better recognize. Mostly a TV writer but his list of credits is thick as hell. Much of it isn't even among the 30 or so items on IMDB. Obviously none of his radiola stuff is on there, which would have made it twice as beefy. He wrote the first Hollywood screenplay with a Native American hero which helped him became an honorary member of the Iroquois nation.

In yet another short-lived career as a stand up comic, I wrote a bit about my extended family. The stuff about papa was complete horseshit. I called him a narcoleptic cripple. It was basically a long way around to get in a stroked out grandpa swimming in circles joke. (He actually could fall asleep anywhere anytime.) All the rest of the set was pretty much 100% true… This is the best way for me to describe the characters at my family night dinners now that I am an adult.

"My Grandma was one of these alcoholics that tries to minimize her drinking. You could usually find her at the bar making her favorite drink… Vodka and vodka. But she would pretend she was pouring 7 up into it. She stand up there like this (back to the crowd) hoping her tremendous girth was hiding the fact that nothing was coming out of the 7 up bottle. Yeah grandma was no little cute, blue haired old lady. She was big and fat and dyed her hair this fire engine red. She looked like a hammered Heat Miser. She would wear orange polyester pants and a bright red vest. Just imagine igniting a giant lawn gnome. To this day if I smell booze on someone's breath, I get this full on grandma pumpkin head visual. Have you ever seen an old person that is really bloated?? There head looks like a fucking pumpkin.. They still have all the wrinkle lines but they are all kinda pushed out. I see grandma around Halloween I get this urge to shove a candle in her mouth and stick her on the front porch.

Everyone has that one relative that's always sick or dying right? That was my aunt Tony. Aunt Tony had Multiple Sclerosis. I guess it was real bad because her pain medication was 2 large Black Russians and a pack of Parliaments an hour. She shook so bad she looked like she was hooked up to one of those old time gut busters with the belt in the front and the motor in the back…and those black Russians were two parts vodka, one part Kailua, and one helpless Ice cube. Sounded like a bell ringing in that glass (dingalingaling) She had no problem lighting her smokes though. That was because her head and her hands actually shook on the same frequency.

Her husband my uncle John was the practical joker of the bunch. Ahh yes… I remember fondly, the time just after a motorcycle accident and he took the bolts out of my crutches. I've seen him try to kick a stick between the spokes of some lady's wheelchair. As a kid he told me he used to grease up the handrails at the old folks home next to his house. "Hip snappin fun for hours." Strangely enough uncle John was the only one I felt really comfortable around. I think it was because everyone else had this attitude like, 'We have a nice normal family'. He knew how fucked up we were. I would see him just looking around and cracking up at this pack of wackos. I wanted to be doing the same thing but I was too busy moving from room to room trying to outrun the severe psychological damage.

My uncle Chet was completely insane. Like he had been locked up a few times in crazy houses insane. But when you're a kid, you have no idea that "uncle Chet's been in the hospital for a while" means uncle Chet was naked in the bushes outside of the neighbor's house with a butcher knife, going to town with a bottle of Vicks Vapor Rub. Chet was also one of those people that stared at you a little bit too long when they talked to you making you feel really uncomfortable. It didn't help that he had this Gene

Wilder in "Young Frankenstein" (Brooks 1974) mad scientist hair do. He also had the thickest coke bottle glasses that made each eye look like a dinner plate with a pea in the middle of it. One year for my birthday he got me a card, didn't even sign it. It said "Congratulations.... It's a boy"... Ok. Still it was a great 13th birthday. We even bonded a little that night. After we cut the cake he cornered me and said, "I would have gotten you a present, but I'm unemployed.... And you'll know what that's like someday...." Thaaaaaaanks.

Now how fucked up do you have to be to be considered an alcoholic in this family. My uncle Mike was the guy that would get hammered then drive his car into a tree, or if he tried not to drink he would have a seizure. Multiple 502's, serious jail time, started the local chapter of MADD's (mothers against drunk driving) nemesis DAMM (drunks against mad mothers) (credit Zane for that one) Never kept a job, sometimes lived in his van.. This guy's life sucked so bad his dog tried to kill himself. Roscoe, loved that dog. He loved chasing his ball, even into the pool. He'd just paddle back to the steps, and then bring it right back to you.

Then one day he just hurled himself off a cliff. Snapped both his front legs. He looked like a megaphone with his legs all taped up and that cone on his head. Unfortunately Mike came home drunk when Roscoe was still healing up and kicked his tennis ball into the pool on his way stumbling into the house. I can still picture that poor guy kicking those back legs like crazy as that cone slowly filled up with water.

I remember one Easter we hadn't even done our egg hunt and Bam! Uncle Mikes having a seizure. He's twitching and flailing on the ground like his nuts are hooked up to a car battery. I'm looking around like oh shit! Not again. Grandma see's everyone is occupied so she has her head cocked back pouring vodka down her throat.

41

Uncle Chet's in the corner trying to win a staring contest with the new dog. Uncle John jumps up and says, "quick, someone throw a martini shaker in his hands!" Uncle Mike finally slows down and aunt Tony gets up all bitter and says 'You call that a seizure!'"

I have never really censored myself in any meaningful way so I didn't have any problem doing that set at the improv or the comedy store, or more often than not some coffee shop open mic.

I could have also written about papa's brother in law Dick Doug. He was married to papa's sister aunt Judy. He was an actor who had also started out in radio. The only thing I ever saw him do was he was one of Punky Brewster's dads friends on an episode of that show. I can't remember if his stage name was Dick and his real name was Doug or if it was the other way around. He would hear something you were saying, then repeat it back to you completely wrong, then give an oooohhh and a chuckle. It was way too much work explaining shit to him. Besides the stuff he was saying was more interesting anyway. Nowhere close to Alzheimer's but he was a little spacey. Mostly he was just a really nice man. There were some other normal people that would drop in on occasion. Most of them were other members of papa's family, not directly related to me, all of them quality people that I am proud to have known.

It turned out that aunt Tony had a very progressive form of MS and she fought it hard. I don't think it mattered how much she smoked and drank. She was a goner anyway. And she was a good mother to her kids, until they had to take care of her. I had my uncle Geoff, papa's son who wasn't around much but was cool as hell. His son was my cousin Ray. He was closer to Michele's age and totally bailed out once we grew up. There was papa's daughter, my aunt Trudy who was an original Venice hippy from the

60's who was my favorite. Her son was my cousin Andrew who has maintained contact with me for all these years. The 4 of us kids were the fearsome foursome. I was younger from them by about 4 years and Michele by almost 2, but I got included with them as we got older. Jessica had Tony's kids close to her age but all that went south when grandma moved in with them. My mom basically called grandma out on the abuse she allowed to go on and grandma disowned her. Grandma was never overt about it but she never really liked Jessica either.

When Grandma and Aunt Tony got sick and eventually died, Tony's kids didn't even bother to call us. It was Dick that told me when each of them had died. I'm sure it was tough for two young adults to care for their ailing grandmother and mother. But a phone call isn't a hard thing to do. Especially when someone is sick.. and then sick and dying. I would have liked to say goodbye. Now I can't help thinking the only reason that they wouldn't let me know is because they had been left all the money in the will and they didn't want to jeopardize their paydays.

Michele had been accepted to the Center For Enriched Studies or CES, a science magnet school that was hard to get into. My mom was desperate for a change in scenery for me but Michele got in instead. This was actually during my 4th grade year at Marquez but because Michele got in, the year after I was offered a spot.

CES was heaven compared to Coliseum Street School, but a pretty run down neighborhood nonetheless. There was much less of a chance of death at this educational institution than Coliseum Street but it was still the hood. Proving this point was a bit of urban artwork that stayed unchanged for both years I was at this school. On the side of one of the apartment buildings someone had written, "Fook Cuz". Now some of you out there might remember the old turn "Fuck" into "Book" trick. I don't think that had any bearing in this case. Same exact color and can stroke all the way through. I always pictured some big assed motherfucker who no one would tell that he had spelled fuck wrong.

When I was there, CES was 4th grade through high school. Now if you ask me, having 4th graders in a school with 12 graders is a recipe for disaster. Nothing really ever happened to me but I do remember a giant ginger kid chasing me every time he saw me. The guy totally reminded me of the giant red monster in the Bugs Bunny cartoons. "My stars, if an interesting monster can't have an interesting hairdo do, I don't know what the world is coming to, bobby pins please…" Loved those cartoons.

I don't know what it was. Every time he saw me he would get this crazy look in his eyes then try his best to chase me down. He never caught me though. I'm not sure what he would have done if he had. Beat me up??, Rip my arms off??… add me to his spider goulash and eat me??

Despite the neighborhood, CES was a really good school. Being a science magnet they drew good teachers and a racially diverse student body. There was no tuition so that meant a waiting list and priority if you have a sibling there. Enter, me.

Michele had been at CES for a year before me and was doing her thing. The place was massive so I only really saw her on the bus to and from school. I had my hands full with some of the kids that the psychologist at Marquez tried to make me be friends with. Yep, they had made the jump by that time too. The boys had remembered me and we were all in the same classes. So we all became fast friends again. Ok that was a joke. The nickname scumbag was back and they never resisted a chance to use it.

I was pretty much left out of everything. I remember they all had retainers or braces and I even felt left out of that as well. I used to unbend paper clips and put them in my mouth like I had them too. The worst one of them all was a kid named Aaron Schneider. He was at least 2 feet tall. Yep I said it... 2 feet tall. He was THE definition of a Napoleonic complex. I was officially a giant next to him. Didn't matter though. He talked down to me, bullied me, and treated me like shit. He made me feel the same way Dick made me feel. So you could say that Aaron was a little Dick.

Well one-day mini-Dick was hitting me and pushing me around. Then, I'm not sure what got into me. Maybe I was tired of being picked on. Maybe I had enough of the world shitting on me. Maybe this was my chance to stand up and not take crap from any Dick anymore. Maybe it was my chance to climb to the top of the mountain and holler for all to hear.. "I'M MAD AS HELL, AND IM NOT GOING TO TAKE THIS ANYORE!!!!" Or maybe it was the fact that a few days earlier I had watched 5 Latin kids corner Chris Stope in front of a classroom, and through the "fuck you whiteboy's" he kicked one in the face, then jumped down the stairs at the rest. He came out all right. So this was one little Jewish kid from the Palisades. What was the worst that could happen??

For the first time, I stood up to Aaron. I grabbed him in a headlock and took him to the ground. He was struggling but couldn't move. His face and my fist were both right there, so I began to bring these two entities together. So I bloodied him up and bent the shit out of his retainer. Then I tossed him a paperclip and said "if its good enough for me…." Just kidding. Not that clever. This was probably one of the first times I didn't feel totally worthless at school. Right there on the playground, bloody knuckles in 1982. That's a great name for a band. Bloody knuckles.

Up until CES, I had one teacher for each grade like most elementary school kids. Magnet schools are set up like jr. high and high schools with multiple teachers for multiple subjects. You would have the standard 6 periods for all subjects such as Math History, English etc. Report cards were the same as well with each 20-week period offering a place for a letter grade, and a place for grades for work habits and cooperation (E- excellent, S- satisfactory, U- unsatisfactory). There was also a very small space for a comment as well.

My English teacher my second year, 6th grade was one Mrs. Margaret Kesron, or Killer Kesron as we fondly referred to her. When I received my report card she had given me an FUU. In the comment space she actually wrote, "This is the lowest F I have ever given in my career as a teacher." So I had that going for me. I was obviously still having a hard time keeping my focus and getting along with the other kids in class.

Michele had decided she wanted to go to public school and started at Paul Revere Jr. High when I was still in 6th grade working on Kesrons last nerves. One of the final times she kicked me out of class, she channeled all of her years studying as an English major, all of her years working with children, and all of the hatred she had for me in her being, into the most Shakespearian referral slip in both length and prose, that had ever been written. She not only wrote 2 full pages on how she could not teach if I was in her class, she also questioned my ability to offer anything positive to the schools community at all.

The dean when I was there was a lady who looked just like a Skeksis from the recently released movie *The Dark Crystal* (Henson, 1982). Part predatory bird, part reptile, part dragon. Which made it pretty hilarious when she kept telling me she wanted me to be crystal clear about how close I was to getting expelled from the school and I probably would have been if it wasn't the end of the school year.

The first day of 7th grade I showed up at CES, went to all my classes, took the bus home, went up to my mother and said "There is no way I'm going to make it at that school." The next day I was enrolled at Paul Revere. The day after that was the fourth day of the school year and my first day at Paul Revere.

The British are coming!!

My first day at Paul Revere was a surreal one. I didn't really know anybody. I recognized a few kids from Marquez, some from Coliseum Street, but for the most part I didn't know anyone. The school was a Jr. high, so it was 7-9th grades. Michele was in 9th and she was the only one I knew so I just hung out around her. She had already found her calling and was very involved in the schools play production class. That year She played the lead in the Paul Revere play productions rendition of *Auntie Mame*. She was awesome. They had a special group of kids in that class. They all would stay acting together through high school. I could tell that Michele had found what she wanted to do for the rest of her life.

Within that first week, Michele told me it was time for me to get a haircut. I buzzed all my hair off and I was beginning to listen to the new music she was getting into. Michele had just found a bunch of mod/ska bands like the Specials, Madness, Bad Manners and the Selector. So where she went, I followed. Besides being my sister she was my only friend at this new and kind of intimidating place. She had always looked out for me but now things were different. I think she knew I had a clean slate socially and she wanted me to make the most of it.

It turned out that if I had stayed at Marquez, I would have been paraded around Paul Revere at the end of my 6th grade year at an event lovingly called "Howdy Day." The

6th graders from all the surrounding elementary schools were brought together for a full day of…. Howdyness, and a quick intro to their new school. I think the most it did was make it easier for the future 8th graders to pick out who they were going to beat the shit out of during the next school year. So, nobody saw me at Howdy Day… then when the next year started, I missed the first few days of school… then I was hanging out with the older kids…. and I was taller than every single person in all of my classes. Everyone thought I was an older kid that was held back because nobody knew who I was.

      Then the most amazing thing happened. People were no longer staring at me, snickering and making fun….They were looking at me all right but for some other strange reason I couldn't figure out. Then over the next couple of weeks it happened. I realized what it was. People actually liked me. No more scumbag nickname, no more being picked on (by my classmates) and no more bullshit. It was the most amazing feeling that I could never fully describe. Suffice it to say that I finally had a place where I could be happy and not scared of any dick, and it was jr. high school! The most awkward time in most peoples entire lives! For me, in many ways, it was a place where I finally felt free.

      It took most of my first year at Paul Revere to truly hit my stride. Trips with Michele to get my hair cut by Keren (who was one of the original Westside skater-punk chicks and probably the inspiration for Michele's wearing torn up rags tied into her hair) I think she is still cutting hair in Venice beach just off the boardwalk. We went to NANA in Santa Monica and I picked out a pair of Zebra skin Creepers and a couple of shirts. Then we went down to Aardvarks in Venice, which was still a true thrift store back in those days for some more duds. A lot of other people in the beach communities were still wearing hang 10 shirts and OP short shorts left over from the 70s. The whole volleyball sports wear fad having just begun, everyone else had on pretty much the same uniform. Side out volleyball shirt, Mossimo shorts. Or if you were a true rebel or a skater maybe some Jimmy's or Stussy wear.

First part of the year, when I was really rocking the mod thing, I even had a black suit thin black tie with fedora rude boy outfit. If you wear a nice fedora, you should rock a smooth looking suit to go with it. I'm not pointing any fingers but when you wear a nice hat like that but dress like a bum it looks kind of silly.

We had yearbooks back at CES so my last one signed by all my "friends" just 3 moths earlier were all addressed to scumbag. Having all of that shit pounded into your head from kindergarten thru 6th grade at home and at school takes a minute to get over. I did however end up having a little bit of help getting through it.

Not long into the school year Rachael Levine had her Bat Mitzvah and I was invited. When the kids are alone I guess it's tradition to play make out games and it quickly became obvious to me that more than one of these chicks wanted to make out with this goyem. When your hormones are just starting to fire and you are a Scorpio like I am, chicks digging you will turn down that "you're a looser" shit right down to just above zero. I had kissed only a couple of girls up until that time. I made one of Michele's friends give me a kiss so I would stop jumping on the bed and go to sleep when she was babysitting me, then Michele's friend Leigh was my first French kiss. But this was my first real, on my own make out session and it was awesome.

The other bit of help I had came by the way of some minor self medication. To this day I still think smoking a little weed is better than any pharmaceutical drugs you could take, but I am not going to advocate for that here. I will say that smoking marijuana was a part of what made my life better when I started jr. high school. Coming home a little bit high made Dicks stink eye way less effective.

I mentioned earlier that I had smoked the stuff for the first time with an older kid named Anthony Tittelli, on a Boy Scout camping trip. Troop 400. While we were out getting high in Vasquez Rocks, (movies like the Flintstones and every off road car commercial ever was filmed there) the rest of our troop had launched a military style raid on another troop camped nearby, injuring several campers and one scout leader. The scout leader had taken a water balloon launcher to the chest at about 20 feet (they can launch a water balloon over a thousand) and was almost knocked unconscious.

If that wasn't enough, our troop managed to take some POW's as well. As fun as that raid sounds, that was the first time I ever really got high so I stand by my decision. Also the fact that the troop was banned from Vasquez Rocks and several older scouts were brought up on assault and kidnapping charges has to be figured in there somewhere as well. (That wasn't really all our troops fault. I mean it says it right there in the goddamn motto… Be prepared!!!)

Since I was no longer cowering in fear at home and feeling like I was actually a person worthy of some happiness, I found some things that I really liked to do. Besides smoking a little weed, I started skateboarding a lot more. My mom had bought me a Dogtown Skateboard when I was 8. It was love right from the start. Skate boarding has probably been the number 1 constant throughout my entire life. It has always been something I could do no matter what was happening around me.

No Dick, No school, no bullshit of any kind could get to me when I was skating. It became my daily escape. There was nothing like smoking a bowl then riding on my skateboard. Palisades Elementary was freshly repaved when I was in 7th grade, like a present all gift-wrapped.

Smooth banks and buttery parking blocks that you could stack on top of each other and grind or board slide till it was too dark to see. There was no judgment when I was skating. There was no pain but the physical and that kind of bleeding is fun. When I am skating, the world just melts away and my focus is singular. For me it was and still is the best way possible for me to truly live in the moment.

I also started surfing and not just during Junior Life Guards. The best days during that first summer would be smoking a bowl, jumping on my skate, grabbing my surfboard and skating down to the beach. Temescal Canyon Road is one of the 4 roads that leads into the Pacific Palisades. It's a perfect ¾ of a mile, downhill run to the beach. You could bomb it with your surfboard in hand and use the board as a block against the speed you would get going down the hill. Block the wind, time that light at the bottom, and then you could, fly across PCH into the beach parking lot. Then it was a quick skate down to first jetty where all the kids who lived around me (and would become some of my best friends) would hang out and surf. Out from under Dicks thumb and doing my own thing. I could get used to this.

Chapter 4

Music, Skate Or Die, Friends, & The Big White Buddha

The music Michele was turning me onto was another huge force in my new life. My first ever concert happened right around the time I was figuring out that I wasn't the loser scumbag I thought I was. It was so soon after the school year started that I didn't really know anyone to take. I actually took a quiet kid I had known from Marquez, Paul Viener. Really nice kid. His dad ran the club soccer team I was never allowed to try out for….and what the hell Paul?? I mean sometimes you need a hack to come take out a player that's giving your team a hard time. Anyway, it was an unreal concert to have as my first. It was the Who's first farewell tour on October 29th 1982 and the Clash opened for them. (Yep, that's right… Ok, my first record that I bought was Sean Cassidy's Da Doo Ron Ron so I wasn't really that cool.)

This was one of the few amazing things Dick did for us. He worked in food service and was some kind of manager at the Coliseum. So Michele invited 3 friends and I brought one. We were the first people inside of the stadium. We sat in the stands for the Who and were against the stage for the Clash. The show they both put on was absolutely amazing!!

The first act was Tom T-bone Burnett. The crowd wasn't too into him. He was throwing drumsticks out into the crowd and the people were throwing them right back at him. Once again if I'm going to be so hard on Dick, I have to emphasize when something righteous went down. It was Michele that connected the dots and realized the opportunity we had, but it was Dick that made it happen. Thank you Dick.

The first small club gig I went to was about a month later. Remember, most girls at that age were jockeying for social position on their best days. Michele, as usual, didn't give a shit about any of that stuff. She saw a way to broaden her little brother's horizons. So my first show was a local mod/ska band called the Untouchables at the Roxy in December 1982.

I had a shirt from the show that had Santa sitting in an oversized Vespa scooter with his bag of presents in back. It had a hole in it and one of the few bullies I had to deal with, Steve Kesron (same last name as my favorite English teacher at CES.. hmm, I wonder if they were related) ripped a huge chunk out of it. I was bummed about my shirt but here was this 9th grade kid, that was one of the uglier kids you'd ever want to meet, who was fucking with a kid 2 years younger that him (actually 3, remember I was young for my grade).

I was pissed off but felt sorry for him as well. I could tell he wasn't going to get any prettier, and he felt the need to fuck with me. Anyway.. He wasn't worth my anger. Besides, before that I had some respect for him. He was a punk way before I was. I was still listening to mod and ska when he appeared to be way into it.

For the show, Luka Johnny Michele and about 10 other people piled into someone's car and off we went to the Roxy. I was folded in half inside of this hatch back that seated 5 on our way down Sunset Blvd. to West Hollywood and a show to remember. I still have the ticket stub. The show cost 6 bucks and the telephone number of the Roxy only had 7 digits. Back then all of Los Angeles, the Palisades, Santa Monica, Culver City, Hollywood, Silverlake, Downtown, was a 213 area code.

The Untouchables you can actually see in the movie *Repo Man* (1984) staring Emilio Estevez, a cult classic and one of many punks favorite movies. A couple of the guys in the band were huge and Emilio's tiny ass was supposed to repo their grandmas car. Anyway it's a pretty funny scene. They end up beating the living shit out of him.

The lead guitarist of the Untouchables was a black guy named Clyde Grimes. He had a brother that worked at the pizza place next to Palisades Elementary where I would skate everyday. Clyde's brother was Marty Grimes of Z Boys fame. Of course everybody remembers all the Dogtown originals and the Zephyr team because of Stacy Peralta's documentary and the Hollywood movie about Dogtown and Z Boys. When I saw the Hollywood movie I was happy when they called out Marty Grimes name during one of the contest scenes.

Even though academically being in a public school was much better for me, I was still having a tough time in class. I was never stupid, I just had a hard time caring about some of the stuff we were learning. There were also more kids paying positive attention to me. Apparently I had a pretty good personality if people weren't busy telling me what a piece of shit I was. Couple that with being bored, much bigger and dressed differently than the other kids made me an easy target for the teachers.... which wasn't always deserved.

If a bunch of kids are talking in the back of the room, you are going to single out the giant kid with two tone hair spiked straight up off of his head. I was also one of probably only 3 boys in the school that had his ear pierced as well, which in those days made you a freak. I had found a safety pin on the ground in music class and shoved it through my left ear. It started bleeding down my neck so the teacher sent me to the office. My mom said she would have it done professionally if I promised not to do that again....so that's got to be the kid who's be causing all the trouble.

My 7th grade Physical Education teacher Mr. Vahn had a special hatred for me. I didn't even really fuck around in his class. So as far as I could tell he just hated me because I stood out. He was exactly like the character, teacher Richard Vernon (another dick named Dick) from the movie *The Breakfast Club*, (Hughes, 1985). He had that "I've seen your type come and go and you are just going to be another piece of shit drain on society," total dick mentality. (He was married to a fairly attractive teacher at Pali High School who I will talk about later.)

The first time you enter a Jr. high School Physical Education (PE) class can be pretty traumatic. It is the first "locker room" experience most boys have ever had. You go from PE being running around outside playing kickball or handball, or if it was raining playing some form of dodge ball or volley ball inside; to stripping naked in front of a hundred other boys. So I'm surrounded by other 13 year old boys (I was actually only 12 until November of my 8th grade year) all of which I was developing much faster than. So I was one of the only kids that had hairy legs. The only other kid that had hair on his legs was an middle eastern kid who was basically already covered in fur. I freaked the fuck out. I actually cried when I got home and talked to my mom because I was afraid that was the next step in my adolescent evolution. Sasquatch.... Lycanthrope.... Wolf boy of Juarez. I ran to the mirror when I got home and realized I was starting to get a uni-brow as well. Couldn't talk to Dick about that stuff because I was way too scared of him.

Once I realized my eyebrows were connecting, I got an idea when I saw one of Michele's disposable razors. I grabbed that bad boy and shaved in between my eyebrows. I probably shaved like that for 3 months before Michele notice some stubble between my eyes and showed me how to pluck them.

As a matter of fact my real father daddy Marcus was the one who taught me to pee standing up. On one of his early yearly visits he saw me peeing sitting down. He stopped me and said, "No son you stand up and hold your pee pee like this. Then you only shake it twice when you are done. If you shake it anymore than that you are playing with yourself." Right..got it dad.. more than twice you are playing with yourself.

Back to Vahns class; So now rather than having massive kickball games and playing butts up like in elementary school, we were doing calisthenics, running laps then lining up military style for our lesson of the day. I'll never forget when Vahn had us doing strength training for some standardized tests. Part of those tests was trying to climb a rope all the way to the top.

At this age, most of the boys were smaller and had way more upper body strength then the girls. So he picked the girl that every guy in my class had a crush on, Fiona. Oh my god she was hot. I couldn't pay that close attention to her on a regular basis in PE because those little shorts we wore would have been no match for my little monster. That would have been way too embarrassing.

Using her as an example he had her start climbing the rope. She only got about 1 pull in then she stalled. Not wanting to let her confidence wane, Vahn quickly jumped to the rescue, cupping both of her butt cheeks very close to the inside of her thighs, where her special place could be brushed ever so slightly with his pinkies. He yelled encouragement into her ear and tried as hard as he could to "help her" get just a little farther up the rope. Pretty much the equivalent of shaking keys in front of us to keep our attention away from the fact that he was finger banging a child. I never thought I could be envious of anything to do with Mr. Vahn….but yes, at that moment I wanted nothing more than to be that grown mans fingers.

Athletically I was pretty well off. I still couldn't see too well out of one eye but that affected baseball the most, which we didn't play. As much as I hate to say anything good about that pervert asshole Vahn, he kind of knew his sports. My balance was already good from skating. I also had size so when we were actually doing the sports part of PE, Vahn pretty much left me alone.

It turned out that everyone who had Vahn had the same incredible story of him groping the hottest chick in the class when it was time to climb the ropes. I heard some years later he stuck his fingers in the wrong little girls hoo-hoo. Her parents were some high-powered lawyers and Mr. Vahn was given the suggestion to retire.

The rest of 7th grade was amazing. Coming into my own as someone that my peers respected and wanted to know. I was truly on top of the world. However, because of classroom shenanigans I was landing in detention or the Deans office more and more… and the dean was a fucking Nazi. He was also a dead ringer for Hitler at 70 if hadn't blown his brains out. Every kid I knew turned his picture into Adolf in their yearbooks. He made it clear to me in no uncertain terms that I was going to be expelled. Most kids who get expelled fill up their disciplinary card in two or part of 3 years. Mine was almost full in one.

Curious to the allure Michele felt to theater I also took a drama class that year. Improv has gotten big these days so I will tell you one exercise that we did that I will never forget. There were two people on stage and two people off stage speaking for the people on stage. The people on stage were just moving their lips. Brandon Lee was on stage with a heavyset girl named Keesha Green. I don't remember who was speaking for Brandon, but Timmy Spain was speaking for Keesha. Brandon began moving his lips and the voices came from off stage. Brandon: "Where you coming from Keesha?" Timmy Spain speaking for Kesha called back in the deepest husky voice he could.. 'Maaaac Donald's' (Brandon) "Well where are you going??" (Timmy/for Keesha)' Burger King.' I felt horrible. Everyone died laughing. It was totally fucked up and I had to hide my head because I was laughing as well. It was pretty bad. Sorry Keesha.

I remember meeting Brandon Lee early in the year and liked him the second I met him. He was an amazingly talented artist and a very funny kid and became one of my best school friends. We didn't always hang out, but the times we did were always memorable.

After my first year at Paul Revere I began my first summer as a kid people wanted to hang with. Which is

pretty huge in a beach town. Mainly because of one thing....
GIRLS!!!! Despite all attempts to sabotage my sexual being
at home, I knew I wanted to meet some girls. Some friends
and I went to one of the many nighttime beach parties at
state (will Rodgers state beach tower 18). It is a very
famous beach volleyball spot where future Olympic gold
medalist Kent Steffes and Karch Kiraly cut their chops. It
was where Chautauqua, West Channel and PCH all met.
We pimped some beer from State Beach Liquor (had
someone of age buy us beer) and made our way under PCH
to the beach.

It was a Friday night, we were hanging out drinking
and smoking, you know, the things normal 13 year olds do.
When all of a sudden Chris came up to me all excited and
said "Dude! I just got laid!!!" I was so jealous! I threw him
a couple of high fives and asked him who he had sex with.
It was Sky. I knew her from parties and the beach a few
weeks earlier. Just as I was marveling at the luck this kid
had he says to me, "Do you want to fuck her?"

I couldn't believe it! This kid just had sex for the
first time in his life and he wanted to sully that magical
experience by asking me..... yeah, you aren't going to buy
that set up. I was just like any other young preteen whose
hormones were just beginning to fire. "Hell yes I want to
fuck her!!" So that was my magical moment. I lost my
virginity on the beach right after my friend had lost his with
the same girl. She was looking to have sex with us and she
had the condoms... and yes, I was 12 years old, she was 14.

Besides trying to get together with girls, I spent a
lot of those summer beach days hanging out with friends at
the jetty. Some of them I had known from the
neighborhood, like fellow pyro Pronger and Boyd, and
some were new friends all together. I would surf there and
hang out with Brandon, Sammy, DK, and many others over
the years. Brandon almost wasn't around very long. He and
DK were smoking a bowl across the street from jetty where

the old Sunspot hotel used to be. On there way back across PCH Brandon got hit in the face with the extended mirror of a tow truck that was driving on the shoulder. Another couple of feet and he would have been underneath that truck.

At the end of the summer right before 8th grade, I met a kid at the Pali High football field one night during various club and AYSO soccer practices named Harley Buckler. I was riding around on my bike and he had just finished practice. We started talking and it turned out he was a pretty cool kid from Brentwood that surfed and was coming from Crossroads over to Paul Revere for 8th grade. He and I have probably 5 groups of 2 girls that we made out with and then switched up over our jr. high school career. I'm not sure how it happened the first time... I think it was actually one of the girl's ideas. But after that, the suggestion was made.... Then it was, "we all switch places when I ring the bell!"(RIP MCA)

I remember making out with a girl and hearing him scream from the other room. He then came running in and hid behind the couch. I was like "What the fuck dude!" It turned out the girl started to wax her braces that were on the inside of her teeth. When Harley asked what she was doing she said, 'If I don't wax the wire it could catch on the vein on your... you know'... At which point he screamed and ran out of the room. No such thing as invisiline back then. It has to be hard to keep a woody when you are getting a smoker from what might as well be a bear trap. Scary shit huh.

It wasn't too hard to rig up chicks because he was pretty popular and his folks were LOADED! His parents were divorced, and both sets of parent\stepparent were fucking rich as hell. They would often go on vacation and leave a huge empty house in Brentwood with a pool and a stocked fridge inside and a garage fridge full of beer outside…. and that wasn't including the beach house.

During a series of winter storms in 1983 almost a third of the Santa Monica Pier was destroyed by massive waves. His beach house was one of those Malibu beach houses that were on stilts over the water at hi tide. I was watching the local news and they were showing the destroyed pier and started talking about houses in Malibu that were being damaged by the storm surf. I grabbed the phone and gave Harley a call. "Dude, is your house in Malibu destroyed?" While chewing on an apple he replied, 'I don't know… hey mom!!' "Yes dear"…. 'Is our house in Malibu still there?' "I don't know honey." 'Yeah dude I have no idea.' I could not believe it. Still a great kid and a huge heart but that was just some shit that I couldn't even comprehend

I hardly ever see him but every time I do, he should give me 5 bucks. A while after we met he brought a girl that he wanted to have sex with back to my house. Him being a virgin and both of my parents working all day made my house a perfect location. Plus she lived just down the street and I had a garage that had been converted into a rumpus room, complete with a fold out couch. This was Harley's big chance. So as the deal was going down I saw my little sister Jessica heading out to the garage. I jumped up and ran out to stop her. I tried everything in my power to casually talk her out of going in there. Nothing worked. I think she knew she had me, and so did I. I knew Harley's chances of following through with this chick would be destroyed if my little sister walked in and said "what's up guys." So she made me pay her 5 bucks to go back inside and leave them alone. If it wasn't for that 5 bucks his "first time" story would have been very different.

I bring up Harley because he introduced me to probably the best friend I have ever had. I had actually met Takeo Stevens when we were both 5 years old at a kid's

birthday party that lived around the block from me. Yuta
Stensil. He was born of a Japanese mother and an English
father just like Takeo. We didn't realize till we were in our
late teens that we had met at such an early age. But Harley
introduced me to Takeo at state beach after we had all gone
surfing that summer before 8th grade.

Takeo's house…. I'm not sure how to explain it…
The negative energy that loomed around my house (minus
Michele's room of course) was equaled and maybe
surpassed by the positive energy at this kids place. First of
all, part of the property used to be owned by Charlie
Chaplin and you could feel the history there. Also Takeo's
dad was a super soulful man and a famous painter. He had
spent much of his life exploring eastern, and other
philosophies that might as well have been Martian to me at
the time.

The house itself was rustic and beautiful. It had a
pool and an above ground wooden hot tub with an aloe
Vera tree twisting around it. Nothing better for soothing
your sunburn after a nice long surf. The place made you
feel like you were at a jungle oasis. The house was actually
3 houses; a hundred year plus old house left over from the
Chaplin property in the back, another one was on the alley
that was turned into a 2-story tall space for his dad to paint
(the door was 2-stories tall as well to get the giant canvases
inside), and the main house was their living quarters.

The studio and main house were all made of wood
to add to that jungle feel. From the back alley you could see
the original Lois Lane from the black and white Superman
TV show sitting on her deck. She was obviously way older
but her face looked the exact same. She always had a smile
and a "Hello boys" waiting for us.

After meeting Takeos dad, he quickly became the
only positive male role model I would ever know as a kid.
He was the only one who would look me in the eye and talk

to me, the only man who ever asked me about things, the only man that cared what I had to say. I don't even think he liked me that much…. or not that he didn't like me, but that he saw this kid with a buzzed head or dyed hair who smoked cigarettes (he saw a vid of us surfing and I had a smoke when we got out of the water) and didn't know if I was the best influence on his 2nd born son.

The first of hundreds of times I slept over at his house I damn near had a heart attack at dinner. As I said before, my mother was the master of the bland, processed food revolution that started in the United States after the Second World War and lasted well through the early 80s. Tasteless food, canned or frozen vegetables, hamburger helper, and foods that were meant to sustain prolonged periods of time in a nuclear fallout shelter. Salt was the only seasoning and occasionally on a particularly frisky night pepper. Lawry's powdered taco mix added to ground beef was as exotic as it got. (Those were actually so fucking good!!!) To give her a little credit we did have homemade pizza night on Friday nights. That shit was so good!! Everybody wanted in on those Chef Boyardee pizza kit nights. Who cares if Dick the dick is there. Everybody wanted some. YUMMY!!

My mom had a serious phobia of fish, but if she hadn't I'm assuming it would have been breaded and fried and looked nothing like it did in the wild. My first meal at Takeos I picked up my fork to go at this pancake looking thing on my plate, cut into it and a purple tentacle fell out. I'm pretty sure my face was on its way to that color too but it had decided to stop on green. I excused myself and went into the bathroom and threw up. I vowed after that meal to be way more adventurous with my meals, starting at Takeo's.

Pretty soon I was eating almost anything Kimsan would prepare. (Kimsan was this old housekeeper and chef for the family) She barely spoke English and could be frequently seen screaming like a banshee chasing Harley around the house with a butcher knife. We would be high, watching a video of us surfing or skating, or listening to some music.. and Harley would go running by with some food yelling for help and Kimsan would be running after him, yelling back and waving a knife. We would be cracking up because she wouldn't let up and the property was so big that you could hear them fade out of range. Then a couple minutes later you would hear them coming back again. Harley would eventually ditch her and then you would just hear her walking around the house, still yelling in Japanese at this little shit that was taking stuff out of her kitchen for the next hour and a half.

Takeo's dad was the first adult male I took notice of actually talking to his kid in what I now understand to be a solid father son relationship. It was mind boggling to me at the time. I couldn't understand what was happening. It was like watching national geographic and trying to understand the social morays of a tribe of head hunting cannibals. I was mesmerized. It was just crazy to me, and I would sometimes be included in the conversation!

At dinner or just walking by after surfing we would actually interact like a father and sons. Not that he felt like I was anything close to a son to him in any way shape or form. He would just talk to Takeo that way and I would just catch the runoff. I didn't realize it at the time that he was the dad I never had.

When I think back on how I looked at Takeo's dad, he was like a big white Buddha floating cross-legged a few feet off the ground with all the answers to the universe. (He had a bunch of those no backed posture chairs that you rested on your knees so it really looked like he was just floating there.) A lot of that was justified because you could sense his energy and knew how thoughtful and soulful he was. Even more mystical to me was that he was a dad that cared about his son and was involved in his life.

Takeo was and has remained the best friend I have ever had in my life. Even though I have only seen him once in the last 10 years. I have never known and will probably never know anyone like him…and it wasn't just me. Everyone that knew him thought he was the nicest kid they had ever met.

One case study on Takeo's soul-ness and the vibe of his house was a 4th of July party in high school where we ate a shitload of hallucinogenic mushrooms in the back yard. There were people at the house when we ate the shrooms. By the time we started coming on we, weren't paying any attention to the house and went out and laid on the grass in the back yard. Then more people showed up, lots more. After frying for a bit someone said maybe we should check on the house? I looked up and there were 9 million people inside and on the deck. There wasn't a single inch of real estate that wasn't covered in bodies drinking smoking and all out raging (Raging; Adj. To party, to drink, i.e. to rage.)

His house was like any other in this situation. Shit could break, shit could get stolen, and things could be fucked. But Takeo's house had some extra-added fun. His house had original works by Ting, Matisse and other artists valued in the millions just hanging on the walls. He had working mechanical sculptures that did nothing that were fragile and priceless! He had quarts and amethyst crystals the size of your leg just sitting on shelves. Not to mention dozens of his dad's multi million dollar paintings stored in the studio.

The next day, not one thing was stolen or broken. Some plants were destroyed, there was a huge cleanup to do, and Laurie Bendwell fell into the koi pond after peeing in the bushes, but besides that the place was completely unharmed.

I came to fully understand who Takeo's Dad was and how important he was to the artistic community when I got a little older. Some time after his death of prostate cancer, (possibly from paint seeping into his blood stream thru his hands) Takeo invited me to MOCA where they were unveiling an exhibit of his work. All the local Los Angeles dignitaries were there. City Councilmen, the mayor, all the muckedy mucks in museum and high society life. I was still kind of a knucklehead so Cheeto and I stood by the bathroom looking up at a giant white wall with nothing on it like we were contemplating some great work of art. Probably 15 people stopped next to us to see what we were looking at before we got bored and walked away.

At one point everyone was gathered around a TV set to watch a taped interview with the artist at his home. I pictured us walking out behind him, surfboards in hand like we did every day. It would have been much funnier if you saw Kimsan chasing Harley out of the house.

I did get a hint of who he was early on when I answered the door and some lady who came to pick up a pair of his old shoes that he had painted in for some auction. The lady was beside herself with joy at meeting him. Takeo's dad's energy and soulfulness stay with me to this day. He passed away the day before my 24th birthday, November 4th 1994.

Chapter 5

1984- The Most Fun Year Of My Life

8th grade. 1984. Los Angeles had the summer Olympic games. I had what was probably the greatest year of my life so far. I was happy, healthy, and ready for whatever came next. Sure I got the occasional tease from the older kids for being much more into the punk rock scene than the year before. Taunts of "poseur" from the 9th graders seemed to come with a nod and a wink, which I thought was courtesy of my super cool sister Michele. Plus the fact that there weren't too many kids in 9th grade that could take me by themselves didn't hurt either. For your social survival you better be damn sure that the younger kid you are picking on doesn't take you out because that wouldn't look very good at the weekly meeting of the bullies.

Michele had left to start Pali High so I no longer had her around at school. Which was fine because she had given me the push in the right direction that I needed socially and for my own self-confidence. I was going to be ok. I would still have her guidance but now as far as school went I was doing it all on my own.

A little while after the school year started, a girl named Shannon brought her best friend from Topanga that went to school over the hill in the valley. Her name was Rebecca Neeland The first time I saw her, she says I was wearing white Jimmy's pants and a white dress shirt with a skull drawn on the back that was ripped and bloodied. Apparently I had just been involved in a pupilial disagreement that went unreported to the authorities. I think it was a mutual fuck you that started with fists and ended with hugs. Bap bap bing... Cool, see ya at lunch kinda thing.

I was in love with her immediately. I got her phone number right away and we would talk on the phone for hours. I still remember her number 555 1168. I know we stayed up the whole night talking more than just once. When we saw each other, we made out and did stuff just short of having sex. I couldn't pull the trigger. I think it had something to do with the fact that she was the first girl I really liked. We dated for a few weeks before she ended up making out with some guy at a beach party. She broke up with me and I was crushed. She was my first girl friend. My first puppy love.

The punk rock music I was getting into (thanks to Michele) was coming from a college radio station out of Loyola Marymount University and good old Rodney on the

Roq. 88.9 FM, KXLU was the college station that had one or two punk rock shows on during the evenings, and KROQ on Sunday nights was all Rodney Bingeheimer. I had never heard such aggressive rhythm and furry all rolled into one. 7 seconds, the Descendants, Black Flag, Bad Religion… Besides the mod ska stuff the year before, I was a certified member of the KISS Army and listend to records like Ozzy Osbournes Diary of a Madman and ACDC. I had never heard music that hit me the way punk rock did.

Michele actually called KROQ and told them they should ditch Richard Blade (regular daytime DJ… you can now hire him for 80's themed parties) and all that trendy new wave crap and give Rodney better and more airtime.

Believe it or not Richard Blade actually called her back! But on my mom and Dicks line. Dick picked up the phone to a thick British accent, "Hi, this is Richard Blade, is Michele there?" Dick.. 'Call back on her phone (click)' Fucking hung up on him!! He actually called Dick back got our number called Michele and thanked her for her input. I wanted to kill her because she bounced around the house talking with an English accent for the next two and a half weeks.

I began coming to school wearing flannels and combat boots. I would bleach my hair, or dye it black and still wore it spiked straight up off my head. There were many times that Michele helped me color my hair, so by the time I was in 9th grade I was a pro.

One time I bleached my hair white and then dyed it sky blue.... not very subtle. I did it this girls house that I had a crush on named Cindee. My mom lost her shit when she saw it and made me dye most of it black. She was afraid that with my academic history, and a head full of electric blue hair it would somehow leave me at a disadvantage in the early 1980's Los Angeles Unified School District.

That year there was a new vice principle or dean of boys, that replace the Hitler gun named Mr. John Miller. Take a wild guess who was the first kid in his office. Yep, yours truly. I'm not sure why I was there but I am sure about what happened next. Most kids that get into trouble lie to try to get out of it. I got into trouble, sat down at his desk and told him exactly what I did. Then I proceeded to tell him the things that I didn't do, or wasn't responsible for, and finally told him why I thought the teacher blamed me for the things that I hadn't done.

I could see it in his eyes. He couldn't believe a student wasn't trying to weasel out of something. Most of the things I did were just disruptive or perceived to be disruptive anyway. I wasn't stabbing anybody or doing anything that bad.

Once we got to be friendly I would also start a dialogue with him about shit I didn't agree with and he actually seemed to dig it. I got sent to him from homeroom for not saying the pledge of allegiance. "Why aren't you saying the pledge Michael?" 'Why is 'god' in my pledge?? This is a state run school, you guys just finished teaching me about separation of church and state, what kind of hypocritical shit is this??' Then he had me research the pledge and I find out 'under god' wasn't even in the pledge until the 1950s.

Little did I know that some 20 years later those same ideas would give way to something I call nazi secularism. The death of Santa Clause. No more Christmas in schools because Johnny and Jimmy dipshits parents are so cool that they can't have some quasi-religious symbolism anywhere near their children. The most religious people I have personally ever come across????... Atheists. The anti religious. The Bill Mahers. Politically correct dickholes. Not to say that I'm a fan of people who are killing in the name of a god or trying to push their values on everyone else. I just have to point out the hypocrisy of an atheist demanding you believe what he believes because he doesn't think religious people should be pushing there beliefs on other people.

Anyway, from that point on Mr. Miller was on my side. I never ratted out other kids but I always copped to my shit and tried to let him know if he was barking up the wrong tree. Mr. Miller kind of felt like a safety net and really let me enjoy the rest of my time in jr. high.

The most fun I had at a Bar Mitzvah was the same year. Andy Melman had what I like to call the punk rock Bar Mitzvah. They had already gotten pretty fun because at quite a few of the after parties there was only me and Huey that were over 5'5" and we were both almost 5'10". So all dressed up in suits, we almost looked like little people. Having the party at some huge Brentwood mansion made it easy for us to find a bar off to the side where we could get drinks for ourselves and other kids. I remember getting buzzed, making out with girls and having lots of fun at every single one of those things I went to.

I never went to a Bar or Bat Mitzvah in the Palisades. I knew there were Jews there because I had been busted for knocking down a cement barrier in the parking lot of the local synagogue. Everyday on my paper route, I saw all these kids having fun on the yard during Hebrew school and I was jealous that I couldn't play. I kicked at that thing until the walls came a tumblin down (that's a wall of Jericho reference right there). I had to have a sit down with the Rabbi and Dick and ended up paying for that shit with money I made on that same paper route.

Before I got invited to Andy's Bar Mitzvah, I spent the night at his mom's condo in Santa Monica. The phone rang right after I showed up and Andy answered it. He immediately started screaming at whoever was on the other end of the phone. "Asshole motherfucker piece of shit rat

71

bastard!!" It was his mom's boyfriend. I was like 'Oh fuck! Shits gonna go down... how am I gonna get out of here?' Then his mom strolled in like nothing had happened and said "Don't talk to Harry that way Andy." 'Fuck you mom, that guys an asshole!' I looked at Andy. "Should I go???" He looked back like I was crazy and said 'no way dude its cool.' I figured it out pretty quickly. After the shock wore off that he talked to his mom that way I realized that they were really close and it really was cool.

What made Andy's Bar Mitzvah different from the others was the after party. Nobody cared who was drinking, the party was actually a party, and all the old people were cool as shit. I think his mom might have had a job somewhere in the Larry Flint organization or something like that. I will say that its very possible that my 13 year old brain just took whatever she really did and that's how it took hold in my head, but I think it was something like that. Regardless if she did or didn't, it wouldn't have surprised me if all the adults there worked in Hollywood, music or porn.

I remember one of Andys friends that I really got along well with was an English punk kid named Truman. Towards the end of the party Truman's dad was talking and dancing with his friends wife. Then his friend, who was absolutely hammered got jealous and started talking shit to him. Truman's dad basically said, "No harm intended sorry man." But the guy grabbed a wine bottle and swung it at his head. Truman's dad stepped back then punched the dude several times knocking him out and sending his teeth skipping across the dance floor. Even with the background noise of the music and the partiers, you could still hear those Chiclets bouncing across the floor like you were throwing dice in an empty warehouse. If the goyem only knew how much fun those things could be. Jesus Christ ..... I mean God Damn!

Another thing that made that year so much fun was I had started hanging out with another kid I really liked who was also into punk rock named John Liberti (Birdy). I don't think we ever went to a punk show together, but we did hang out a lot of weekends in Westwood or Hollywood (Mostly Westwood). I would take the number 2 RTD bus to his parents house on Sunset Blvd. right at Capri on Friday afternoons. They had a pretty huge spread and he lived in a back house by the garage. I only ever saw his folks from a distance. I knew they were older but didn't know much more about them than that.

I always pictured them thinking that they better hurry up and have a kid because his moms biological clock was ticking pretty loudly. Once they had him they ended up with a little buyers remorse and they just put him out by the garage. I'm not sure if any of that was true but it did seem to me that he was pretty much on his own. So we would hang out, listen to GBH, the Exploited or Abrasive wheels, (we had something of a UK punk thing going on at the time) and then hop the bus to Westwood.

There was a family of seemingly lost kids that hung together in Westwood. Back in those days if you were a punk, then you were basically considered by society as a social reject. If you looked that different you couldn't walk 50 feet without someone talking shit to you, or getting into a fight, or having the cops stop and harass you. I wasn't the social outcast that a lot of these kids were, but I felt a kinship with them just the same. At home I was a reject. Most of my life I had been an outcast in every possible way. I knew how to embrace the fact that I was different.

A bunch of us kids were hanging out one day during school hours. There was Mya, Aaron, Birdy, me, Jason, Caroline, and Andrew. Birdy and I were the only ones from Paul Revere, the rest were from Emerson in Westwood, West L.A., or were just homeless kids. Andrew had a blonde Mohawk with black roots and was wearing a

heavy flannel jacket. Jason was a black kid with a skinhead,
which was very different back then; it was all afro's and
jerry curls on all the kids we knew. He also had a thick
safety pin in his cheek for so long that if he pulled it out he
could shoot water out of the hole it made. I had dyed black
hair sticking straight up off my head and a leather
motorcycle jacket. Birdy had a buzz cut and some punk
rock T-shirt or another. Caroline had a shaved head with
bangs and was also wearing a torn up flannel.

Birdy and I had ditched school, which just meant
staying on the bus past the school to its last stop in
Westwood. We were all eating at Pizza Hut and Aaron,
who was one of the homeless kids, was fucking around and
lighting the torn pieces of Caroline's flannel on fire. She
would pat it out, then tell him to fuck off, no biggie. After a
while we got kicked out. Kicked out for being
different…that or the fact that we had been in there for 2
hours and ordered maybe 3 slices of pizza between 8 of us.
We were pretty much just sitting in there smoking
cigarettes. We must have been a sight. A large group of
punks in 1984 Los Angeles was not a common sight
anywhere but at a punk show. It's not like today where
every kid you see has his hair dyed and piercings or tattoos.

Aaron lit Caroline's flannel on fire again when we
got outside and a gust of wind took that little flame and…
FOOM! She went up like a Christmas tree in March. Public
Service Announcement…. Attention stupid people…
Flannels are flammable!! If that concept is hard to
remember, the two words almost sound the same…
FLANNEL…. FLAMMABLE!!

Birdy and I just stepped back, Andrew jumped in
and tried to pull her flannel off but a tiny flame landed on
him and he freaked the fuck out. Way bigger balls than us
but once he had fire on him he jumped back and started
putting himself out. So now there were flames 2 feet above
Caroline's head going up her back and she was flailing

around basically cooking right in front of us. Some Teamster looking motherfucker pushed through the crowd that had gathered, threw her on the ground and started rolling her around to put out the flames.

At that moment some passing woman saw this full grown man throwing this shaved headed little punk rock girl onto the ground. Not seeing the flames she started beating on the Teamsters back screaming "Leave that girl alone!!" Totally oblivious to the fact that this dude had just saved this girl from a most painful and horrific death. The lady must have smelled the burnt flesh or seen her body smoldering because she ducked out of the crowd real quick as Aaron started running for it himself.

A few minutes later we were saying goodbye to Caroline as they were putting her and her barbequed back into the ambulance just as a cop car with Aaron in it pulled up to the scene. A cop got out to talk to a couple witnesses and held us as well. Aaron was all smiles trying to wave to us with his hands cuffed behind his back. He was one of the homeless kids. I think that was the last time I ever saw him.

Birdy and I took the bus that next week to Westwood ditching school again to see Caroline at the UCLA Medical Center burn ward. After laughing for a bit at the whole crazy scenario and getting the full story of how the doctors had to scrub the melted flannel out of her back, then keep scrubbing the open 3 degree burns twice a day so they didn't scab up and get infected, Birdy and I headed out to all American Burger on Westwood Blvd for some lunch. The only problem was as our elevator was going down, the doors opened and two cops walked in. After a floor or two and some light conversation by the cops, I thought to myself, Fuck! Ok here we go…. 3..2..1.. On cue, one of the cops turned to us and said, "Aren't you boys supposed to be in school right about now?"

If you didn't know the UCLA burn ward has its own version of a jail. Actually it was more of just a room with a desk, a phone and no windows. The cops questioned Birdy first. "What's your name son?" 'John'... "Ok John, what's your last name?" 'Smith.' I busted out laughing. I couldn't help myself. I wasn't prepared for it. He used his real first name so I thought he was just going to fess up but the first thing that popped into his head to trick this officer of the law was the last name Smith???? Maybe his parents did wait too long to have a kid. Fucking retard.

The next thing the cop did was call our school. I knew that Mr. Miller wouldn't be too pissed off at us. He definitely had to give us detention. He could have suspended us but I knew he wouldn't. That was a no brainer. Visiting a friend who was severely burned in the hospital? Now that I think about it... that should have been a free pass.

Birdy and I also had PE together at school one semester and would pretty much bail the class on the same days so we could hang out and smoke cigarettes on the tennis courts. If you know the layout of Paul Revere Jr. High School in Brentwood, you know that the tennis courts are at the farthest end of the school. Up above the banks that can be seen in the Dogtown and Z boys documentary. If they ever repave those bad boys you will know where to find me every Sunday.

The PE teachers had to know we were up their smoking and just didn't care. It wasn't that big a deal. These were the days when Palisades High and actually most high schools had smoking areas for students that were over 18. So one day we were sitting on opposite sides of the court smoking when I pulled out a razor blade and showed it to him. I pretended to cut my jugular and bleed out and we both got a big laugh out of it. Then I went to work cutting a little cross onto the back of my hand that still stands to this day (that was basically my only "cutting" incident and I more did it to be funny.) If I was smart I would have done what some of the other hardcore kids were doing and rubbed some India ink into it and I would have had my first tattoo. I showed Birdy and he laughed then walked over and took the blade from me. He sat back down at the other end of the courts and started to go to work.

Some 20 minutes later, I checked the work he had done and was impressed to see that he had carved the exploited punks not dead, just like it was written on the album cover, into his arm. My little 1-centimeter cross, seemed even sillier after seeing Johns work.

That same PE class, when I did dress up, had a pretty cool benefit. Crystal Rand. She was a year older and unbelievably hot... And sometimes didn't wear a bra or underwear to gym. If she was sitting the right way you could see up her little gym shorts and see her no-no spot in all its glory. There were many of us that took note of Crystal each and every time she walked by. So it wasn't surprising that half the yard was watching her as she crept up behind me at the drinking fountain and pantsed me to my ankles.

Amid thunderous applause I started chasing after her. She was heading back to the girls locker room but had about 50 yards to go. I caught up to her and grabbed the back of her shirt to slow her down, but that worn out cotton shirt just ripped right off into my hand. The applause turned to wide-eyed silence as she ran the rest of the way to the locker room shirtless trying to cover her already ample breastessess. And the towns' people rejoiced. All was well in the valley. I saw her afterward and tried to apologize but she was laughing too hard. She took back the shirt and tossed it into the trash. I am pretty sure I was responsible for many a boner that day.

Back to the classroom I was very much enjoying the girls in my classes as well. Texting being some 20 odd years away, we wrote each other notes on paper, many of which I kept. I could blackmail TV personalities, authors and a slew of soccer moms with some of the shit we wrote to each other. I was writing to a bunch of girls I was crushing on, a couple I felt I was in love with, and a bunch I just wanted to bang. (Which could have been every female at that school including some faculty.)

I was a horny little Scorpio who had just gotten his first chance to take his penis out of the shop. I actually only had sex with a couple of girls from our school and those were more just crimes of opportunity. I did scam on quite a few (yes making out was called scamming for us back then). Ewe!! That sounds really gross now. Sounds like you should take a shower in bleach if someone scammed on you. Anyway, I was in love with Cindee, Kelley, Becki, and Lisa. (Becki was above the rest) I had a crush on Joanna, Traci, Yvette, and Tracy. There were also girls I wrote to that were just friends like Shannon, Katie and a few others.

Many of the letters I still have from these girls are all about having sex with me. Ok maybe I should preface that with the fact that I would just casually throw into a letter something like.. "Hey, we should have sex as friends." So then it would turn into responses from them that said, 'So when are we going to have sex?' Maybe I should be trying out that old gem again. I can't remember the last time I had… nevermind.

Just about every weekend from this time on, someone's parents would be out of town and there would be a party there with plenty of beer (sometimes multi keg parties) lots of pot and many, many pretty girls. One particular party I went to very early on pretty much shot down the whole Hollywood mystique for me. It was a party for a young actor, at an old actor's house. We walked right in the side gate of the party, Mickey looked around and said "Hey look! The fat chick from *Truths of Living* is here." She ran out of the room crying. I felt kind of bad. When I went outside to take a piss later I saw her sitting on a curb crying and telling her friend that she couldn't lose any weight because it was part of her contract.

The parties were great because Madonna's like a virgin had just come out and many of the girls dressed like her and by the end of the year were acting like her too. Parents!! Kids do mimic their idols….. and all us boys could say was "thank you Jesus!" I mean this was nothing like the scandals I've seen lately about kids wearing a certain bracelet signifying the fact that they will do anal, but it came pretty damn close. Madonna was a slut, so some of the 7th grade girls thought this was a cool thing to be. By the end of my 8th grade year, one 7th grade girl sucked a dick, so they all had to do it. Same thing happened at the beginning of my 9th grade year.. One 8th grade girl got laid at a party, and then they all had to do it. I have to tell you it's kind of weird when you hit your sexual peak in Jr. high school.

Some friends and I formed a band around that time that was an answer to the Madonnabie lifestyle. The short lived FSD (yes kids… Fluorescent Socks Denied.) Yeah, we were hardcore (ha). Josh Adam Jason and me on vocals. I still have contact with Josh and Jason thanks to Facebook but I have no idea what happened to Adam. The only original song we did was about a club that was at 321 Santa Monica Blvd called …321. If you want to know what 321 was just picture Breakin' 2: Electric Boogaloo, the dance club years.

Chapter 5-B

Hitting The Clubs

Michele still liked mod and ska music but she was way into her own grove. She listened to reggae, punk and anything that she thought rocked... You could hear the Damned, the Sex Pistols, Siouxsie and the Banshees the Smiths the Dickies or any number of other bands playing in her room. She would make mixed tapes off of KXLU and Rodney on the ROQ. She would request songs then tape them on her stereo. Her style was ever evolving.

Besides dying it she began tying shredded rags into her hair as well. Weekly trips to the thrift shop trying out every crazy thing she could think of doing. Cat eyed glasses, little flapper hats from the 20's vintage mink stoles. When she dressed up as Cruella DeVille from 101 Dalmatians one Halloween, she didn't even need to go out and buy a thing for her outfit. She was the coolest. It all worked.. ..and if it hadn't worked, she wouldn't have cared.

She was oblivious to the fact that some people saw her as crazy. All she was concerned with was living, and loving life.

Then, one day I came home and she had a crazy look in her eye. She told me she had found a new band that was the gnarliest band she had ever heard. She played me the first track by a local L.A. band called the Red Hot Chili Peppers. The song, "True Men Don't… Kill Coyotes". This band had the hardest hitting punk funky bass lines I had ever heard in my life. I had heard solid popping bass lines in funk before that had intrigued me, but this was something completely new. It was almost like the bass lines were battling the guitar solos for dominance. Most previous bass I had heard kept the beat. This music kept it, wrapped it up in barbed wire and jammed it down your throat!

Michele took me and our neighbor Rob to my first of many Chili Peppers shows soon after at Fenders Ballroom in Long Beach. Fenders was a great place to see a show because it felt like you were watching your favorite bands in a friends basement. If you went inside, closed your eyes and ran straight forward, you would bash your shins on the stage. That place made the Whisky in Hollywood look like the Coliseum.

The Chili Peppers had been signed not long before, so there were EMI promos for the band all over the place, some of which I still have. I think it was their record release party. They played after Channel 3 and Cathedral of Tears. When the Peppers took the stage the energy was unreal and I was hooked. I read a review in the LA Reader not long after, that described their sound as "bone crushing mayhem funk". That pretty much summed them up for me.

Michele and I saw lots of their shows together. One show I didn't go to was at the Roxy on Sunset. It was a show still promoting their first album. Michele went to the show, then went back the next day and asked the manager if she could have the posters that were up in the window.

81

The guy sold 2 of them to her for 5 bucks each. I have the one she gave me framed in my living room.

Power Tools.

One of the first of the new breed of big LA underground nightclub hotspots was club Power Tools….and no it wasn't a gay leather bar. It got that name because it started in a rented warehouse downtown that had a sign out front that said "Power Tools". They ended up moving around a lot because the city kept shutting them down. It was one of those places that you sometimes didn't know where to go until you met someone in a parking lot and they told you where it would be that night. Michele and her friends would say they were sleeping at someone's house then just go all-night and party, occasionally bringing her little brother with her. I'm not sure if it was 21 and over or not, but I remember getting in sometimes and not getting in others.

If you made it inside you could see famous actors, musicians and nobodies alike all rubbing elbows. This was before TMZ, bottle service and VIP rooms made those big Hollywood clubs kind of shitty unless you were famous or knew someone. "I'm a total douche who's on a horrible reality show that glorifies the worst in humanity, so me and my entourage of total fuck nuts get priority in this dump over everyone else." Power Tools was the exact opposite. They had VIP rooms but if I remember correctly anyone could go in them and were encouraged to do so.

After a while, Power Tools settled down into the Park Plaza Hotel, which sounds much more glamorous than it was. First of all it was across the street from MacArthur Park. Back then MacArthur Park was one of the most dangerous places in all of Los Angeles. Second of all, the old gothic looking hotel was basically falling apart.

Michele took me to what was probably my favorite Chili Peppers show there with Rob and some other people. They got right in and this time Michele couldn't sweet talk her way into getting her brother in. She looked at me and said "Good luck!" I was on my own.

There was no way I was going to miss this show, so I had to figure out a way to get inside. The Park Plaza looked more like a castle or a gothic fortress than anything else. If you were able to walk through the front door you would be greeted by 30 ft. ceilings and a marble staircase leading up to the main room. On each side were banquet rooms that could serve at least a couple hundred people each. The rooms were blocked off with giant oak tables flanked by chairs on both sides.

First, I snuck past the security guarding the outside of the building. Once past them I found a broken window that I could silently pull the glass out of. Once inside I made my way to the banquet room and hid behind a curtain. I could see the promise land and almost taste it, but could also see the security guards watching the crowd and the banquet area. Then I noticed the pattern. They didn't want anybody going near the banquet area and stopped most people before they could make it to the chairs to sit and smoke. Once the guards were looking the other way I made my move.

I ran as fast as I could, stepped on a chair, put two hands down on the table and vaulted over the about 4 feet of barrier and landed right in one of the chairs on the other side. As I was landing, one of the security guards turned around and yelled "Hey!! You can't sit over there!! Get back inside!" WOOHOO, I'M IN!!

The Butthole Surfers played first. They had been around for a while and were doing some interpretational shit that my 14 year old brain couldn't comprehend. Either that or it just sucked. All I remember is the singer standing in front of two tom toms beating the shit out of them with clothespins in his hair. During their big finale he shook his head back and forth really hard and showered the crowd with them.

When the Chili Peppers started up I made it to the front of the stage, right in front of Flea. His bass playing was so fucking amazing I always had to be right in front of him so I could rock out to the fullest. Michele having the world's biggest crush on him would always be right there too. So I was right next to her when they started playing. We were losing our minds jumping around like maniacs. I saw a shoe on stage so I threw it at the drum kit. Michele yelled something at me and punched me like 5 times in the arm. Ooops! I just threw away her shoe. I don't know if you've ever lost a shoe at a punk show, but it's a great way to get Hepatitis C or spend the night getting stiches at the emergency room (or both).

Michele actually got Fleas attention and got him to try to get her shoe back. It was hilarious. He couldn't find it. They had a running dialogue going for almost a minute while the band was waiting to play their next song. "Over here??" 'No its over there!!' .... "Over here??"...... 'No back there!!' He finally found it behind the drum kit brought it out and handed it to her while the rest of the band was wondering what the fuck is going on.

The stage had this intricate arch that went from the floor to the ceiling. About half way through the show I think it was Dave Navarro from Jane's Addiction (they used to play the club before anyone knew who they were) started to climb up it. He got to the top up above the band and got stuck. He was up there the rest of the show. He was up there till the lights came on. I have no idea how they finally got his dumb ass down.

On the way back to the car I ran ahead because I was so full of adrenaline I couldn't contain myself. I ran into two Latin gentlemen who jumped up and asked me, "What set you from?" Now remember, this was the early

80's; Dr, Dre was still dancing around in a sequined doctors outfit and a brand new Music TeleVision station (actually only played music videos back then) was just playing songs like Kajagoogoo's "Too Shy Shy", so the ways of the hood hadn't yet successfully infiltrated the suburbs. I replied 'What???' "What gang you from man, what set?" 'Ehh.... None? I live by the beach, I just came to see a show.' I'm surprised I made it out unscathed. People would get mugged or stabbed on those side streets on a nightly basis. When Michele and Rob and the crew caught up we hit the green machine (moms van) and made a beeline for home.

For people who didn't grow up in the 1980's or earlier, the world was a much bigger place. There wasn't the free flow of information that the Internet age allows. Nightly news moved relatively rapidly but was basically 3 channels competing over the same 5 stories they could fit into the national news hour. Every other story and culturally significant event moved at a snails pace. There was no 24 hour news cycle. As a matter of fact, after about 2 AM, television turned off! They said, "That has been your broadcasting day... goodnight." Then that color bar came up and all you heard was.. a high pitched.. booooooooooooooooo.

Not long after the Power Tools show, Michele took me to one of the greatest gigs of my life. 45 Grave, Social Distortion and the Damned at the Santa Monica Civic Auditorium. If you like punk rock and zombie movies and have never seen *The Return of the Living Dead*... SEE IT!!! 45 Grave, the Cramps, TSOL, and The Damned among others lend their sounds to the movie. Oh and Linnea Quigley dancing naked with her blood red short hair in the graveyard was one of the hottest things this little kid had ever seen.... and still ever saw!!! It didn't hurt that she

85

was still butt naked when zombies came out of the ground and ate her on a vault.

So we walked into the Civic and were greeted by Dinah Cancer of 45 Grave singing "Do ya wanna party?! Its party time!" And oh yes…. party time it was. After 45 Grave, Social Distortion came out. They played everything they could have possibly played. I was standing on the stage in front of one of the side stacks of speakers. It was easy to get on the stage because there were no barricades back in those days. Most shows, like the ones at the Civic, relied on large quick footed bouncers that kneeled by the edge of the stage like Wimbledon Tennis, ball boys waiting for someone to linger on the stage to long. See, stage diving was fine. It was standing up there like you were part of the band was not. So if you reached for the mic or just stood there like an asshole, they would chuck you back into the crowd. Not like today, where if you make it over the barricades, the yellow jackets immediately throw you out the side door and your show is over.

So while in front of the roughly 8 foot tall speakers, this skinhead kept climbing up to the top, then jumping off feet first wearing what appeared to be steel toed combat boots. I couldn't believe what a fucking dick this guy was. This asshole was damaging people. Then this old guy standing next to me (he had to have been at least 20. Lined himself up underneath the skinhead and swung his foot out football kicker style right when the skinhead jumped. Now I know you can see a million nut shots on the interwebs but I am hear to tell you… this was the greatest nut shot of all time. He almost came to a complete stop when that dudes foot came into contact with Mr. skins skins. The scrotal assault of the century to be sure.

One of Social Distortions last songs was "Telling them." The guitar started playing, everyone went apeshit, then once the band all joined in I couldn't sit still any longer. Time for my own stage dive. Unlike Mr. dickhead skinhead I ran across the stage and dove head first and rolled part way into a summersault so I would easily land on top of the crowd. From there I would get carried overhead until an opening let me get my feet back to the floor. Those few seconds you are on top of the crowd you really get the best view of the band you've had the entire night. Too bad it never lasts that long.

The Damned headlined the show and they were incredible. A first generation punk rock band cut from the same cloth as the sex pistols the clash the dead boys and the like. They were the one of the few punk bands back then that had a truly theatrical stage show. Fog machines, Dave Vanian wearing a cape and black makeup, Captain Sensible wearing bright red pants white sunglasses and a Scottish golf hat. Even punk rock bands had some kind of uniformity to them. These guys were all over the place. Rat Scabies banging away on the drums wearing a full length black sparkled tuxedo coat.... it was unreal. And the music... the music you just need to hear for yourself.

I soon found Michele by way of the pit. It was not called a mosh pit back then and if you ask me, whoever came up with that name needs to be beaten with a sock full of nickels.... THE SLAM PIT!!! That's what they were called. If you are ever with a punk or someone who was into the scene back then and you somehow bring up anything related to a show and describe the pit as a mosh pit, you will be forever seen in that persons eyes as a knucklehead. They will know that at best you are someone who started paying attention to that kind of music after some Limp Biscuit or Corn show you went to in the mid 90's. Needless to say, all musical conversations you have with this person, they will take them with a grain of salt. Anyway, the PIT at an early punk show is one of the most amazing phenomena's I have ever experienced. Pure controlled aggression.

Addicted To Tragedy

(I recently heard one of the members of Bad Brains say that they started the term Moshing. If that's true then its more legit than I thought but that term wasn't used by anybody in the LA punk scene in the early to mid 80's. I still cringe when I hear it.)

The Slam Pit

Let me first take a moment to describe the perfection of fluid energy that was the slam pit. For it to reach its full potential, it has to be in a bigger venue (like the Santa Monica Civic). If it has the numbers and the room to grow it can turn into an F5 tornado. Pure adrenaline, pure rage, pure fury, but as fluid as a river you stopped to soak your toes in. Everybody moving in one direction exuding as much energy as they have. Arms flailing legs stomping…. Sometimes you go with the flow; sometimes you try to go against the grain (never successful for long). That's like peeing in the wind; you might try to tough it out for a minute but at some point you are going to have to turn around. At best you can stay swimming in one place…..at worst you end up searching the ground for your teeth at the end of the show because you read somewhere that if they got knocked out whole, you could put 'em back in and they just might stick. Only problem is you might find a tooth, but odds are it wont be yours.

If a man goes down (or woman for that matter) immediately hands go down to bring the fallen to their feet. If that man stays down everyone will trip over him and 1 will turn into dozens in a second. In my eyes it is perfection of the human condition. Mass output of human energy coupled with survival instinct of the whole and progression of the mass. It's truly a beautiful thing.

The pit always went in a counter clockwise direction. I wonder if it goes in the opposite direction in the southern hemisphere like toilets and drains? Some of the kids were cranked on speed, but I will attest to the fact that it was not necessary. Some pent up rage that needed an outlet will do just fine. 14 years of Dick worked for me.... Ok let me rephrase that, 14 years of living with Dick did it for me. Any way, pits kind of lost their luster when Nazi skins started to come to shows standing at the edge of the pit and punched people in the face as they went by. They would come from Orange County or the Valley just to get into fights. Lots of riots fewer shows and a bunch of bullshit pretty much killed that part of the era for me.

In the later 80's lots of shows would be cancelled because of skinheads fighting or any other number of gangs. Some riots were fun, when it was the punks against the cops. Those were the way it should be. As a young punk kid there was nothing better to battle against. But that punks against punks stuff was just the dumbest shit ever. Thanks, kill the scene...great idea. Every venue is going to want to have shows when all their windows are kicked out half way through the night. Fucking dickheads.

There are many coincidences going on with my writing. Two nights ago I went to the first of three Goldenvoice 30th anniversary shows and saw X and Social Distortion. I think all the same people were there from that Damned show in 1984 because I felt young. If they had all gone on the road together they could have called it the Balding Walker Crutch and Wrinkle tour.

I have been to a lot of Social Distortion shows over the years. I even wanted to be Mike Ness when I was a little kid. I don't remember them playing that first album at all for the last 20 years. I'm not sure what the deal with that is. There has to be some kind of story there but it just seems like pulling teeth to get that guy to play any of it.

The 30th anniversary show they started with the air raid siren RRRRRRRRRRRRRRRRrrrrrrrrrrrrr (everyone knew what was coming....) ATOM BOMB!!! It was a short set, but they probably played 90% of that first album. Many people in the crowd must have felt the same way I did because every time they played songs off their first album, all you could see was a sea of smart phones recording the song. Every time they played something new…. they all went away. It was pretty fucking funny.

Since I heard Michele playing Social Distortions Mommy's Little Monster, they have been my favorite band. That is my favorite punk record, and probably means the most to me. Even having said that….. and the fact that they played so much of that first album….. the night belonged to X. John Doe Excene Cervanka and Billy Zoom were just absolutely killing it. What a fucking show. It was truly amazing. Another cool thing was they were auctioning stuff off for charity and one prize, valued at 1000 dollars (not sure how they got that number) was 10 original Goldenvoice flyers, 7 of which I own myself. They also had a poster sized PIL Olympic flyer (which I also own) advertising the show. That whole thing seriously made me feel like a kid again.

L.A. Street Scene Music Festival.

Fuck Coachella!!! And you young punks stay off my lawn!! More than 500 bucks a ticket for 3 days of crap bands with maybe one or two you might want to see that are no doubt playing at the same time?? No thanks!

Before Coachella… before the warped tour…before even Lollapalooza… we had the LA Street Scene. That is my gold standard for what a music festival should be. There were like 15 bands playing on multiple stages on the streets of downtown Los Angeles and it couldn't have cost more than 10 bucks to get in. I want to use the word alternative to describe some of these bands because punk or ska couldn't cover them. Now, it's hard to use that term because alternative is what has become the mainstream.

90

Back then, you had all your standard genres. Rock through classical. Punk, being still only a grade schooler, was evolving and turning out shit that couldn't really be classified.... and the best of it was coming right out of LA.
.

Not only did you get to see raw punk in the streets by bands like Nip Drivers and Agent Orange, but you could have also checked out Jackson brown, a beat box contest, Buddy Rich, Richard Pryor, a rap battle, a dance contest, Chris Iasac, a goat milking/clown show and about 20 more acts and bands (and if not for a riot that started during Fishbone, The Circle Jerks and Fear). That was September 28th 1985. The next year we got all that, and our 10 bucks also brought us front and center for Jane's Addiction, Fishbone, the Untouchables, and a special guest that we knew would be there.. The Red Hot Chili Peppers.

We drove downtown with Rob, super excited for the show. For Michele, that meant dancing her ass down the sidewalk. For people of my generation I will ask you, for your own understanding of my sister, not to picture Molly Ringworm dancing on a table in *The Breakfast Club*. Rather picture people on the side walk quickly getting out of the crazy girl, dancing like she's all alone in her bedroom's way because someone that strange in downtown LA just might whip out a knife and go all stab-happy on you.
Then, eyes closed, she unknowingly danced right up to a veteran of the streets Vato, with his wife and kid in a stroller. Zoot suit pants half way up his wife beater, suspenders, thin chain down to his knees, with a hair net and tattoos (tattoos being pretty much the domain of sailors, gangsters, bikers, and prisoners at that time).
Michele spun out of a move and stopped right in front of the family. The Vato put his arm up to make sure she didn't fall into them and replied with a simple, "Excuse

me homes"..... Now.. on its face that is a nothing moment... But Michele turned and looked at me with the biggest smile you could imagine and utter excitement on her face. I totally got it, and I will never forget it.

See, someone had used the term properly, outside of the confines of our little white bread community. We kidded around, talking like that all the time.... This time it.. was real... it was a legitimate use of the phrase, by someone who should be using it...and Michele was so excited. Not practice use of the phrase like we did with each other all the time.. "Aaaeeehh homes... come 'ere homes... get off me homes." Mimicking Cheech and Chong.. This time it was legit. No other words were spoken; we all knew, and we all laughed.

Michele got that excited look a lot. She loved living and loved experiencing new things...and didn't hide her excitement. I think it was pretty much around this time that I realized what it was and what it meant. Being beaten down by Dick (lets not forget Dick) kept me from being comfortable with the crazy out of control happy energy that Michele lived. Her unbridled energy no longer embarrassed me or made me uncomfortable like it did in elementary school. Now I wasn't just comfortable with it, I fucking loved it!

So we found our way into an underground bar and bought some 32 oz beers, had a couple of those, then made our way into the Street Scene itself. I had figured out the quickest way to get us through any crowds we encountered. I would simply yell out "woman with a baby!" (which there were many). The crowd would part and through we would go. Even if they got pissed there was little they could do because we were already long gone.

I was a little buzzed from the beer and about 15 years old, but this is what I remember. We saw Fishbone, Jane's Addiction and the Untouchables. We had to run between stages because I think Fishbone and Jane's overlapped by a little bit. The Red Hot Chili Peppers being the surprise guest played toward the end of the night... and they went off!! It was an amazing show. Anthony Kiedis, Hillel and Flea were more than up for the challenge and threw down an earth-shattering performance on the streets of Downtown Los Angeles. Michele had a camera and in the middle of jamming during a song Flea looked right at her camera..... still popping and thumping his bass, and smiled ear to hear for a picture. What a show... they absolutely killed it!

Riots can start for any number of reasons. I think this one started not during a punk show, but during of all bands Midnight Oil. Not a crowd favorite apparently. First beer cups started flying out of the crowd at the stage.... then some scattered bottles that had been snuck in.... then too few riot cops tried to break up the crowd with no success... and then all hell broke loose. The riot cops were chased off and the punks celebrated their victory by trashing anything they could get their hands on. All the while the riot cops were regrouping with reinforcements and planning their attack.

If you could promise me a full on battle royal with cops after seeing bands like that on the streets of Downtown Los Angeles.. I might shell out a couple hundred bucks just to bear witness. But it has to be that good old apocalyptic, kids vs. cops type of shit. No prisoners taken by the cops accept the ones that were too badly injured to run away. I had never been hit in the face by a horse, but after seeing the Mounties roll right over and straight trample people; I didn't want to find out how it felt. I didn't see any ambulances for the injured, just Paddy wagons. (After fact checking I am not sure that I might have gotten this riot confused with another from around the same time) Hey, I'm part Irish, shouldn't I be offended by the term paddy wagon? Shouldn't I have some ginger Jesse

Jackson suing the police department for racial insensitivity? (I had a 40 potatoes and a whiskey joke in there but I don't have enough Indian in me to feel comfortable making holocaust or slavery jokes so I cut it)

Michele had followed the Chili Peppers to the point that she was getting invited to parties they were going to. She even played me an answering machine message from Anthony telling her to come to a party with her friends and to bring their "most edible undies." This was very soon after the Chili Peppers had released there second album *Freaky Styley.*

Somehow, someway, Michele found out they were making a video for the song "Catholic School Girls Rule" and got some friends of hers and me to be in it. (I brought my friend Brandon) Overnight I found myself standing on the basketball courts of the Chili's alma mater Fairfax High School. Most of the scenes there were just of Michele and the other catholic schoolgirls doing what they do; jumping rope, playing hopscotch, hula hooping and just running around like crazy. Then for some scenes they were singing the chorus.

Here's a little trivia for you. If you see the video, the first and second time you see the catholic schoolgirls, the middle one is Keith Morris of the Circle Jerks and Black Flag (Flag) in drag. Anthony wasn't at the shoot, but technically, I was hanging out with Flea, Hillel Slovak and Keith Morris... How fucking cool is that!!!

So the chicks were doing their thing and they wanted some cutaway shots, so Flea started improv-ing some freak out scenes at the little hotties just beyond the fence.... and I was standing just off camera! Best day ever right???? But wait.... There's more.

The second part of the day we went to a studio that was done up like the inside of a catholic church. This was our part. Just about every time they are playing the chorus, you see 6 choirboys, me, Brandon, Gene, Steve, Tim, and Phil. As the song begins, the camera rolls down the isle to focus on us singing, "Catholic… school girls rule… Catholic school girls rule!" (I'm in the middle of the back row.) They were also filming scenes of the churchgoers dancing in the isle. You can see Michele pretty clearly in a couple of those. They also had a bedroom scene where Michele, Allison, and some other girl were all filmed falling over each other laughing and fighting over a playgirl magazine. During that time I was pretty much done filming and was just hanging around the set.

I was tripping out on how fucking cool this whole thing Michele had hooked me up with was, when two guys walked by talking about how they wanted to smoke a joint. Now, I knew I was only 15, but I also knew I looked older and would probably never have an opportunity like this again so I spoke up. "Can I come with you guys??" Flea turned around and said, 'Sure'. Oh did I not mention that the "guys" were Flea and DH Peligro, drummer for the Dead Kennedys? At that point in my life.. and maybe even today, if I could have hung out with any musical figure and smoked a joint and shot the shit, it would have been Flea.

After hanging out and smoking a "gorilla finger of indo" as Flea called it, we all got up totally baked and spilled out of this small sound room like we just fell out of Jeff Spicoli's van in the Ridgemont High School parking lot. (*Fast Times at Ridgemont High,* 1982)Totally cracking up and bumping into each other with smoke billowing out behind us. We were still in the hall of the studio and we walked past an open door where an Asian guy was thumping and popping his bass. He was good.

We stopped and watched for a second, then Flea asked him if he could try his bass. He played a smooth line with some funk at the end. Then he handed the bass back. The other guy upped the ante and played a little more complicated riff then handed the bass back to Flea. What

95

unfolded was one of the most epic bass battles the world has ever known. DH and I were just absolutely mesmerized. By the end there was hooting and hollering and high fives all the way around. We were all jumping up and down and I was just another one of the boys. Thank you!!! Thank you Michele! Thank you again for another one of the best moments of my life.

So the end of 8th grade and the summer after was a combination of going to punk shows with my sister, and hanging out in Santa Monica canyon at Takeos house. I was skating and surfing as much as I could and living every day to the fullest! I'd like to read that back to myself… one moment please…. Yes indeed. 1984-85 was pretty much the greatest year of my life so far…. but it has to get better. I'm only 14 years old! I have so much more to look forward to!!!!

Chapter 6

Outsiders, Acid, & Grease

9th grade came around and now being the older kid, I felt like I could do no wrong.

I remembered well the ribbing I had gotten from the older kids when I showed up to school wearing mod and ska stuff and band shirts in the 7th grade, then punk rock stuff later on. I got it… it kind of sucked, but like I said, usually not too mean spirited. Besides, Michele had gotten some of the same shit from the same people as I did. Now there were 3 people I teased a little bit, and I do mean only a little bit. One of them was a year younger and his name was Mitchie. I didn't give him too much shit but just enough to make him apparently want to kill me. I do remember calling him a punk rock mon-chi-chi. Remember those things??? "Mon-chi-chi Monchichi, oh so soft and cuddly…" Ok, maybe I did need my ass kicked. I couldn't help it! He was a dead ringer for one of those damn things!

The other two were in my grade, John de Salvo and Mark Fox. Now I had seen Mark Fox the last day of school in 8th grade. He was wearing his trademark penny loafers complete with penny, argyle socks, khaki shorts, pink polo shirt and a sweater, wrapped "tad" style around his neck.

First day of 9th grade he came in as hardcore punk looking as you could possibly be. Shaved head, spiked leather jacket, combat boots complete with chains and rags, flannel around his waist and cool guy attitude like you wouldn't believe….. It was like he looked at the cartoon guy on the circle jerks album and used him as his new fashion consultant; and the new kid, Johnny fishface de Salvo. Dude looked like a fish. A grouper or a big mouthed bass or some shit like that… and for some reason they had it out for me!!

I couldn't have cared less and would respond to any sneering I got from tweedle dee and tweedle dipshit with a quick "what happened to the top siders?? I like you much better in the pink polo's. I don't want you to get a cut from those spikes you got there, make sure you be careful now sunshine."

I apparently had a roll of confidence going, which Mark did not. Even he and his fish faced cohort together couldn't mount any kind of offence beyond giving me some aggressive stink eye. Having been raised by the king of stink eye they had no chance of bugging me in any way shape or form.

That was the extent of my "bullying" of those two. I will say however that an older kid was on the bus once and he was a Mexican greaser, straight out of the outsiders. John was standing and He and I were sitting when the greaser looked over at me and said, "Should I hit him??" (Nodding to John) I want to say my response was 'Whatever' but it very well could have been 'Sure.' John got hit in the stomach, looked away, held back tears like a champ, and I felt like a world-class piece of shit. It had such an affect on me that I can remember it like it was yesterday. I should have said 'Hell no! Leave that fucking retard alone.'

I never saw either one of them after 9th grade but apparently I had planted the seed of deep-seated hatred in Mark that he must have watered on a daily basis until it grew into a mighty oak of pure unadulterated hate. Had that hate filled tree been felled and used for lumber, it might have built an entire city of hate. Had that tree been mulched and used for fuel, it could have powered a rocket of hate to the furthest reaches of the hate nebula…. Sorry just wanted to see how far I could take that one. Now this didn't end well for Mark and not by my doing.

I think It was sometime in 11th grade, Mark brought a bunch of older Hollywood punks he had befriended in the years since we met. There must have been 9 or 10 of them, definitely two carloads. They showed up at a huge party where I was supposed to be. It was a party that everyone from the Palisades was at, but I wasn't. Now when the party was breaking up, Mark dressed up like a cartoon villain, was waiting for the cars to come down the street. He had on a black leather trench coat, cane in hand, friends in tow, and was pounding on every car as it got jammed up by a stop sign at the end of the street. "WHERE IS MICHAEL FRIEDLANDER?!!!!" DO YOU KNOW MICHAEL FRIEDLANDER???!!!

Unfortunately for Mark, he pounded on my friend Josh's older brothers car. Now Josh's older brother was two years older, but still smaller than me. He had just happened to be giving his friends, the Yamamoto brothers a ride home. The Yamamoto brothers were even more badass then they sound. Being raised around all white people they were schooled on martial arts from a very young age. Their patriarch wasn't going to have any of his children picked on by the white kids in the neighborhood so those kids were raised on the art of beating ass.

Mark pounded on the hood of his car, "Do you know Michael Friedlander??" D's brother said 'yeah that guys my brothers friend' Then Marks famous last words... "Get out of the car!" All 4 brothers jumped out, 'Yeah we know Michael Friedlander...what up!?!'and so began the beating at cold mountain. (I wanna saaaay top of Kenter Canyon?)

This is all hearsay but I heard it only lasted a minute, which is forever when you are in a fight, but what is not in dispute is that Mark, and all of his friends were laid out on the ground. To the point that they had to drag these guys out of the street so the cars could make it by. Cane, broken... bones, broken...blood, flowing. I wish I were there to see it. I never saw or heard of Mark again.

This one I'll have to talk to my cousin Andrew about. My cousin Andrew grew up on Rialto in Venice. He was about 4 years older than me, so he was a young teenager there in the late 70's. He knew or went to school with all the guys that would eventually become pretty serious gangsters.

Apparently my "punk rock monchichi" comments were not appreciated by Mitchie. He informed me that his friends were coming to school on Friday to beat my ass.. I believed him. I called cousin Andrew, told him the date and time and asked him if he could help me out. I didn't show up to school that day but my cousin and his van full of Venice OG's did. Now I have to check with Andrew because my memory is a little hazy on this one. One of two things happened; Either Andrew drove up, all his homies jumped out and all of Mitchies friends ran for the hills. Or more than likely Mitchies friends were the younger generation Venice gangsters, and my cousin had brought the older. Then laughter and high fives were thrown all around. I'm pretty sure that's what happened because Mitchie did become a pretty serious Venice gangster and everything was mysteriously cool after that.

Because surfing and skating was so important to me when I was growing up, I have to say a quick word about the scene. Back then, surfers and some skaters were extremely territorial. If there was 15 miles of beach break, or a big place to skate that wasn't a bust, you could pretty much be anyone and go there and ride.

When you are talking about a jetty or a small break, or a skate spot like the pavilion in Venice, you might get your ass beat or worse if you are fucking around down there. I was quick to throw around my cousins' name and nickname. "I'm cool, Wamba's my cousin. Conan's my cousin." I was only 14 or 15 but it wasn't uncommon for five 20 year olds to throw a 15 year old a beating because he didn't belong there. I'd go down there with him on occasions when you knew a lot of skaters would be there. I saw Christian Hosoi (who Takeo was childhood friends with) Scott Oster, Jesse Martinez, Aaron Murray, Chris Cook and Eric Dressen among others, skate down there.

I would like to say I skated with them but I pretty much only skated with Eric Dressen. He grew up in the Palisades and was friends with Michele. I had skated with him many times at Palisades Elementary and we went to Paul Revere together. We reconnected in the mid 90's and still hang out on occasion. He is tattooing in Hollywood now right down the street from my work. Maybe its time for some more ink.

Besides these two instances, being bullied in elementary school and treated like shit by my stepfather kept me pretty grounded once I started to have a lot of friends. One girl named Marilynn made it a point to tell me just a couple years ago, how much it meant to her that she saw me as a popular boy and that I was nice to her. She was tall and a little awkward and had some pretty frizzy hair. I saw some guys tease her so I reached out to her and was nice to her just because I could relate to her pain and I wanted her to know she was not alone..... Ok if your bullshit meter is going off you are only partially correct. That stuff was true, but I could also tell this chick was going to be smoking hot when she grew up and I was right!

When I first got to Paul Revere I became pretty good friends with a guy that I would be good friends with for a long time named Chuck. Chuck was in Michele's grade and was friends with her too. She inspired Chuck to loose the Mark Fox 1.0 gear (purple polo's etc) and had a pretty big influence on his life just like mine. He was used to a house where you can't sit on the furniture and he had a stepmom-ster instead of a Dick.

He picked up that license to be anything you want and ran with it. So by my 9th grade year we were really good friends. Now I could write a hundred stories about the booze and drug fun that we have had together, but that would be another book. Most of it was harmless, weed and beer.. Sometimes hard liquor, rarely cocaine, super rarely hallucinogens. The later I will write about here. I mean, you can't write about growing up in the 80's without a couple stories about LSD.

9th grade; LSD

Chuck and I decided to see Disney's Fantasia at the Beverly Plaza on two hits of purple pyramid. We ate the acid and got into chucks shitty yellow pickup truck with about 3 other people, one of whom is a cop now. This was back when it was legal to have unrestrained passengers in the back of a truck in the state of California. We pulled up to the Beverly Plaza, parked, and went straight to the video games. After playing for a while I realized that I was totally coming on. The last movie had just let out so we were swimming through an ocean of people on our way to sit and wait for the next show.

On the way into the movie there was an old man walking out with a cane and it fucking looked like this guy was melting right in front of me. His skin was dripping off and making a pool around him on the floor. I knew I was hallucinating so I was keeping it together, but I couldn't take my eyes off him. I was coming up to him from the side so I could only see one half of his face. Then in passing each other he turned his head and I saw the other half of his face. He must have had some kind of lip cancer because the lips and lower cheek on the left side of his face were gone. All you could see was his teeth from the front all the way to the back molars. Scarred up tissue and a big smile was all I saw. I screamed as loud as I could. It scared the shit out of me. This dude was a monster and I knew that I was really seeing what I was seeing. I would have probably been less freaked out if the crypt keeper sat down next to me and asked me for some of my popcorn.

Chuck and the older guys I was with covered my mouth and dragged me into the movie and we found a place near the front to sit. We walked past rows of rocking theater seats and ornate couches; it looked more like an Opera house than a movie theater. Everything inside the place was red. So to me it looked like the walls were bleeding. Now I'm not an advocate for LSD (although I think it should be mandatory for every person on the planet to eat hallucinogenic mushrooms or peyote to expand their mind at some point in their lives) but that was one of the radest experiences ever. That movie was made for tripping.

After the alligators danced with the hippos and you actually got to see the face of Satan, the movie let out and we jumped into the back of chucks truck for the drive home. Future cop, me and this guy Richard decided to smoke a bowl on the ride home. As we were riding and smoking we suddenly realized a cop was following us. I thought out loud, if he hasn't pulled us over, he must have not seen us blazing.

You have to understand we were facing him in the back of the very small bed of a small truck. We were less than 10 feet away, looking right at each other, fried out of our minds. Just then, as if we couldn't be any more freaked out, Rich noticed aloud that it was a k-9 unit. He can smell it! All I could think was we are so busted!!!

Chuck had to have seen him by this point. He had to be tripping just as hard as I was as well. He made a turn onto a small street and the cop followed him. Right then I thought the world was going to end and I was resigned to spending the rest of my life high on LSD in jail. Chuck slowed down and pulled to the side of the road as the cop slowed, then punched it around us and took off to what must have been a more important call. Scared shitless we all screamed and high fived and freaked out at the fact that we didn't get busted then made our way back to the Palisades.

Then as we were driving down San Vicente, the whole cop thing must have gotten the best of old Rich. He started standing up in the back of the truck pounding on the roof of the cab and yelling at Chuck to slow down. That must have made driving while frying on LSD very difficult.

Chuck yelled back "I'm doing 35 miles an hour!" This was when the speed limit on this part of San Vicente was still 45. Now, if you want to get pulled over while driving on acid, there are a few ways you can go. You can speed, which will draw attention to you. Or you can drive 10 to 15 miles per hour under the speed limit, which will attract much more attention.

It quickly deteriorated into Rich demanding to be dropped off at home. We tried to talk him out of it, telling him his parents were going to know he was frying his balls off, to no avail. We got back to his house by driving slowly on side streets so he wouldn't start freaking out again. We pulled up to his folk's house and could see them through the kitchen window.

We asked him one more time to change his mind, but as soon as we stopped he was out of the truck and walking up his front steps. It was like watching an accident about to happen. You know it's happening but there's nothing you can do about it. He walked into the kitchen where his parents were and I think he just grabbed the first thing he saw and started to mess with it. It might have been because he was a Brit or that it was the first thing that he saw, but he started to make tea. We watched his parents close in, checking out his pupils, then freak out on him as we bailed. Note to kids out there, no matter how bad a trip you are having, going home and making tea with the folks is not going to make it any better.

The next story involves some more purple LSD during the same year. Chuck picked me up from Paul Revere and we drove with 2 carloads of guys to Disneyland. Now I was tall for 9th grade, but I was one of the shortest guys that went that night. The only guy shorter than me was a guy named John. He was also the only one not frying on acid as well. So from personal experience, back then if you went to the happiest place on earth with an anarchy shirt on and a mohawk, you were denied entrance. But if you went with a bunch of fried out of their mind giants, its "Right this way gentlemen."

The whole trip somehow turned into a bunch of jokes about John. Right before we started going on rides we went into the bathroom because I had to pee. There are two things that you don't want to do when frying on acid. Look in the mirror, and watch yourself pee. I looked down because I freaked out looking in the mirror and saw instead of one stream, what looked like 20 simultaneous streams of urine. Ok, this rides no fun! I don't need to see that, off to adventures thru inner space (the People Mover).

The People Mover is a very slow ride. The coolest part for us was when we entered the room with the giant eyeball looking through the microscope at us. John decided to stand on top of the car and act like an asshole. So as we were tripping on all the molecules flashing around the room we saw John loose his footing and fall off the ride. You just heard his cry 'AAAaaaahhh, then a good two count, before you heard him hit what sounded like a stack of metal poles then several other unknown surfaces, then the ground.

If you don't know, sometimes the smallest things are funny when you are on those kinds of drugs. This was not a small thing. We were dying we were laughing so hard. We laughed the rest of the ride, got off, and then laughed hysterically at the exit of the ride. Just when the laughter started to die down, a service door opened right next to us and John spilled out, shirt torn, covered in blood grease and dirt and the laughter began all over again. John being fully into the new wave Ton Sur Ton fashion, was wearing all light colored clothes so every grease spot and blood stain looked like it had a spot light on it.

A few years after our Disneyland acid trip, the park got into trouble because the People Mover had a small model of the ride on the side of the building that only had white people riding it. Too be fair to Disneyland it was a pretty white bread ride. Moved super slow not very exciting. Unless you were frying on acid and your friend almost kills himself.

Space Mountain was the next ride we rode. An indoor roller-coaster in the dark. It was fun as hell but all we could do is crack up because whoever was sitting behind John pretended to spit on the back of his head. John turned around pissed off and said "What the fuck did you do that for?" Someone else chimed in, 'Yeah, look what you did to his hair!'….. See… the 1980's Ton Sur Ton fashion was often accompanied by zig zags and shit shaved into the trendy kids hair. Think Vanilla Ice but not as….. edgy?? Again, Just sort of funny…. Frying??? Funniest shit you have ever heard in your life.

We rode It's a Small World and all I wanted to do was hang over the edge of the boat and play with the water. All those little fake kids singing were way too creepy for me to handle. Halfway through the ride I realized that if the world was really so small, why was everybody so segregated on this ride? I was ready to jump ship and integrate the world when God actually spoke to me. He said that he would stop the ride if I didn't get my hands out of the water. After that, we hit Pirates of the Caribbean and a few more rides and went through the Haunted Mansion last.

We were screaming when the floor started to sink and scared the shit out of some corn-fed family from the Midwest. They grabbed their chubby kids and stayed pressed up against the walls and waited for us to get on our cars before they came out of the house. At the end of the ride we passed a mirror and a hologram ghost was sitting between Chuck and me. I screamed like a little girl as Chuck took a swing at him. There being no ghost Chuck whacked me instead. Thanks… dick.

Making our way home from Disneyland, I was sitting shotgun in Chucks shitty yellow truck. Half way home he gripped the wheel super tight and started repeating, "The lines are still straight, the lines are still straight!" See, apparently the whole world flipped upside down on him while he was driving on the freeway and thankfully, the lines were still straight. Now this is the point where I tell you never to drive and do drugs. Actually it's all relative. If you live in the middle of nowhere fuck it, knock yourself out. It's safer than texting or putting on makeup in the city. (Ok you shouldn't drive fucked up at all.)

When you hear about people having a "bad trip" on any sort of hallucinogen it is usually preceded by an overwhelming feeling that usually turns to dread. Most trips lasting upwards of 8 hours this can be a a very long, serious bad one. If you are something of a shitty person, it's easy to have a bad trip because the mind expanding nature of the drug could have you looking at yourself and not liking what you see. So if you are an asshole I don't recommend that you do mushrooms acid or peyote. (You should be forced to do them but I don't recommend you do it voluntarily.)

I had an overwhelming feeling at one point on the way home from Disneyland. I was looking at the moon and it became a black panthers eye. Then after the panther head was swirling in the sky for a minute, it slowly became the panther's toenail. Now for that to be so, the size of the panther would way out grow the size of the sky.

Momentary freak out as my head fell back in a vain attempt to see the rest of the panther. Staying in those "freak out" moments is what gives you a bad trip. I shook it off and when I came back that song.. "You spin me right round baby right round like a record baby right round round round," by Dead or Alive was playing on the radio. I still can't hear that song without feeling a little bit like I'm that 14 year old kid frying on acid with Michele's and my friend Chuck. (if you want to see some good plastic surgery disaster [DK] photo's Google Pete Burns, singer, Dead or Alive.

Paul Revere.

Back inside the classroom I had a couple teachers that I really liked, like Mr. Schwick. He wasn't full of shit, wasn't stupid, and never came off condescending like so many teachers did. He didn't give a shit what I looked like and I dug his history class. I had him first period so I was probably baked in his class more than I was not.

One thing I never really did was drink at school. That was for weekends and parties. I remember one time a girl named Caroline came into his class hammered. She didn't make it more than 15 minutes before BWAAAAA. She vodka and orange juiced everywhere. Now he had to know what was up and could have had her suspended but he just had a friend of hers help clean it up and sent her to the nurses office with a note that said she was sick.

On the other end of the spectrum were teachers like Mrs. Wood. She was about 900 years old and hated everybody. Thankfully for us (and probably her too), she complained about a bunch of black girls making noise outside of her classroom by referring to "Those colored people" not being able to keep quite (or something equally offensive) and got canned mid semester. It was 1984 so you could still have movies like *Soul Man* and *The Toy* but couldn't say shit like that in the classroom. *Soul Man* starred the very white C Thomas Howell in black face, trying to get a minority scholarship to Harvard, and *The Toy* stared Richard Pryor and was about a young rich white boy who bought himself a black man: who incidentally wasn't going to sue the newspaper arm of this rich white guy's company for its no hiring blacks policy, but was going to sue because they weren't going to hire him as a cleaning lady because he was a man. Go 1980's! Yeah!!!

At Pali, Michele was in 11th grade and their student body president was a guy nick named Zippy the Pinhead who worked for SST records. SST was formed by one of the founding members of Black Flag, so they had a lot of great punk bands on their label. Meat puppets, Sonic Youth, the Minutemen, Husker Du, and of course Black Flag. Michele told me he also got Henry Rollins of Black Flag to do a spoken word in the play production room. Instead of standing on the stage, he stood on a couple desks, one of which Michele was sitting in and read from there. I still have a booklet he gave out after the reading. It was some cool shit. If this was what my high school experience was going to be like, bring it on!!!

Before 1st period was homeroom. My homeroom teacher for all three years of Revere had about 20 years on old Mrs. Wood. She was so old... ("How old was she???") She was so old she coulda been Methuselah's great grandmother....great grandmother... Thank you ladies and gentlemen, thank you. I'm here all week. Mrs. Schultz. She kinda looked like the blonde Nazi in *Raiders of the Lost Ark*, half way through melting when they opened the ark at the end of the movie. To put it nicely, I didn't like her and she didn't like me. Which was cool... it was just homeroom. Just a few minutes a day; morning announcements, pledge of allegiance, then off to first period.

One particular morning ole Schultzie lost her shit. She jumped up and started screaming "That's it, I'm not going to put up with you any longer!!!" I took off my Walkman (precursor to the disc man which was the precursor to the iPod) to see who or what she was yelling about. Shaking way more than her usual tremors, she filled out an office referral, walked right up and set it down on my desk. I picked it up totally confused and read it... "Student said 'Fuck You' to me." I said 'Are you kidding me?? I said nothing at all!!!' We bitched at each other for a minute then I had to suck it up and go down to the office.

When I got down there I sat down in Mr. Millers office and told him I had zero idea what she was talking about. I had my head phones on so I couldn't even tell him if I heard someone else yell it and I got blamed for something I didn't do. I had nothing. But because of our history and because that was totally out of character for me he had no choice but to believe me. I mean come on, there is no point or joy in yelling fuck you to a teacher! It's instant suspension or expulsion... and you don't get anything out of it!! I mean how can you get inside a teachers head and screw with their world by yelling something stupid like "Fuck You?" He knew I was much more creative than that.

I should have been expelled but wasn't. Miller took me out of my homeroom class and made me his office assistant. Hanging out in the office, bringing summonses to students, it was awesome. Schultzie was furious. She freaked out on Miller in front of me and demanded to know why I wasn't expelled or at least suspended from school. He tried to calm her down and tell her that there was a chance she was mistaking and that I was out of her class forever and she would never have to deal with me again. That must have been enough for her because she just walked away.

I graduated Paul Revere by the skin of my teeth. I had just barely passed my classes and got the maximum amount of "U's" (Unsatisfactory) and had way passed the limit on how many times you could be sent to the Dean. So many times that I truly felt like all those ladies in that office were friends I would be leaving behind. I would miss them giving me shit for smelling like cigarettes when I was just smoking them to cover up the sent of weed.

Thank god for eye drops that get the red out. My mom actually came to the school and brought Mr. Miller a bouquet of balloons that barely fit inside his office and a giant thank you card for helping me graduate. I miss that guy. I wish I could track him down on Facebook but John Miller???? If he is still alive and on Facebook, I would be going through about 2 million profiles looking for him.

Paul Revere graduation was held down the street from my house at Palisades High School. I wore a blue plaid jacket my mom made, a pair of red and black bondage pants and blue and black Creepers. When they called my name, I got a big cheer from all of my friends... I also happened to get a cartoonish amount of cheers from my sister and her friends. She had to have made every single one of them promise to scream as loud as they could for me when my name was called. She was wearing a bright pink wig so when I looked up into the crowd I had no problem picking her out. I got the loudest response that day. I was proud… sort of.

My real father made the trip to see me graduate and he had to hear his kid using some Dicks name and getting a rousing applause. Part of me felt like an asshole. I knew it wasn't my fault but it didn't really matter. My dad and Dick didn't like each other. And Dick knew my dad was there. At the time I felt like Dick was probably happier that my dad had to hear his named called over the loud speaker rather than being happy that I graduated.

Around this time Michele was still on the YMCA swim team, which I had abandoned many years before for the beach. We were both in that pool since the time we were babies. Michele made it to the height of swim team fame by having a local punk rock band write a song about her called Swimming on Hot Ass-fault. The band was a bunch of young teenagers that played gigs at the infamous Cathay De Grande in Hollywood. (Being driven to gigs by their parents because they were too young to drive.)

Michele had tried to time the light at El Medio and Sunset at the same time a car was doing the same thing. Without laying blame, the two met and lets just say Michele lost. My mom came up to me and told me that Michele had been hit by a car, she was all right but she was going to get her from the hospital. I freaked out and took a swing at a broken window in the clubhouse we used to play in. A piece of glass stuck in my hand and gave me a pretty good scar. Turned out the car just clipped her and she just had some road rash, from swimming on some hot asphalt.

The summer after 9th grade was an elevated version of the last two summers; more surfing, more skating, more parties, and more shows. Towards the end of the summer, Michele had a friend who was going to film school and wanted to film a completely dubbed version of Grease 2. Michele asked me to do it with her and her friends and it was a blast. Acting with my sister, hanging out with the older kids, dressing up like a greaser and running around Palisades Park….. it was great!!!! The highlight for me was I got to grab her super hot friend Alyssa's ass. I grab her ass; she turns around and slaps me. I kept fucking up the end of the take so I could do it again. Take one… Take two… take three.. Ok, got a boner I need a few minutes.

These chicks are going to be at Pali with me next year?? Lets get this shit started!!!

Chapter 7

Pali High, Parties, Davis, Catalina, & Attempted Manslaughter

Making the jump to Pali High was just like coming home. First of all, my real dad built the place. My grandpa Nick (his dad) was the foreman on the job and my dad and some of his friends were busting rot iron under him. I also lived 2 blocks away so the school had been my playground since I was old enough to cross the street by myself. On a usual day we would be down there playing a game we called bike tag. Pronger Zoyd and some other neighborhood kids would usually play on the second level, which made for a lot of blind corner collisions complete with bent BMX's and little bloodied bodies.... You're it!!

I got to see Michele and her friends again every day. She was now a senior and was still super involved with acting at school; be it play production or Thursday Theater (student run shorts performed on Thursdays in the play production room). I am ashamed to say I only saw a couple of the Thursday theaters. They were brilliant. Some of the funniest shit I have ever seen live. I couldn't make it to see more because.... I don't know.. I was busy, I was too cool, I was an idiot. Michele, Kristina, Phil, Colleen, Chris, Mike, Josh, Anna and a couple others would put on the most amazing shows.

Those guys also won many Shakespeare festivals where all the schools would compete against each other. Every time they went they would win. Their captain was Mrs. French. Vicki French. She had some kind of thyroid problem so her eyes always looked like they were bugging out of her head. She was an amazing teacher and Michele and her loved each other to death.

The plays they would put on were extraordinary. Not your average shitty, "do I have to watch this?" type of high school play. I have seen many high school plays over the years so I know what I'm talking about. (I know that could sound pretty fucking creepy but it will make a lot more sense later.)

If it wasn't completely clear before, Michele was going to be an actress. And not any, run of the mill actress either. In a group of amazing talent, she had shone bright like a diamond. She had more charisma, stage presence, and star quality than the entire town of Hollywood these days. And of course I am biased but there are hundreds of people out there who would agree with me completely.

My academic path continued much the same in high school. While Michele excelled in the classroom and was her usual eccentric self out in the world, I split my time at school between doing the bare minimum to get by and entertaining my classmates and myself. I wouldn't really call myself a class clown.. I was more of a fine clown craftsman. Take for instance Ms. Krepps. Poor Ms. Krepps.

She had super frizzy hair that looked like you could carve Mickey Mouse in it like the shrubs at Disneyland. Her style of eyewear was giant, thick, super wide glasses. She would wear the same purple shirt denim skirt combo ever day of the year. Now I don't know if she had 7 of the same outfit or if she washed it every day or more than likely just once a week.

That lady was wound so tight you were constantly covering your face because you thought her head was going to explode. I'd like to think I was there to make her realize the error of her ways…. Teaching high school when you are wound so tight that if a mouse farts you hit the ceiling, is going to lead to a brain aneurysm or a heart attack for sure. She would start by pleading with us to pay attention. Then she would scream for a second. Then she would cry. I actually feel a little shitty about that one. All I really had to do to fuck with her was say her name. Ms. Krepps…. Ms. Kreeeeepps. Ok, maybe I was a bit of a bully.

On the other end of the professorial spectrum was Mr. Ronald Lane. I loved that guy. See, he and I had an understanding. He totally got it…and he was a very smart man. You have to be smart to be funny. Most of his class was all about the work. But sometimes you need to blow off a little steam….and sometimes shit is just funny. If I was blowing off steam in his class I had to be careful. If I said something stupid he would turn it on me and the class would be laughing at me. On the other hand if I said something that he thought was funny or somehow appropriate, he would let me have it.

It was only a matter of time until I couldn't control my mouth and disregarded our unspoken rule. He waited for me to finish up whatever brilliant social commentary I had for the class that day, then he closed his text book on his desk and stood up to address the class.

He began; "Rarely do I get a chance to work with a…. a really special student. A student who really reaches into our hearts and inspires us all." He picked up a pamphlet off his desk and held it up… "This, Michael Friedlander, I am presenting to you." He handed me the pamphlet he had just shown the class. The cover of pamphlet read *High Goals For The Underachiever.* The class went absolutely nuts. Fucking brilliant right?!!??? As I prepared for my acceptance speech I realized that there was no way in hell I was going to get a bigger laugh than he had just gotten. I held my pamphlet high, thanked Mr. Lane and my classmates, took a bow and sat the fuck down. I knew there was no beating that one. Sometimes you have to know when you've been bested.

I had Mr. Lane for a creative writing class in 10th grade as well. On January 28 1986 our class (along with just about every classroom in the country) watched the Space Shuttle Challenger take off because the first civilian, a schoolteacher, was blasting off with the crew. A little more than a minute into that historic flight the thing blew the fuck up. A fuel filled rocket kept going straight so there was more confusion than anything else. The classroom was silent. After a minute I said "Well that's not supposed to happen." So much for Teachers….. In… Spaaaaace! (where are my mupets fans at… Pigs in space???? No?? Ok.)

Besides being my creative writing teacher, Mr. Lane was my English teacher as well. He was also the teacher advisor for the school newspaper the Tideline. After seeing some of my work, he asked me if I wanted to be on the staff. That was unheard of. To have a 10th grade kid in a class of mostly seniors running the school newspaper just wasn't done. A chance to finally do something academically that I really enjoyed! Boy did I let him down. I wrote the minimum number of articles to pass the class. I don't think there actually was a minimum before I got there. I wrote one article on skateboarding and one on the B football team that I also played for.

There was another teacher that really liked me and I'm not sure why. He was the coach of the aforementioned B football team, Mr. Del Monte. You will remember him from the first of the Disney movie series *Gus* the field goal kicking mule (McEveety 1976). Ok maybe not as familiar as *Air Bud* (Smith 1997) or *the Computer Wore Tennis Shoes* (Butler 1969), a young Kurt Russell's breakout vehicle, but it existed.

I think he was only in the movie for a second. I think he was the kicker that gets replaced by Gus. Anyway he made me an offer I couldn't refuse. It was the beginning of the school year. The B football team had been practicing for about a month and their games were about to start. He said if I transferred onto the team I would fulfill my PE obligation for the year and I could put on pads and just wail on people. So began my short lived career as a high school football player.

He put me in as starting left tackle on defense. We were good for a B team... really good. Our first game we played in East LA at Garfield High. We beat the shit out of them and were celebrating on the bus getting ready to come home. Apparently I didn't get the memo because as we started to pull out of the schools driveway the bus driver yelled "Duck!!" and everyone hit the ground. I remember getting halfway through the thought of 'what the fuck' then the bus was in a hailstorm of rocks and bottles. I guess that was better than gunshots. Go East L.A.!

Once I was on the team I had to show up for practice 6th period. Normally extra school would have been fucking awful but I knew that this was a special experience that I would never be able to do again. Despite my size and the fact that I was pretty damn athletic, there was no chance for me to ever play JV or Varsity. Those two coaches were straight out of central casting for *Varsity Blues*. They were the prototypical high school coach-jock-cop-meathead-fucknuts. There was no chance a punk kid who dyed his hair and looked different was getting a shot with these pricks. Coach D told me they scouted me but didn't like my "attitude." Whatever. Go snap a towel at a child's behind ya kook.. One of the coaches was also the dean of boys. I got to know him on a whole other level.

The B team is like the 10th grade team, Junior Varsity 11th,, Varsity 12th. Of course if you are a great player you play above your grade. So most of the B teams have their better players playing JV or Varsity. That being said, we won every game we played. At one point, we went 10 quarters without even being scored against. Ok that's not entirely true. Jordan high, which is in Watts, consistently had a high number of players scouted by colleges and some even made it to the NFL.

They played their JV team against our B team and beat the shit out of us. It was like playing against grown men. Jordan's Varsity team was only the best of the best high school athletes in the city. That meant everyone else was on JV. Our asses, thoroughly kicked. So that loss didn't count because they had to forfeit for playing the wrong team against us.

We ended up with a 5-0 record. I ended up being named second string all league left tackle. That sounds pretty cool, but that just meant that out of the 6 teams in our league I was the second best at my position. Doug Lachman ran right through the hole Lou and I would make on other teams punts and he still holds the record for blocked punts in a season to this day. Al Bundy eat your heart out. You know what, that's not too shabby for a guy that never played football except in the park with friends.

The privileged, prototype of the future, Pacific Palisades High School had other good teachers and bad teachers.... and really bad teachers. When you hear people complaining about tenure and entrenched teachers that you can't get rid of, they are talking about teachers like Mr. West. West was a drunk that kept a bottle of booze in his desk and was not afraid to whip that bad boy out and take a chug right there during class. I saw him during lunch one day throwing up in the Kentucky Fried Chicken parking lot. He was definitely over high school children and was just waiting to retire or die. Mrs. Daniels smoked pot with the kids. I liked her a lot. Never smoked out with her but I was a Teachers assistant for her a couple times. She ended up getting canned and becoming a resident of ghost town, which ill explain more about a little later.

I still had some friends I made thru Michele that were seniors like her, but I had made a couple of my own as well. One of them was a former "greener" named Pat. (Greeners were stoners who got their name from hanging out at the village green, which was a triangle of grass and benches in the middle of town.) I had a curfew, but it didn't matter what time pat came home so there were many nights that I slept on the floor of his room. He should have been brain damaged because the top screws on one of those old school, metal, child bikes seats came out and his dad drove him for about a block and a half bouncing his bare head on the pavement. Pat had gone from stoned greener, to a glam rocker that quit smoking weed all together by the time he got to high school.

For those of you that don't know what a glam rocker was, think Poison or Motley Crue or Hanoi Rocks. He had long blonde feathered hair, bracelets half way up both arms and a Ford F250 pickup that I may or may not have passed out and puked in. After he retired that truck (probably because it smelled like puke) he got a mustang 5.0 that we got to over 100 mph at some point every weekend, often racing somebody or ditching cops.

There were more than one or two times that we probably should have died in that car. Flying up San Vicente doing 120mph, seeing the light was red at 26th street, and downshifting to 80 with no chance of stopping if there is cross traffic. I think it was the little smile he gave me when we saw that the light was red. The look was.. If anyone is crossing San Vicente its either T-boning them at 80, tree at 80 or gas station at 80.

Pat took me to my only glam rock show I ever went to. It was Rat and Poison at the Long Beach Arena...... Oh shit! I just got that.... Rat and Poison.... Rat Poison!!! I never thought of that. 22 years after the fact! Huh. Pat was dressed in his full glam rock regalia and I had on a flannel and combat boots. We drank beers on the way down there in his Jacked up pickup and for a while outside in the parking lot. I was pretty much hammered when we got inside. I was so shit housed that all I could see was hair makeup and spandex. I was grabbing every ass I saw thinking they were all women. Quite a few dudes turned around to give me stink eye. I either pointed at Pat or just laughed out loud when I figured out it was a dude.

After walking thru the crowd for about 5 min I actually had an old security guard stop me and yell "Quit groping.... Ehh...Everybody!" Now there were two things to note about that statement. #1- I had never heard of the term "groping" in my entire life, so it took me a good 4 or 5 count before I realized what he was talking about....and #2- he had to hesitate before saying "everyone" because he was not sure which of these people were women and which were men. That all being said, those motherfucking transvestites put on a seriously good show. Loved both bands and had a great time…from what I remember.

During school, Pat would also get me out of some of my classes that had teachers that didn't really care if I was there or not. He would pop his head in and say "Shop class, parts run!". It was somewhat legit, because for auto shop you sometimes had to go get parts for whatever car you were currently working on. Only thing was... I didn't have auto shop. One day we grabbed the school president Reginald Peterson IV and told him we were going to go get some food at jack in the box. He had an off period so he jumped into the back of Pat's truck and off we went. It had just rained so we drove him up into the Santa Monica Mountains on fire roads.

We went through the highlands, past skull rock, and hit all the muddy spots we could think of. It was about 25 minutes of serious off roading and then donuts in the empty muddy lots. I can't believe he didn't fall out. By the time we got back to school he was covered head to toe in mud. He is now an accomplished lawyer somewhere in Southern California now so you're welcome.

Pat and I were so different, maybe that's why we became such good friends. When I was young I always joked that if I ever ran into myself at a bar, I would have gotten into a fight. I consider Pat, Chuck, and Takeo, to be some of the best friends that I have ever had.

Now that I was in High school, parties on the weekend became a whole new experience. Some parents let their kids have huge parties (obviously not mine). Other times it was someone left alone or staying at the other parents house and just throwing an unsanctioned blow out. It was a no brainer to take the hit of being grounded for a while if you could be known as the kid who threw the coolest party of the year that the cops had to shut down. Kids staying at dad and step moms while Mom is giving them a hundred dollars a week to feed the cats and make sure her house is secure while she and her boyfriend are on vacation. On her way out the door she might yell back, "Don't have too many people over honey!"

If I were to be in that situation, that idea could be subjective. I could see the logic in a kids head start to work itself out. "How many is too many? Too many to fit in the house?? I've seen her fit over a hundred people inside alone! So If you figure that if you used the spacious back yard that's at least another 150.. Plus not everyone is going to be able to stay there the whole night so that's another 200 rotated in and out... So maybe I will be safe with about 400 people." With a huge mansion, you might even get away with it. But if its that one night where there are no other parties to go to, and everybody from the Palisades, Brentwood, Santa Monica and Malibu shows up... The shit show will ensue.

Most kids knew at least one person from all the different schools in the area. On any given weekend there would be one or two parties from each school, some at multi million dollar mansions, sometimes wide open, sometimes with hired thugs or off duty cops working security. They were all over town. Palisades, Brentwood, Malibu, Bel Air, the Riviera, Mandeville canyon, Kenter canyon, Santa Monica or Malibu. It was not uncommon to have a party with 20 kegs of beer and have the beer run out....early! When those parties got broken up, it could be a few cops asking people to leave, or a bunch of cops and total mayhem.

I had a lot of groups of friends, none were closer than the kids from my neighborhood. The ones I lit the bluffs on fire with. The ones I played bike tag with. Those were my boys.

One house we partied at a lot was up Rockingham in Brentwood at the Vons house. Mark and his little sister

123

Audrey. I had made out with Audrey a bunch of times but she would never sleep with me just because she banged some of my friends. What kind of excuse is that?? I think that's a reason why you should have sex with me.

Anyway I was pissing on the side of her house one night she was having a big party and I realized I was standing right in front of her neighbor with my dick in my hand. I was like "Oh shit, sorry." He said 'Oh no, don't worry about it, just throwing out some garbage.' I was talking to OJ Simpson. It was funny because now that I think about it, I could see the air conditioning unit behind Kato's side house that OJ supposedly ran into after he allegedly killed Nicole. His kid Jason was in my grade. He punched me in the face for no reason in Mr. Diggs science class at Revere. Kid had some serious anger issues. Without getting too into it, it looks like his dad did too.

If there were no parties at anyone's house, there were custom-made party spots at the top of every hill in the Palisades. Lets start with the top of Lachman Lane (Named after Doug Lachmans family, the kid who thanks in part to me still has the record for blocked punts for B football at Pali.). The top of Lachman had one of the most beautiful views of the city on the whole Westside. You could see the ocean all the way to Palos Verde's, and inland all the way to century city. At the top of the hill there were empty lots, carved out and level, and there were at least 10 of 'em. Each one could fit 10-20 cars parked over looking the city…and that is not even including the cul de sac at the top.

Most of the time the neighbors would only know something was going on up there by the constant stream of cars going down the hill at the end of the night. We even had some bands play just up the mountain at Skull Rock. Skull Rock is a giant skull shaped rock up above Lachman Lane in the Santa Monica Mountains. If you didn't have a serious off road vehicle….. I take that back. I drove my moms 2 wheel drive GMC Jimmy up there one time. I totally forgot about that. There are houses blocking every way we used to drive up there now. It's still a nice hike from the bottom of Temescal Canyon. I suggest it if you get the chance. If you are feeling adventurous you can chill out in the eye socket of the skull.

The top of Capri we called the top of the world. Up there you could see all the way to downtown LA. At the very top was a plateau that was covered in giant boulders . If you made it up there you could also see the valley, but you couldn't have your car up there or music….besides, who wants to look at the valley?? (There was a healthy rivalry between the beach kids and the valley kids.)

You couldn't really party at the top of hills in Brentwood because most of those hills already had houses built all the way to the top. Which was eventually what happened in the Palisades. The final death nail for those spots was when about 15 cop cars, a bus and a helicopter blocked off the bottom of Capri and shook down every carload of people partying up there. Kids were busted for cocaine, pot and alcohol…. and how they got busted is beyond me. I get maybe the first or second car but don't you think you might want to get rid of your shit if you see what's coming?? Or is that just me? The top of all the hills were patrolled by cops and built out after that, which thankfully wasn't until about 5 years after I graduated high school and had already left town.

At parties for the most part, I kept up my old routine of mostly drinking beer and smoking pot. Again cocaine was way too expensive for me and we hardly ever had any. If I did do coke, I would find myself in the most fascinating conversations with someone I was sure would be my best friend for life. When in reality I was in a conversation that meant less than nothing with someone I knew was a

125

pretentious asshole that I wanted nothing to do with. It also sucked doing it with friends because once I did a line, it would be all I wanted to do. Forget the girls, forget the party… when are we gonna do another line?

Plus the fact that I didn't really do pills meant no easy comedown. Curled up in a ball intently studying the inside of my eyelids as the sun rose, wishing I was dead wasn't very fun for me. Looking back that might have been the way to do it. Lots of people die fucking with pills coming down off of other drugs. Most of those famous Hollywood people that die too young are victims of that shit…and a whole lot of people nobody has heard of as well.

It wasn't just me that pretty much just stuck to beer and weed. Most of the kids I knew pretty much just drank on weekend nights and only really drank beer. Rarely were kids hammered and puking their guts out. The kids that did that on a regular basis were in AA by 11th grade or shipped off to rehab by their parents. I'm not saying we didn't put away a shit load of beer and get hammered on the weekends, I'm just saying that the kids that did that every day or were drinking a lot of hard alcohol were the exception not the rule. There was way too much fun to be had to live like that.

Marx was the main drunk in our little group. A great guy… totally normal, until he had one beer. After that he was like…. "AAAAAAAAAAHHHHH". After his 3rd DUI he went to AA and has been sober ever since. His first DUI he got passed out at a red light. His second, he rear-ended another car in his VW bus. With no seatbelt on, he went through the windshield, onto the back of the car in front of him, passed out. Not knocked out…. PASSED OUT! His last DUI, one of the cooler neighborhood cops was breaking up a party and telling everyone to beat it. The cop saw him getting into the driver side of his car and told him not to drive because he was too drunk. His response??

"FUCK YOU PIG!!!!" The cop told him again… 'Have someone else drive your car, I'll arrest you if you try to drive out of here.' Again, "FUCK YOU PIG!!!" Marx started up his car rolled it about a foot and the cop turned on his lights, walked up to his door and took him off to jail.

.

11th Grade

11th grade was more of the same for me except Michele had been accepted to UC Santa Barbara and was starting her first year in the dorms. I was sad to see her go but knew she would be having a great time in a new adventure… College.

I had a few groups of kids I hung out with at school. That made it cool because when any kind of bullshit was going on in one group I could just bail and hang out with another. When you are in high school and there is drama in your click, you have drama. "So and so fucked so and so's boyfriend." "So and so was talking shit about so and so." 'Soooo… I'll see you guys later…' and off I'd go.

I would also take full advantage of the fact that I lived so close to the school. It was a perfect place to go smoke weed. Mom and Dick still working days made it almost too easy. On one occasion I remember 2 joints a pipe and 2 bongs being passed around in my back yard during a ditch session of one class or another.

One time I brought over a bunch of friends from my football team and guys I had known from Coliseum Street School. In other words a bunch of big inner city black kids. I brought them thru my house to the back yard so we could smoke some of my kind of weed. This being before Snoop Dog and Dr. Dre were talking about the chronic, the only kind of weed you got in the inner city was shitty Mexican weed that just gave you a headache. They had never seen the kind of crazy good Indica bud that I smoked. But they

127

had all disappeared. I couldn't find them anywhere. Then I realize that my little dog Mocha had them pinned against the fence in the back yard. I couldn't believe that they were afraid of a little wimpy dog like Mocha.

It didn't dawn on my sheltered ass that most dogs in the hood will eat you if you come in their yard. They are there for protection, not as much as for a fun family pet like most in the suburbs. So if the dog is a little smaller, the bite wounds won't be as bad, but that's probably as good as it gets.

I apologized real quick, locked up Mocha and brought out some purple stinky sticky herb that looked like a turd that god would lay. (Sorry, stretching for metaphors) I packed a fat bowl and passed it around. I don't think I have ever seen a group of people that high before in my life, because me and my other friends were used to smoking that shit. These guys were used to smoking shitty shit. And these guys smoked it like it was the shitty shit that they usually smoked..... and shit.

After that I had to herd these stoned kids back down to the school and hope we didn't get busted. That must have been a site for some of the old white people who lived in between my house and Pali High. A large group of black kids laughing hysterically, falling all over each other walking past their houses back to the school.

Hanging with the guys around my neighborhood in the daytime almost never involved drinking beer. We were way too busy taking advantage of living life by the beach. Having said that, there were occasional day parties or times we drank beers at one of our outdoor spots. Sometimes it would be down by Sunset beach at Safeway getting some beers and hanging at Casa La Mar overlooking the beach a few hundred yards up the coast.

One day we had decided to drink some beers and were getting people to buy them for us. We had run out of money and Damon Hughes volunteered to try to walk out of the store with beer, like he had just paid for it. We had the car parked on sunset and were watching over a wall that was about 4 feet tall on our side, much taller from the Safeway parking lot. All of a sudden Damon came running out with an 12 pack of bottles in his hand. Two guys in suits that must have been managers or plainclothes cops or something, were running after him. He threw up the 12 pack to me, knowing full well there was no way he could jump the wall as well. He knew that he was going to get caught, or lose the beer. Not wanting us to lose the beer, he tossed himself full body on top of a grenade.

Not knowing what to do for him, I caught the beers, jumped into the car, and then drove back up the street to regroup at Jack in the Box. None of us even noticing Zoyd wasn't with us anymore. Before we could figure out what had happed, Zoyd came walking back to the car with a big ole smile on his face and then Damon came running up from a cross the street laughing. It turns out right when the shit went down, Zoyd calmly started walking down to the front of safe way. Right before the suits dragged Damon inside (who was trying desperately to get away) Zoyd ran up and nailed all three of them football style with his shoulder. All three went down, Damon popped up first and ran off. The suits turned to Zoyd and yelled at him, "What the hell are you doing?" He played dumb and said, 'Oh, I thought you guys were just beating that kid up... Sorry about that.' Fucking genius!!!! Love both of those guys.

I didn't have much time away from the Palisades during high school, but If I was away on some sort of vacation or trip, that was when drinking a little more than usual felt a bit more acceptable. A couple of those outings involved a kid who showed up at Pali late from the east coast named David Strickland. We took a couple of trips

129

together, one being a soccer tournament in Davis and another was a quick jaunt to Catalina Island.

Davis

The soccer tournament in Davis California was sponsored by the AYSO. I drove up there with Strickland, Stony, and Suarezburger, all friends I knew from school. If you don't know Davis, it is somewhat of a nerdy college town whose symbol was an old timey bicycle with the huge wheel in the front and the little wheel in the back. You were in fact greeted by a statue of said bicycle right when you entered town. We started the trip by stopping at the liquor store and buying a couple of cases of beer for the road. I was 16 and everyone else was 17. I was driving my moms GMC Jimmy to the tournament that my little sister Jessica was also playing in. Because Jessica was playing, she drove up there with my mom and Dick.

On our way back to meet the rest of the team at Pali High, we spotted our teammate Mike being driven down to the school in his dads new Porsche. I was behind him and he turned illegally in front of the school to where the team was meeting. We followed. He stopped short leaving us diagonal in the street in his blind spot, he looked over his right shoulder and started backing up. Not seeing us at all he took the front right bumper of my moms car and dragged it from the back panel of his car all the way through the door up the entire left side of his car. Great. We hadn't even left yet and we destroyed a Porsche.

The whole trip was super fun, but an absolute drunken mess. We bought vodka in those plastic handle bottles and would walk around drinking them looking for parties and hiding them in the bushes. We were driving to practice one day and Stony said, "I think we stashed a bottle in the bushes around this IHOP". We drove by and could see it out in the open under the IHOP window. Stony jumped out of the car ran up to the window which had several old ladies enjoying their Rooty Tootie Fresh and Fruity breakfasts, grabbed the bottle, took a big swig and screamed at them through the window. They were mortified.

The only establishment we didn't end up getting kicked out of was this college bar down the street from the hotel. Our cheap fake IDs worked but Strickland didn't have one. We passed back Suarezburgers ID and it worked no problem. After getting sufficiently hammered, I took the cigarette I was smoking in the bar and asked Stony if he had ever played chicken. He said, "How do you play?" I said 'You put your arms next to each other like this, then you drop a lit cigarette in between them and the first one to move their arm is a chicken.'

The only problem is when you are that drunk you don't really feel your flesh melting. So we all played, and we all got burns to prove it. Most of mine are covered up by tattoos. Poor Strickland got keloid scars pretty bad. At the end of our last game he got this bored look on his face, then picked up the lit cigarette and put it out on the back of his hand. He still had that one pretty bad when we met up again years later.

We went back to the hotel room to sleep it off but Strickland wasn't done yet. He begged Suarezburger for his ID until he finally threw his wallet at him and yelled "Don't fucking loose it!"

The next morning we had our first game. First thing Suarezburger did was ask Strickland for his ID back. He checked his pockets and said "I don't have it." 'What the fuck do you mean you don't have it? You better fucking have it!' He kept yelling at him the whole way back to the bar. Strickland was just laughing the entire time, saying he didn't know where it was until we were on the street next to the parking lot and he said, "Look its right there." Sure enough, it was sitting in the middle of the parking lot right out in the open. We could see it from the car.

Now again, I was never the best soccer player on the field, but if you wanted the best player on the other team taken out… I was your man. This one kid on the other team was tall and skinny and had the sickest mullet you have ever seen. He looked like Joe dirt with a perm, but tall. He gave me an elbow about 10 min in so I pushed him away. He got up in my face so he had to die. After picking him up and body slamming him onto the ground, I had a referee and two line judges blowing whistles and running towards me all frantic. It looked kind of funny because he wasn't getting up and everyone else including me was just standing there. The ref blew his whistle about 5 more times with a red card over his head right in front of me. Like if he blew the whistle hard enough it would somehow punish me more. Red card. Out of the game and suspended for the next.

There was a giant black kid on the other team that had amazing footwork and was fast as hell. The only problem was when anyone on our team went near him they got sent flying. He wasn't playing dirty or anything like that, he was just so big and fast that it looked like he was steamrolling everyone. The refs didn't know how to call him so after giving him a yellow card, they red carded him and he was out of the game as well. After he made fun of the guy I body slammeds hair, we ended up sitting together making fun of all the people on both our teams. Cool kid.

The next day's game was the one I had to sit out. Mom and Dick had already planned to come to that game so they could watch our team. The other team jogged out onto the field with military precision, complete with a 'hut' on every other step. They ran into a circle and began calisthenics while their coach barked out orders from the middle in between tweets of his whistle.

Then, over a rise that separated the field from the street, the faint sound of a ghetto blaster… Then our team comes falling all over each other carrying vodka (water) bottles to the tune of 'Mary Mary, why you buggin' (if you don't know, it was an 80s RUN DMC cover of the 60's tune by the Monkeys.) Just picture the beginning of any Jackass movie.

The kid who had the boom box we called soul man because he looked exactly like C. Thomas Howell in the movie *Soul Man* (two *Soul Man* references??? I smell Pulitzer).

Our pregame regiment consisted of some people stretching but most of us lying on the ground watching the clouds go by or totally asleep and snoring behind our sunglasses. I think one of the guys was even puking from drinking the night before. I didn't even have my uniform on because that was the game I was suspended from so why bother.

We had one real player. Well one and a half. Suarezburger was actually pretty good and we all could play our positions, but our main weapon was Irwin. He was an amazing player and was tough as well. He got cleated by one chump who couldn't defend him in that game and should have gotten stitches. It was into the white meat or bone. All I know is there was a hole in his leg, the shit inside was white, and it was nasty. He limped for a minute then shook it off. Not like pro soccer players today. I would watch that sport a little bit more but when those pansies fall on the ground when someone brushes by them it infuriates me. They need to up the fines for these guys taking dives and ruining a pretty cool sport.

Strickland and Stony were in rare form. Strickland had his hands on his knees for the first half of the game just trying not to fall over. The second half he would walk a few steps toward the ball, then the ball would get kicked somewhere else and he would walk a few steps that way, then rest again. Finally Irwin past the ball to him, Strickland one touched it back, then threw his hands up in the air and walked around the field for the next 5 minutes like he had just scored the winning goal in the world cup and the crowd was screaming his name.

Stony was playing goalie and just talking shit to everyone and cracking himself up. You couldn't help laughing when you heard Stony laugh. First of all he was a 6'4 inch Mexican with blond California boy sun bleached hair. If you closed your eyes and listened to him he sounded exactly like Tigger from Whinny the Pooh. Same exact laugh at twice the volume of any voice on the field. He was talking shit to and about the other team, the ref's, the linesmen... even the parents sitting on the sidelines. Shit that wasn't even that funny but once he started cracking up and woohoo-ing even his victims were shaking their heads and laughing.

Every time Stony got his hands on the ball he was talking shit to whoever shot it. "Little challenge 'cause you've got nothing! My moms got one leg and she could hop circles around you!" Right then, hand-ball by one of our defenders.... penalty shot. Time to humble the dude with the big mouth. A penalty shot is basically a free goal. You stand 12 yards from the goal with no defenders. The goalie has to stay on the goal line and not move till the ball is kicked. It's basically a sure goal. But Stony didn't quit. Stony just took the opportunity to take it up a notch.

The kid who was taking the penalty shot was the other teams top forward and was smirking because he was about to shut Stony up. As he walked up to the ball awaiting the refs whistle to shoot, Stony started to yell….. "AAAAYYYAAAAAHHHHHH, this is what I'm talking about!! Lets see what you got!!! You gonna whiff this one or do you got something for me. I'm thinking you are gonna whiff it." Then, as the ref blew his whistle, stony grabbed a big handful of dirt and started screaming and rubbing it into his face. The guy on the other team ran up to the ball and kicked…. right into Stony's hands. Totally psyched out. Complete choke. Needless to say Stony's mouth went into overdrive after that. Even people on our side weren't happy he stopped the goal. They were like, 'Oh no!' Knowing there wasn't a chance in hell he was going to shut up now.

For Irwin's sake, lets say we won that game. I have no idea if we did or not but I'd like to think we did.

That night there was a banquet for the whole tournament grades 6-12. We showed up hammered and got thrown out almost immediately. People were still walking in and Strickland went up to a girl that couldn't have been older than 13 years old, totally fucking around he started asking her if she wanted to be a model and telling her he could make things happen for her…. A man that must have been her chaperone walked up and slapped Strickland right across the face. I was on the ground laughing as hard as I could as Suarezburger ran to stop Strickland from killing this dude.

He grabbed him around the waist and tried to calm him down but that wasn't going to happen. Strickland ended up dragging him across the parking lot as he unleashed an obscenity laced tirade about how he was going to kill him and his family and then sneak into the funeral and beat the shit out of them in there caskets. After howling in the parking lot for about 10 minutes, we finally managed to get him back into the car and we hi tailed it out of there.

The next day our team was summoned to the tournament office, which was a bunch of benches in the park next to the soccer fields. We were told by tournament officials and campus police (who also thought they would tag along) that we were kicked out of the tournament and no longer welcome in the city of Davis California. There was about a two second pause, then Strickland spoke up and said…. "Its because were black isn't it…" They didn't find that funny. The cops escorted us back to our hotel and watched us drive out of town. In total, we were kicked out of 3 restaurants a bar, a banquet hall, a hotel, and a tournament. When all was said and done I had driven 600 miles and destroyed one Porsche to play 10 minutes of soccer….and it was the greatest tournament I ever played in.

Catalina

A couple of months later, Strickland, another friend Josh and I, took a quick trip out to Catalina Island. Only 26 miles off the Los Angeles coast, Catalina is the perfect place to go for an overnighter. We wanted to get an early start, so we were going to take the Catalina Island Express at 8:30 in the morning. This was back in the day when the fastest boat out there took about 3 hours to get there. We all slept at Josh's house and got up at 6 am to make ourselves a screwdriver for breakfast. Josh's brother dropped us off in San Pedro and we jumped right on the boat and started drinking Bloody Mary's to get the party started. We put away quite a few cocktails on the trip over and made it to Avalon at about 12 in the afternoon.

We exited the boat on a wooden dock in the middle of the harbor (Now a days you dock on the far left side of Avalon on the shore). The old dock had a bar on it in between the boat and the shore that was basically just a tiki hut with a painted red line you couldn't take your beer past. 4 or 5 beers later, it was about 1:30 and we were hammered. Technically we hadn't even made it onto the island yet.

We stumbled off the pier and onto the island. We then walked up the street and came across a liquor store on the backside of downtown Avalon. Across the street was a parking lot with a bunch of tricked out golf carts (the vehicle of choice in Avalon). Strickland saw the keys in one so he jumped behind the wheel and tried to start it up (not knowing it took two keys.) He kept messing with thing trying to get it going when a lady walked up to him and asked him what he was doing. He offered a simple reply. "I'm stealing this golf cart what does it look like I'm doing?" The lady said something else to Strickland who gave up and walked back over to the liquor store where josh and I were cracking up.

Josh and Strickland walked into the liquor store and began checking out their sizeable collection of porno magazines (remember Al Gore was still some 10 years from "inventing" the internet so liquor store porn was much more abundant back then). I was hammered and had no use for a hard on, so I just sat on the ground out front. After a minute I realized that the two dark figures that had just gone into the store were two cops.

They came out of the store with Strickland and Josh and one of the cops said "There were 3 of you, where is the other guy?" Now it would have been nice if they at least hesitated but they both at the same time pointed right at me. I'm not sure if the reality of the situation had sunken in because they were both drunkenly giggling as the cops walked us to the parking lot across the street.

We were pretty much fucked from the get go. "Where are you boys staying?" Josh said 'We don't know.' Oh yeah, did I mention our plan was to meet up with some random chicks and stay wherever we could. Even crash on the beach if we had to. Great plan.

Then after downplaying Strickland's admitted attempted grand theft auto (that's right, there was enough money put into those things that they counted as cars) the cops started asking questions about our prior records. Now, here is something of an extended side story..

137

The story I am about to tell you flashed drunkenly through my head in the blink of an eye. This all happened not too long before this Catalina trip. Earlier in the year I got wrapped up in something that I really had nothing to do with. I was the passenger in a car that was in a car rally. We would have these a couple times a year, where we would get about 15 or 20 cars of 4 or 5 people and have a scavenger hunt. Everybody would put in 5 or 10 bucks each and the rally master would go buy beer with it and wait at the finish line. Winner takes all. The winner could take all but it ended with just a big party for everyone.

Things on the scavenger list would be like, a street sign from the highlands, a cocktail menu from the house of lee, a bar napkin from the SS Friendship; the gay bar right next to state beach. Back in the eighties gay was still sort of a dirty word. The way people acted you would have thought the napkins would have been bright pink or have flowers all over them or be covered in sparkles or have the power to turn you gay, but they were just plain white.

One of the items we needed was part of a sign from a state park. Temescal Canyon was right there in the palisades so our car, driven by my old friend who later became a cop, went driving up the road.

Quick story, inside a story, inside a story. There was an old man that lived next door to two brothers I knew named MR. Stewart. His wife was a fixture in the Palisades who you could always see walking all over town. You could never miss her because she looked exactly like the wrestler George the Animal Steel in drag. He was the guy that would eat the padding on the ring in the middle of a fight. For no reason besides the fact that I looked different, dressed different and had a skateboard, he hated me. When I say I did nothing to this man, I lived 5 blocks away from him, I never talked to him, I never did anything to his property, I never spit on the side walk out front of his house… the only thing I ever did was skate past his house from the bus stop every day and look different. Years of walking by his house with dyed hair ripped jeans, flannels and combat boots began to take their toll on the old guy. He had enough. He began calling the police on me on a regular basis. He told them I was dealing drugs and loitering in front of his house and up to no good. I didn't even know he was calling them because I never did anything wrong and the cops never bothered me.

So when we were driving up Temescal during the car rally, old man Stewart was walking down the road after taking a little hike. We got part way up, about to where he was and there was a gate blocking our path. We realized we couldn't get through and someone also realized it didn't have to be a state park sign, just a sign from a state park (aaahhh loop hole). Just as we figured this out, Stewart walks up to the passenger side of the truck and starts shaking his walking stick and yelling at me. We all start laughing and future cop who was driving, flips him off, peels the truck out and we take off.

Stewart thought he had me. He called the cops and told them we had tried to hit him with the car. This time the cops had something to investigate so the next day they showed up at Pali to my English class, which I just happened to be ditching. It's funny the way kids react to you when the cops show up for you at your classroom. It's totally different when the cops come to address the student body. Getting on the intercom and telling the student body that you can't drive the wrong way on the street in front of the school on your scooters because "it's the law!" was met with thunderous laughter echoing through the halls. But a cop interrupting a class and asking to speak with a specific student was a totally different story.

My parents got wind from the school that the cops wanted to talk to me so my mom took me down to the

Purdue station. She talked to an officer on the phone before hand and explained to them that I wasn't driving the truck and that I hadn't done anything wrong. The detective was cool and told her that they just needed me to come down and make a statement.

We drove down to Purdue and the West L.A. police station. I started talking with the same nice detective and my mom about what happened when he realized I was a minor and that someone else had to handle the interview. He splits and a few minutes later detective Hokanson walks in. Fucking dick to the core. He tells me to come with him so I start following him and my mom starts walking behind. He sees her coming with and turns to her and puts his hand up in her face and says "Lady, you are going to have to wait out here."

Hokanson takes me down to his office and sits behind his desk. He spends equal time starring at a file (no doubt full of all of the complaints from Mr. Stewart) and then at me. He starts, not with any questions about the incident that happened, but about my earring. "Why do you have that thing in your ear? Does that mean you are some kind of a queer?" It was obvious he was asking the questions just to hear himself talk, so I said nothing. Pausing to look at the file between questions he continued. "The only people I have ever seen with hair dyed like that are what we refer to as societal rejects.... is that what you are?....... a reject?........" After another long pause he continued. "What makes you want to dress like that?..... You like people thinking you are a degenerate, unprincipled loser?" I wanted to say, 'Yes sir, yes I do. I bought this ensemble at the Jr. *degenerate unprincipled loser* boutique right next to the *fuck people like you* outlet store.' I tried to tell him he had the wrong guy but he saw the way I looked and knew that I had to be a fuckup and I needed to be punished.

I knew the drill with people in authority that were total closed minded pieces of shit. The type that has his head so far up his ass that it hits a worm hole of space and time and comes back out in the 1950's. They have a habit of writing off anyone who is black, brown, gay, or not their version of an upstanding white American. If you fall into any of those categories, the best thing you can do for your safety is shut your mouth and avoid eye contact, like deep down you know all the things this piece of shit is saying are right.

Finally he finished his paper work, shook his head at me with disdain (like Dick loved to do) and said "Ok, I'm done with you." One of his subordinates comes and gets me and I asked him where they were taking me? As Hokanson walked away down the hall he barked back "booking!" I was completely blown away. I yelled back, 'For what???' As he got into the elevator he turned and looked me right in the eye and said. "Attempted manslaughter," as he pushed a button and the elevator doors closed.

So detective "Suck Mydick" was gone and the other guy took me down and began the booking process. I was photographed and finger printed and entered into the computer. He looked at the paperwork then asked me why I had been arrested. I told him what Hokanson wouldn't listen too and as he was pausing to process the information I gave him, another cop in a suit ran in and whispered in his ear. He stopped what he was doing and said, "Come with me."

I was led down a hallway to the elevator. This time we went up… all the way up to the top floor. We ended up at a door that read "so and so, deputy chief of police." As the door opened I was greeted by my mom crying in a chair and my step dad Dick, mad as a motherfucker, and for once, not at me. I have talked enough shit about him so I will give credit where credit was due. He was great. Before the deputy chief could even get the question out, Dick said, "Yes we would like to lodge a formal complaint!"

It got even better for me because apparently Hokanson had been such a dick to so many people that he was actually disciplined. We got a phone call that said he was suspended without pay. Unfortunately we also got a call from Chief of Police Daryl Gates himself the next day. He had set aside the suspension and was required to let us know. Dick!! If you don't know Chief Daryl Gates, he was the police chief during the Rodney King beating and became synonymous with police brutality.

OK ok ok, back to the original story. So this whole clusterfuck goes through my head while the cops are questioning Josh and Strickland outside that liquor store on Catalina Island. I knew if I was honest when they questioned me we might get off with a warning. I also knew I was photographed fingerprinted and entered into the computer, but nothing had really happened. I didn't do anything wrong. I had to be honest because if that shit showed up and I didn't say anything they might think I was lying to them. So this is what happened.

To Josh; "Have you ever been arrested?" 'Yeah I punched in a movie theater window.' To Strickland; "Have you ever been arrested?" 'Yeah for minor in possession of alcohol.' To me; "Have you ever been arrested?" 'Yeah for attempted manslaughter but it was nothing.'

In my drunkenness it totally made sense. Strickland and Josh burst out laughing hysterically and literally rolling around on the ground. Then I realized how that sounded as the handcuffs were going on my wrists. I began to try and explain myself but it wasn't helping my cause. "I didn't kill the guy... No wait, I wasn't trying to kill the guy... I mean I wasn't the one who tried to kill the guy.. I mean I was there but I didn't really".... Yeah it didn't get any better from there.

I was brought to the same jail that my real dad had spent time in. They used to have rugby tournaments on the island that he and his friends played in. They had to stop having them there because the jail wasn't big enough to hold all the players that got in bar fights after the games.

We were obviously underage so my mom had to take the ferry over the next day before they could release us. We slept in a barrack with a TV set waiting for my mom to come to the island to get us. Boy was she pissed. She still gives me shit about that one to this day.

Back at home, hitting the bars with Strickland was always a blast. He was good for at least one or two fall down laughing moments a night. One night, all the kids in my grade (who had fake id's or could sneak in) were having beers at the Gaslight in Santa Monica. Strickland went up to this 75 year old bar fly who looked like he had been drinking gasoline on the face of the sun for the last 30 years. He started telling this guy how his dad was Bruce Lee and he had shown him the tiger claw right before he died. He said it was only know by him, a couple of shaolin monks and Angela Lansbury. He was holding his hand like a claw and doing the whole WHOOOOAAAA, thing in the old mans face. The old man got up and yelled "You arrogant bastard!!!" and took a swing at him. Strickland was laughing before the punch half landed on him and he fell on the ground howling as someone apologized for him and everyone got back to having a really fun night.

I finished out 11th grade just having fun, skating and surfing and partying on the weekend with friends (and just getting by in school). Senior year was coming up and I couldn't have been more psyched. I had no idea what the next year would bring, but I had a feeling everything was going to fall into place once my last year of high school got going...and then it began...

Chapter 8

12th grade, Senior year. This is going to be the best year of my life!!

Finally, my senior year of high school, I could not have been more excited. I always knew that I didn't put enough effort into school so I was cool with going to Santa Monica City College and seeing what happened from there. That meant no pressure from grades, so I could do what I had to do to pass, and focus on enjoying my last year of high school.

For a person like me that didn't have the greatest self confidence growing up, it was really amazing to be not only socially accepted, but to have as many friends as I did. Jr. high and high school are such awkward points in most people's lives. I was on top of the world. Plus I had my whole life in front of me! This is going to be the best year yet.

I was missing Michele even more, but I was super stoked for her because not only was she starting her second year at UC Santa Barbara, she had just been accepted into their bachelor of fine arts program for theater with an emphasis on acting. Only a few select spots opened up for this program every year. Out of the 15 or so thousand students, there were about 10 places available. You had to audition to be accepted and would be trained for an enduring and artistic life in theater. If you make it to the end you are individually prepared for national auditions into Master of Fine Arts programs, regional theaters, Shakespearean festivals, and acting companies across the country.

She loved theater and plays but Hollywood couldn't be far behind. Fuck Julia and Eric Roberts that shit was going to be me. I am going to ride my talented sisters coat tails to a career in Hollywood if I got bored with my life. Watch... Check this out... Eh hmm eh mmm... "Charlie.... they took my thumbs man... they took my fucking thumbs!!" (*The Pope of Greenwich Village* -1984, Stuart Rosenberg) Pretty convincing right?

I got a chance to see how she was living when she brought me up to Santa Barbara during the beginning of the school year. She was renting a house on El Sueno Ave in Isla Vista with 4 other kids from the school. The tent from their failed camping trip still up in the back yard. They had a camping trip planned the weekend before, but something

145

kept them from going. So in true Michele form, they had a camping trip in the back yard instead. They set up a little fire pit, pitched a tent on the grass, and spent the night drinking beer, roasting weenies, making s'mores and telling ghost stories.

Michele had picked me up from the Palisades and drove me in her recently purchased Dodge Dart Swinger, back up to Santa Barbara. She had a fresh bruise on her cheek from her job just south of the university at a place called Donavan's house. Donavan's house was a place for mentally challenged youth. One of the cast members of a show we grew up watching had a kid there that had tried to eat her face. Ok not really but he was a bit bitey and had gotten her pretty good. She loved that job and loved those kids.

This was my first actual college experience, apart from crashing UCLA parties in Westwood. Like with most things, Michele had forged her own path as a college student. She made her own friends earlier in the dorms and now in her theater classes and some just on the street. She made one friend by chasing her around on her bicycle for a week yelling at her that she was going to make her stop and talk to her. After figuring out she wasn't a complete lunatic, they became really good friends.

Michele took me around campus, showed me the theater department where most of her classes were, and then all the spots the students hung out. I stayed over Friday and Saturday night and we partied like college kids. Drinking beers by the beach in the late afternoon. Taking a quick power nap then beers and shots late into the night.

After a bunch of rocking out to the Peppers, Siouxsie and the Banshees and what ever else she was playing, she told me that she was having the time of her life. She said that she was doing exactly what she wanted to be doing. It had a serious affect on me. I mean what the hell do I want to do? I had no direction and never really had a

Dad to ask me all those questions about how I was going to plan out my life.

I quickly snapped out of that thought and got back to how stoked I was on how excited she seemed and how cool all her friends were.

After a fun weekend in Santa Barbara we headed back for home. On the way driving back, we were singing songs like we had used to do in her bedroom when mom and Dick were fighting. But now we were listening to X and the Dickies and just rocking the fuck out. It was a beautiful early fall Sunday afternoon. Michele had to be back in Santa Barbara that night so we took the 101 back home. It was a little faster than taking the coast and she just had time to come inside and say hi then turn around and head back up to school. Pretty cool for her to do for me, considering how intense her theater schedule was that semester.

We made it back to the house and went inside. Michele gave Jessica a huge hug and had the same thing for mom. Mom's eyes lit up when they talked about the new theater program she was in. I had never really seen that before. I think she was seeing her daughters future unfolding and it awoke something inside of her. Something good… something very foreign to her…something happy. She went and said hi to Dick, who stayed in his easy chair and maybe mustered up a "how's school" but that was it.

A couple of weeks later it was November 5 1987, my 17th birthday. I had gone on a bunch of dates with a girl named Tina that I really liked in the few weeks prior. I thought this girl could be my big high school relationship. Maybe this would be the first girl that I really loved that I would also have sex with. She was one of Michele's best friends little sister so it was perfect in more ways than one.

One night I took her to Hakata for sushi and had an amazing time with an amazing girl. After eating and having a few beers I took out my black zippo adorned with a black panther and lit a cigarette. I asked her if she knew what a totem was. She had no idea. I explained to her the concept of a spirit animal. I told her that I thought that this was mine….. Ok I know it sounds super cheesy but that's some deep shit for a 17 year old in 1987.

Tina was a virgin and I was fully aware of this fact. I wasn't taking that shit lightly. As far as I knew I wasn't anybody's first and really didn't want that responsibility. But Tina was different. I cared about her, I liked her as a person, and I loved her as a woman… a 16 year old woman but a woman none the less.

We had been dating for a few weeks when on November 7, 2 days after my birthday, I took her to Huey's birthday party. Huey was the kid I was able to get drinks with at the Bar and Bat Mitzvah's all those years earlier. I had known him since first grade. He also happened to be on the wrong end of the phrase, "its all fun and games until someone loses an eye."

Huey's dad was cool and let him have a little get together for his birthday before we all went to a huge house party in Brentwood on lower Rockingham where all the boys were going to be. I brought Tina, thinking at the end of this night we might actually be doing it. We had made out so many times with no follow through it felt like even she was going to say.. "Dude! Throw down already!!" It was fucking time…. For fucking.. No, that would really have been much sweeter than that….her first time and me really caring about that, and her.

It was still early in the evening and I wanted to smoke weed. I figured I would grab David DeKernion and smoke a little with him in my car before we left for the party. DK was cool on another level apart from the rest of my neighborhood friends. In a world where it was all "surfs up bra…. lets go skate…lets scam on some chicks, lets smoke some weed WEEWW!!!" He was the type of kid who would have a real conversation with you. "How are you Fred, (yes my actual nickname, from Red Skeletons Freddy the Freeloader) everything good at home? How's your sis?" This time, since we were both high school seniors, UC Santa Cruz was high (pun intended) on his mind. As we smoked out, he started telling me about how he and Brendo were going to school up there and how awesome it was. The next 20 minutes were spent with him telling me everything he did on their trip up a couple weeks before (around the time I was in Santa Barbara). About the literally legendary surf and Derby skate park. (There were no skate parks anywhere at that time. The only one near me was Marina Skate Park and I think it was Bruce Jenner that bought it and filled it in with dirt 10 years earlier and built a gym on top of it… Dick.)

He said the campus was in the middle of a redwood forest, and there was elf land. There was a place called fucking elf land. A place right in the middle of campus that looked like wood nymphs and fairies and shit should be running around. "Some chicks walk around campus totally naked…. Naked!!!". I had never seen him so animated and excited. Not about naked chicks on campus but the whole deal. I looked right in his eyes and said, 'It might take me a couple years, because with my grades I'm going nowhere but city college right now, but I will be with you at the University of California at Santa Cruz at some time in the future…. You had me a skate park'.

His eyes got wide again as he put out his hand and said "promise me" we shook hands. 'Promise' I said. We got out of my car and went inside to hang for a little bit longer and then say our goodbyes. DK was going to pick up Damon Hughes and meet everyone else at the party.

DK had gotten me so excited about Santa Cruz that I probably talked with Tina about going there for a half an hour. Ok so some talking and some making out. I looked over at her smiled and said "We are probably missing a pretty cool party." She smiled back and nodded and off we went. As we drove down Sunset past the Riviera we slowed down for an accident. The cops were there, there were a few people standing around but I couldn't make any of them out so I just kept driving. I looked at Tina and grabbed her hand and said "I hope we don't know anybody in that shit."

We got to where the party was, parked my car, got out and maybe made it 20 feet before Zoyd ran up to us screaming "DK's fucking dead!!"

DK had picked Damon Hughes up at Craig's house on Capri. Damon put on his seat belt but the shoulder strap wasn't working. DK didn't have his seat belt on at all. They had turned onto sunset, drove about two blocks then DK looked over at Damon and said "Feel the torque of the grand prix" as he hit the gas. Those were the last words DK ever spoke.

Some woman turned left, right in front of him and they slammed right into her. DK's chest was crushed by the steering wheel. Pieces of Bone tore thru his organs causing him to bleed out internally in a relatively short period of time. He died sitting there, right next to Damon. The faulty shoulder strap had caused Damon's head to fly free and slam into the dashboard causing a scar that never went away. DK's wasn't speeding, or drunk, it was just an accident. The girl turned right in front of him. There was nothing he could have done (That is what I knew from being with him right before but was confirmed by the police report). This was the first time I had ever experienced death. I didn't' know what to do. My friend who was sitting next to me an hour earlier telling me about his plans for the future, a future I was going to be a part of, was gone and never coming back.

I was in shock. Everything in my life was put on hold. School, Tina, family…. I hung with the boys just grieving. We walked to DKs funeral at Corpus Christi Church. I saw his family right when I walked in. I saw his sister and his girlfriend sitting in the front row. I listened to his girlfriend Linda speak about him. I could not imagine what they, and his mom and dad were going through. It was the most painful moment in my life. I spent the next week in a daze. I couldn't comprehend what had happened. I mean I had a couple pets die but no people close to me. I had no father to ask questions or to lean on. I could try Michele, but she was away at school. I didn't feel right laying all this heavy shit on her. I didn't want to be a burden when she was enjoying herself so much and everything was going so well for her.

Twelve days after DK died Michele came thru town. She and some friends stopped by the house on their way to see U2 and then drive back up to school. I was in the back yard with a couple friends still trying to wrap my head around the fact that DK was gone. I saw Michele with a couple of her housemates, people I had just met a few weeks before. I don't think either of us knew what to say. We looked at each other, she gave me a nod and then walked out the door. The nod was meant to comfort. We didn't really need to speak. With that one gesture she had just told me that she loved me, and that no words will suffice.

Even though I was a hack I managed to play for the Pail high varsity soccer team. (Probably because Zoyd and Paul pestered the coach till he let me play) We only lost once or twice, and I broke a guys arm from Venice, our cross town rivals in our final game. After practice the next

151

day after the U2 concert I came home to my mom crying. She told me that Michele had not made it home from the concert, and that her roommates hadn't either. She told me a car had driven off PCH into the ocean right past the Ventura county line matching the one they were driving. There were no survivors. Mom said that she and Dick were going to go and identify Michele's body and make sure that is really was her.

Belaying the shock and horror, my first thought was why the fuck should Dick go?? Fuck that guy!! I should be the one going!!!! He treated her like shit. When she and her friends stopped at the house on the way to the concert, he didn't even get out of his chair when she tried to introduce her friends. I could see him from outside. He barely looked up while Michele said everyone's name… everyone that would be dead within the next 8 hours. Fuck that guy!!! But then the reality of the situation set in…. and I stayed as together as I could for my mom. When they left, I ran up to the garage to hit it as hard as I could, like I had done so many times before, but just collapsed on the ground and cried.

If you have ever taken the beautiful drive along PCH between Malibu and Santa Barbara, you are familiar with the giant sand hill on the right shoulder just past the Ventura County Line; and if you have ever seen a car commercial with the pacific ocean as the back drop, you are familiar with the point right before that; the giant rock that is standing alone on the ocean side of the road. There are a couple of swooping curves that feel like they run out over the water right in between those two landmarks, right next to the surf spot that breaks like 5 times a year called Supertubes. The first time you drive them you can't help but think "I wonder what would happen if I didn't make this turn?" That's where they drove off the road into the ocean. The evidence suggested that the kid driving fell asleep at the wheel hit the mountain on the right side, then shot across all lanes and flew off the cliff 30+ feet into the ocean. Michele and one other person were found inside of the car. They dragged the bay and found one more kid, the last one was never found.

Over my lifetime I had pictured everyone dying; Friends, neighbors, Jessica, grandparents, strangers, my mom, Dick (duh), but Michele dying never even crossed my mind. I guess it was something that was just too much to even think about. I mean she was my safety net! Nothing could ever happen to her! She was the one that made it ok to go out and be who I am. Growing up she tried protecting me from Dick every chance she had. She took the role of my mom and stepdad who were too busy fighting with each other or pretending everything was fine to be real parents to me. She was my best friend. Growing up it really felt like she was my only true family….. she was my big sister. She was the brightest spirit of anyone, even to this day, that I have ever known. How could I ever imagine someone that strong and full of life being taken away? I guess I never thought of it because it was just too much to imagine.

After my mom and Dick left for the Ventura County Coroners office I do not remember how I got there, but the first place I went to was my spiritual home, Takeo's house. Takeo, Greg and Buckler were in the hot tub after surfing. I walked up and said "Michele is dead"; the serenity of the most soulful place on earth to me was instantly shattered. No one said a word.

I wish I could make this a feel good, come from adversity story but that's not what it is. If I had died and Michele was writing this, it probably would be…but it's not. I'm not that strong. I'm not that self-confident. I knew in my heart that the truly special child was dead and I was all that was left. So this is more a story of how a 17 year old kid, trying to find his way in the world, survived when the only person that really mattered to him was ripped away at probably the most important point in his life.

When Dick and my mom came back, my mom nodded yes. She handed me a fairy ring that was badly mangled. The front was fine, but the back was so twisted you could never fit it on your finger. It was practically folded in half in the back but that fairy was perfect. She and her friend were probably pretty badly damaged from washing up in the car on the rocks over night. It went from road, to cliff, to rocks and ocean so there was no beach. Someone fishing spotted the car in the water the next morning.

I knew about my mom's brother, killing himself, as do you from the beginning of this story. I also knew about her abuse as a child and that she stayed with a man that was a piece of shit so she could take care of her children. I knew that Michele was .... let's face it… the brightest, most talented, most gifted, most giving, and most anything else you can think of her three children. I knew that my mom saw in Michele the person she thought she might have been able to be if she hadn't been so beaten down physically and emotionally when she was young. I knew that losing a child on its own has to be one of the hardest things any parent can go through but losing Michele had to be different. So I knew I had to be there for her. Otherwise I would have blown my fucking brains out right then and there.

I am not saying that to be dramatic. Those were the only two things I could think of. Blowing my brains out, or living so I don't add more pain to my mothers' life. Thankfully I didn't let selfishness win out. I thought, I can't see my mom hurting any more than she already is. I guess I have to live.

Act II

Chapter 9

Survival Skills When You Are On Your Own, Sensational Murder

I put the FUN in funeral. Michele's service was at the Palisades Presbyterian Church… The one where we went to midweek (church group) as little kids.. The same one where I might have peed in the orange juice on a Sunday or two with Gene Roca when I was 5 or 6 years old (I think the Sunday School teacher just opened the door and let me loose when I got too crazy for her to deal with). My mom asked me to make the playlist for the funeral so you could say I DJ'd in '87. Michele would have wanted it to be a huge party, but I kept it pretty mellow. The service wasn't really for her. As far as I was concerned it was for my mother. The Red Hot Chili Peppers had just released the *Uplift Mofo Party Plan,* and the album just happened to have on it the mellowest song they had ever done…a song called 'Behind the Sun'. It was a beautiful song that was almost tailor made for Michele's service. If you haven't heard it I highly recommend checking it out.

The main other song I remember from the service was another one of her favorite artists who also died way before his time. Bob Marley's '3 Little Birds'. That song will still stop me dead in my tracks if I hear it. The chorus if you don't know goes like this. "Don't worry.. about a thing.. 'cause every little thing.. 's gonna be all right." At the time it felt like Michele talking to all of us trying to let us know that everything was gonna be all right. I'm not saying I was channeling Michele I'm just saying that in that church, when that song went down, you could feel it. (It is in a car commercial now…. So much for that.)

I rounded it out with some Cat Stevens, or Yusulf Islam or whatever the fuck his name is now. She really liked him. That was one of the artists we had the most fun singing when we were little and mom and Dick were fighting. Parents yelling at each other in their room… 'Peace Train' downstairs in Michele's room.

We walked the 5 blocks to the church passing my fellow fire starter Pronger's house and then Zoyd's house. They were both on their front porches with some members of their families. Not really much you can say. Gave a nod, and on we went. Michele would have liked it more if we had the tradition of full jazz marching bands following the family like they do in New Orleans; Everybody dancing there way to the funeral. Celebrating someone's life with a real party. I think she would have really dug something like that. But again, the service was for mom.

The service itself was beautiful. There were tropical flowers that I had never even imagined existing surrounding a picture of Michele at the front of the church. Michele's good play production friends Josh and Phil sang 'California Dreaming' by the Momma's and the Poppas. It was another song she loved.

One of the most memorable parts was when her friend Michael Lee did an interpretive dance that was one of the most amazing things I had ever seen. I know. Interpretive dance...not very manly. (He was a gay black kid) But his dance was literally his heart breaking set to music done with movement. He kept collapsing on the ground crying and forcing himself to get back up and continue on. It was one of the most beautiful things I have ever seen in my life. Thank you Michael Lee.

After the service we finally got down to doing what Michele would have wanted us to do in the first place….. PARTYING!!! This is an all out celebration of my sisters life!!! We walked back home from the church and started out with things we had at the house, but what really made it a party was the stuff people brought.

As far as I'm concerned, here is the hierarchy of what to bring for an event like this. #1- Alcohol and ice. This is also the one type of party where the guests should be doing all the thinking…and its easy! Whatever you like to drink….bring enough for at least 3 people. That will end up taking care of all the liquor, wine, and beer lovers and hopefully leave enough for the family to have some left over. Ice- because even when you plan a party to the last detail, you always end up sending someone out for ice. #2- Food. We could use food for the party but also nobody is cooking in this house for the next couple of weeks so if you could bring something that will last a few days in the fridge you might keep us from starving. #3 Flowers. We will probably have flowers from the service but its still nice to know that you are thinking about us…if you are thinking about us and are a little more on the ball, you will go more along the lines of #1 & #2.

All the people from the service came over, as well as people from the neighborhood and also people that just thought Michele would like to see them there. So many friends and family, it was the most amazing fucked up party you could imagine. Even my dad had flown in from Chile to be at the service.

I had a bunch of booze in my system so it was time to smoke some weed. I was walking out of the house with Takeo and my dad said "Don't hold out on me son." So that would be the first time I ever smoked weed with my dad… And not just a joint or out of a pipe… We were ripping bong hits out of a 3 foot bong in Takeo's dads minivan.

It was the perfect party for Michele that had its drama as well as everything else. One of Michele's friends Tracy had run out screaming into the night. You could hear her howling through the neighborhood when you went into the front yard. My only other solid memory of Tracy was our neighbor Rob, me, Tracy, and Michele sitting smoking cigarettes in the emergency room of St. Johns Hospital. Tracy had cut her leg at a show and thought she was gonna die. Some hobo was sitting next to us nursing a foot that closely resembled a mangled tree root. The hobo, dead hammered, leaned over to Tracy and said, "Hey Madonna….. HEY MADONNA…. Ilikeyouyourpretty." He said this all in one word as he fell out of his chair and passed out on the floor.

Tracy was a little crazy anyway and the whole Michele getting killed thing just sent her over the edge. When she finally came back to the house I was filling up my cup with ice cubes in the kitchen sink. She burst through the front door, ran into the kitchen and grabbed a butcher knife out of the drawer. Screaming, she raised it with both hands like she was going to plunge it into her chest. Dick came running in from the other room and tackled her to the ground and got the knife out of her hands. She was screaming and crying uncontrollably and Dick had her pinned to the kitchen floor trying to calm her down. I was still dropping ice cubes into my cup one at a time…. "That oughta do it," I thought to myself as I stepped over the two of them to get back to the bar. I wasn't even trying to process that shit so I just poured my jack and coke then made my way back out to the party.

That was pretty much the night….lots of drinks, lots of condolences, lots of sorry for your loss. My tears flowed the entire night, but I was so numb it was as if they were coming out of someone else's eyes. I did feel very sad but the numbness was like some biological imperative that kept my head from exploding and spraying everybody with my sorrow (Sorrow is not the right word. I don't think the right one exists).

Paramount Ranch

A day or two later was when we spread Michele's ashes. Most theater kids love the Renaissance Fair and Michele was no exception. She would go almost every year all dressed up with a bunch of her friends to Paramount Ranch in Agoura Hills where it was held. Paramount Ranch is right next to Tapia Park just east of the hills above Malibu. Tapia Park was were moms brother uncle Brock killed himself and where his ashes were spread. It kind of sucked for me because I had worked for Dick at Paramount Ranch so it didn't hold the same allure for me, but again; not for me, for my mom.

Cremation is probably a little different then you think. The body is not placed into a furnace, reduced to ash then placed in an urn. The furnace is not hot enough to do that. The body is placed into the fire until the only thing left is bone. The bones are then sent through a series of ball bearings that pulverize the bone into tiny fragments, and that's what ends up on the mantle above your fireplace.

The family and I went up a trail to a bench at the top of a hill at Paramount Ranch. Aunts uncles cousins grandparents, all there to spread the ashes of our fallen loved one. We didn't need to spend the extra money on an urn so I was carrying the velvet covered brass box that contained Michele's earthly remains. I took the box out of the bag. In the most somber of moments, I held onto it, looked up to the sky, then at my surrounding family, then went to open it.

I flipped the box over a few times, then looked at my cousin Andrew and said, "How the fuck do you open this thing?" He took the box inspected it, put one of his keys in the crease and promptly bent it in half. The next 20 minutes could best be described by watching that Sampsonite luggage commercial from the early 80's. A bunch of monkeys jumping up and down on the luggage trying to damage it or to get it open. We finally managed to open it by stomping on and bending the shit out of the thing. By that time we were all laughing hysterically.

After the laughter died down we all began grabbing handfuls of Michele and spreading her around. When I dropped my second handful I saw something in the ash that stopped my heart. I saw a bright pink piece of bone. I almost immediately realized that Michele's dark fuchsia hair dye had stained some of the bone during the cremation process. I was fascinated, horrified and relieved, all at once. I say relieved because there was a scandal in the news at the time about crematoriums burning multiple bodies at once and giving families parceled out pieces of everybody. Now I knew this clearly didn't happen to Michele. So I stared at the bright pink pieces of bone as I walked away with the family down the hill away from what was left of her body.

That wasn't going to be the end of that. A couple days later I went back up there and grabbed a rock with a depression in it and some of the pieces of Michele including several pink ones and brought them home. I still have them and that brass box all bent up to this day.

Surviving the first year.

Because I had made the decision to live, I had to make it through the first year. I only had my memories of Michele and a scant few other things to help me out. One of which was an experience I don't fully understand. I guess you could call it an out of body experience.

After we spread Michele's ashes, I started to light a candle in the window of my room every night. I put it right by the ledge that she and I used to smoke cigarettes on or just hang out and talk. One night I was looking at the candle, then all of a sudden I saw the candle from outside. Then picture Google Earth pulling back from the view of a house. That's what I did. The feeling of motion was amazing…and the entire time, I could still see the candlelight. So after pulling back from the house to the city to the country to the planet… I could still see the candlelight. Then the feeling of motion was even faster as I zipped across the solar system, then the galaxy, then the universe and still, I could see the candle light. I shook my head and I was back in my room, staring at the candle. Some crazy shit right? I have never felt the power of acceleration so intensely as I did that night sitting alone in my room. Never.

I took about two weeks off of school because that seemed like the standard amount of time you take when your life blows up in your face. Now where was I??? Oh yeah, Senior year, feeling great about myself, got my whole life in front of me…this is going to be the best year yet!!!… Oh fuck me.

So now I'm supposed to start figuring out what I want to do with my life? If anybody asked me what I wanted to do, I would think to myself, stay alive so my mom doesn't get hurt anymore, then tell them to go fuck themselves.

Scholastically I was one referral away from being suspended for a long time or maybe even expelled. At Pali if you fill up your disciplinary card, you are out. But because Michele died they flipped my card over and let me have that side as well. I had a no bullshit teacher for science in 10th grade named Mr. Pierson. He was known for being a hard ass and lets just say we didn't see eye to eye. You were supposed to get him for a semester as a senior and then a super mellow very nice and smart teacher named Mr. Anderson the second. They gave me Anderson both semesters. So I never got to dissect a frog, or a fetal pig, or a hobo. I'm not sure really what they got to chop up but I never did it. I guess somewhere there's a frog that got a few extra years because my sister didn't.

Teachers for the most part didn't know what to do with me. Neither did the administrators. They didn't even have me sign up for my mandatory year of language. I guess they thought the fewer difficult classes I had the less likely they were going to have to pass a failing kid. I also never took the SAT or any other placement test. I did have a pretty tuff government class with Lord Bailiff. Michele had given me the heads up on Mr. Bailiff and so when he called on me the first day of class (before she was killed) I responded "Yes lord Bailiff?" The class laughed out loud and was sure I was going to get reamed by him. But all he said was… "Yeah, I like the way that sounds."

He was a ball buster and most kids hated him but he was occasionally good for a laugh. One day a kid named

Robert who had exceptionally big and wild hair that had about 3 or 4 too many angles on it, was sitting in his seat listening to Lord Bailiffs lecture with the rest of us. Mid sentence on the three branches of government Bailiff stopped and asked, "Robert, where does one go to get a hair cut like that?" We all just busted out laughing.

I mention Mr. Bailiff because he was the one teacher that didn't let me slide on anything. He told me that he was very sorry for my loss, but that I had to do everything that everybody else had to do. He said he understood that I might not be able to make all the deadlines everybody else has to make, but by the end of the course I had to turn in all the work. At first I was like "Well fuuuuck you!!!" I mean how dare he? Doesn't he understand what I am going thru? But another part of me realized what he was trying to do for me.

He was trying to make me see that no matter what happens in your life, you still have to push forward. I knew what he was doing and on some level I appreciated it, but couldn't really act on it. I couldn't wake up and be like "ok time to put this behind me and press on with my life." The best I would be able to do was limp sideways and maybe fall forward every once in a while.

Old Mr. Vahn from Paul Revere had a much younger wife (I wonder if he met her when she was climbing the ropes). She taught photography at Pali. Someone came up to me one day and told me that she was using Michele as a "see what happens when you drink and drive" example. Great idea. First of all, I didn't know if anyone was drinking and driving, and second the girl you are talking abouts little brother is still at the school where you work. I went straight to her classroom and walked up to her and said "do not EVER, mention my sisters name again!" I think she tried to apologize but I just walked out of the room. It's all right. She got hers a couple years later when her husband got busted for feeling up the little girls at Revere.

Michele and I still had our same telephone number. Yep, back when it was only landlines. The rich girls did have car phones and pagers but cell phones were so expensive and so heavy that you could kill someone if you dropped one on them. I wasn't much help to Michele's friends. It wasn't like today, where someone puts up a Facebook post about someone dying and then everybody knows. I would get calls... "Hi, is Michele there?" ' No, she's dead.' " Oh my god! I'm so sorry." 'Yeah, fucking sucks, bye.' I was way too busy being hurt. I didn't have time for anybody else's feelings.

Lots of people would tell me they were sorry, which must have been a very difficult thing for them to do. Actually none of my little sister Jessica's friends could relate to her and they all dropped off. She was 5 years younger than me and still at Paul Revere. The people that came to support her were kids that were from the inner city.

I think the reason why was they were from a rougher area. They probably knew someone who died or were affected somehow by death. They weren't afraid to say, I'm sorry for your loss, then reach out and hug her. Those were mostly her friends throughout high school. I think it made death too real for all her friends from the Palisades. I don't think any of them had the courage to do that for her. Which isn't really a bad thing, they were 12 or 13 year old kids! They just didn't know how to do it.

My very deep hurt would quickly fluctuate to anger. I wanted to hate everybody that was alive because Michele wasn't. I managed to control a good deal of it but sometimes I couldn't keep it inside.

People would say they were sorry for my loss, but then some people would have to fuck it all up by following that with a very sincere, "I know how you feel." Now, if you were one of the unfortunate people who said that to me back then, let me apologize to you now. Having apologized because you didn't deserve my rage when you were just trying to be supportive, let me now also say, you are a fucking idiot! No you don't know how I feel! What because your cat died? Or maybe your grandmother had a heart attack and keeled over? Not even close! Those things are supposed to happen! Even if you had a sister that basically raised you… the only true family that you felt that you had… had died in the exact same fucking way, on the exact same fucking day at the exact same fucking time, you still don't have a clue how I feel! So if this were a "how too" guide to providing moral support to someone who has experienced a loss, this would be where I would say, "Choose your words wisely."… and your shoes go on your feet and a hat goes on your head.

On the subject of stupidity and what you might not want to say to someone who has experienced a loss, a couple years later, Tony Demani's (Michele's grade who I dated) little sister came up to me at a party and said that she totally understands me….. "Why, what ever do you mean Sandy??" She proceeded to tell me that she had taken a couple of psychology classes in college and she knows exactly what is going on with me. Again, apology to Sandy… The fact that you cared enough to think of me when you were studying and were trying to empathize with my plight is an amazing thing. But the nice, 'I understand your pain and am here,' vibe that you might have been going for was completely lost on me. All I could think was you have to be the dumbest person on the face of the planet. Lucky for you you didn't pass me that gem right after it happened. Oh god… I just found out she is some sort of therapist now.

Back to the days and weeks around the funeral. I don't' know if you have ever seen the sunset during the fall in the beach communities around Los Angeles, but they are something to behold. On a usual day the Santa Anna winds have blown every bit of smog and pollution out to sea. It being fire season you can usually get a bunch of smoke blown out across the horizon. You also have an unobstructed view from the mountains out over the pacific. The only thing the Santa Ana's don't touch is some high level clouds. When the sun begins to set those high clouds catch the lower end of the color spectrum casting out the most gorgeous yellows oranges and reds, to violets, then dims to the black of night.

Those sunsets remind me vividly of that time in my life. The slight Santa Ana wind building up off the desert makes a nice hot dry off shore wind. If you were surfing it would take the tip off of every wave and make a mini rainstorm complete with rainbows. It is truly an amazing time. I can't remember the last time I surfed during that time of year. I like to say the waters too cold and I don't like wearing wetsuits. Sometimes I think being in the ocean… and being that happy is just a little to hard for me to deal with.

Next up, Thanksgiving….Ahh family gatherings 5 days after a "you've got to be shitting me" death. Back at grandma's, aunts uncle's cousins, the whole gang was there. I looked at my aunt Trudy (Andrews mom) and whispered, "Lets start passing all the food to that end of the table." After a minute everyone from my grandmothers end of the table had both hands full and everyone else was pointing and laughing out loud. It was a nice break from the shit show. All I remember from the rest of that night was everybody crying. Christmas wasn't much better. "It's the most wonderful time of the year!" Yeah, that was the day I found out why so many people kill themselves during the holidays.

After that... New Year's!! My resolution??? I resolve not to brain myself with an ice pick. Thanks. There was a pretty strong Santa Ana event that year. Stronger than it had been in the last few.., Huge fire danger, 30-40 MPH winds, gusting even higher up to 70 or even 80. That first trash day after new years, all the Christmas trees are out at the side of the road. Who can tell where this is going? That night, everyone that had a pickup truck grabbed it and we were all off to pick up as many dead Christmas trees as we could.

We brought them all to Jetty, our local surf spot (which would later become the set of Baywatch). We lined them all up, probably about 30 trees in all and someone tossed in one match. Within maybe 2 or 3 seconds all 30 trees were fully engulfed in flames. Cars on PCH came to a stop because that many trees fully engulfed burn so bright that it looked like daytime. You could have seen that shit from space. Almost as quick as it lights up, with nothing else to burn, it goes out. Now unlike the bon fires that the future TV show got to have, ours were illegal for some reason so once that shit went out we all jumped into our trucks and bailed.

Back at school

I was having good days, and bad days as the year moved on. Towards the end of the school year we had graduation rehearsal, where the counselors divided the class in half on the bleachers inside of the basketball gym. I happened to be on the other side of the gym from my old friend Brandon Lee. Over the years we had become really good friends, (he's the one I brought to be in the Chili Pepper video shoot) such good friends that we could crack each other up from across the gym without saying a word.

Now I was cracking up when Mr. Weinstein who was maybe 70 years old was calling out the name of every student in our senior class. He had a microphone and it was mandatory that you show up for this thing if you wanted to graduate so they didn't care that everyone was talking. When it got close to your name you listened up.

Then he got to my name, but instead of calling my name, Michael, he called Michele's. "Michele Friedlander.... Michele Friedlander.... Michele Friedlander....Michele Friedlander".... By the time another counselor realized what was happening and ran up and grabbed the mic away from him, the entire auditorium was sitting silent, staring right at me. I stood up and walked to the back door of the gym and went outside. I walked back and forth for a second then followed up on the punch that never happened when my mom told me Michele was dead. Only instead of the garage I hit the cement pillar that ran up the side of the gym. A pillar that my dad probably placed the rebar in while my grandfather was watching.

I hit that motherfucker as hard as I could then walked straight up to my moms office right up the street 'cause I knew right away that my hand was broken. I didn't feel any pain but I knew that concrete is a lot harder than bone and I couldn't unclench my fist. Apparently it was a nice flush punch because I did minimal damage to my knuckles. I broke the bones in the middle of my hand. I guess it's called a boxers break.

I got a cast and have some pictures of me with it on in the yearbook. It didn't even fix it. The doctor said he could re break my hand and I could wear a cast all summer. Lets see when I need my favorite things to do like skating and surfing now more than ever I have to have a cast??? No. Fuck that. As a matter of fact it's still broken right now. Swells up sometimes when I am doing repetitive shit like writing... you're welcome. Oh and I know you are dead now but fuck you Weinstein.

Brandon's birthday was in March, right around St. Patrick's Day. So his brother Tex would get us a green keg of beer every year. There is one pic in the yearbook with my broken hand, the rest I have are from his 18th birthday that year. One pic had me Branden, Tex, Chris Dowling, Christian, Teak Dyer, Scott, Kristina, Tracy, Tracey, Suarezburger and I think that's it. Chris is awesome in it because his head looks like a penis.

So the two hottest girls in high school were Danielle and Teak. Maybe another Danielle as well but she was sort of quiet around me. That was two Jews in the top 3, for all you white supremacists out there. Suck on that for a minute or two. The Danielle's were awesome, but Teak was something else.

Not only was Teak beautiful, but also she was one of the most down to earth people I had ever met. It was also pretty great that her dad lived on San Vicente in a huge house, and was out of town quite frequently. She and her brother would have huge parties at least once every month or two. One time she had a few hundred people over on a Friday night and just some close friends over on Saturday night. Rod (her dad) wasn't coming home until Sunday.

To get a good picture of Teaks house, it was pretty classy 80's modern style decor. There was some really cool modern art, and then there was definitely some, "what the fuck kind of shit is this?" art too. For instance, there was a metal cow in the back yard. A full sized metal cow. There was a staircase that didn't go anywhere as well. On said staircase was a giant cement ball.

If you have ever seen *Beverly Hills Cop*, you might remember Balkie from the TV show *Perfect Strangers* playing the effeminate worker in the modern art shop in Beverly Hills. Eddie Murphy... excuse me Axle Foley can't believe the crap that's in the shop and how much money it costs. "How much is this piece here?" 'One hundred thirty thousand dollars.' "Get the fuck out of here!" 'No I cannot.' The piece he is talking about is a bunch of mannequins sitting at a set dinner table that has mannequin heads spinning in circles on their plates. Teaks folks had bought a smaller version of the same crap, for an equivalent price.

So after surviving yet another hundred plus person party on Friday, I walked past this thing on Saturday and the flannel around my waist hooked the leg and pulled it off in a way that made it not want to go back on again. So she ended up getting busted for having people over and breaking their hideous mannequin modern art crap all because of me. What a dick.

I had met a girl a year younger than me at Pali that would be my girl friend for the next year and a half named Serena. She was a champion for dealing with me as messed up as I was. Just before my high school graduation, Teak and some of her girl friends threw a birthday/graduation party at the Carousel on the Santa Monica Pier. I was with Serena, trying to get Teaks attention but things were a little too crazy. The party was getting broken up because everybody had booze and the Carousel people knew we were in high school and were freaking out. We were all trying to figure out where to go and I gave up on Teak, turned to Serena and said I'll just talk to her later.

I woke up the next day, the day before my high school graduation a little early. People had been calling…. lots of people. Something bad had happened, something happened to Teak. Her body was found at 6:30 AM in the bathroom of a business complex on Sunset Blvd. She had disappeared from a party and was found apparently sexually assaulted and shot.

I'm not sure what really happened. What I do know is she had a run in with a Mac Guard security guard named Rodney Garmanian and he shot and killed her. (Yes, her dad was a Rod too) We had all been drinking so I knew she had to be at least a little tipsy. They crossed paths and then he probably tried to take advantage of her. She resisted, he persisted, she beat his ass and scratched up his face, and then he shot her several times and killed her in the bathroom by the Great Western bank in Pacific Palisades California. He was later observed nervously smoking cigarettes in the Mobile station parking lot across the street with scratches on his face. Teak was then found dead in a building he patrolled and he was arrested. In his subsequent trial he was also found guilty of attempting to use his contacts to kill the judge and lead detective. We also found out later that there were sexual harassment complaints against Garmanian and he wasn't fired, he was just moved to a new area.

The guy that owned Mac Guard was a real winner. The week after Teaks death he took out a full page article in the Palisades Post expressing his condolences to her family….in the first paragraph. Then he went on to say thank you to all of his MANY supporters and talked shit about people jumping to what turned out to be the correct assumption. He was a scumbag. Teaks parents sued him. The terms of the settlement were not made public. I heard it was a lot.

We were supposed to be excited for graduation. We were supposed to be putting on our caps and gowns, heading down to school, walking across the stage, then walking off to the rest of our lives. Prongers sister was in my grade so the party they had planned that was supposed to be in celebration of our graduation was morphed into a happy graduation/sad good bye to Teak. The 30 or so kids from our class that came by had a drink to toast the end of Teaks life and the supposed beginning of our own.

Before making our way down to the football field we all shared a couple of sharpies and wrote messages to Teak on top of our caps. I have the traditional picture of me receiving my diploma and shaking the principals hand with a smile on my face. You can't tell that there is a message of love to Teak on top of my cap. I don't know if she could look down and see those messages but it felt a little better to put it out there. Maybe her soul had to roam the Palisades High School football field until her name was read aloud and she could be set free by the sacred act of high school graduation.

Almost everyone's names were read…almost everyone graduated…almost everyone survived… The class of 1988………. No but seriously….how fucked up is that? What a way to graduate! Writing notes to Teak on our caps because we couldn't say them to her face. All because some limp dick wanna be rouge, fake cop, tried to rape the nicest, hottest, coolest girl in our class, got his ass kicked instead so he shot and killed her.

I just happened to have an incident with Rodney Garmanian about 3 days before he murdered Teak. We were rolling a car that was done up to look like a can of Coors Light silver bullet onto the quad for our senior prank. All of a sudden there were security cars everywhere and we all bolted. My dumb ass was pretty drunk at the time so I got caught pretty quickly. The real cops got our names and let us go. On the way out I extended my hand to the security guard who cornered me, shaking his hand I said nice grab. I was shaking the hand of Rodney Garmanian….the hand that would pull the trigger on my friend Teak in less than 72 hours.

Chapter 10

The Death Of Fame, The Fame Of Death

I know everyone says that a person they knew that died young was a super special person. I also know a lot of the time that's bullshit because assholes die too. So do ordinary people. It just so happens that Michele *was* going to be a superstar. She *was* larger than life and an exceptional person that loved everyone and everyone loved. Teak *was* the hottest, super cool girl in school. DK *was* one of the most soulful kids that we hung out with (and the smartest).

I didn't go to Teaks funeral. I was too upset. I couldn't watch Teaks brother crying as people talked about how amazing his sister was. Those wounds were too fresh.
I knew that Teaks funeral was going to end up something of a scene. I wouldn't be able to see her close friends and family mourning the loss of a loved one. I would only see a bunch of people crying about someone they didn't even really know. I know I should have seen it as a show of support and love. Everybody loved Teak and thought she was a beautiful person. I knew I wouldn't be able to help seeing those people that didn't really know her as a bunch of fucking vultures. Using Teaks death as some sort of social tool. In my head it was going to be like a scene from that movie *Heathers (1988 Lehmann)* that had come out earlier in the year. "This is going to be the best funeral yet!" It wasn't "teenage suicide" but it was the next best thing.
I also knew there were going to be reporters there. Besides being another funeral in this small town, it was a pretty big story. I knew if I went I would end up in jail if someone started snapping pictures of me. Reporters don't give a fuck. They just want the story or the shot.
I will never forget a little over a year later, watching the news and seeing reporters trying to be the first one to get a reaction from a parent that was at the airport to pick up their child from a Syracuse College semester abroad. Pan Am flight 103 that was blown up by terrorists over Lockerbie Scotland. Reporters literally ran up to this poor woman yelling "How does it feel knowing your child is dead?!" The lady had no idea what had happened until that moment. You could literally watch her world get destroyed in the blink of an eye. She crumpled to the floor sobbing uncontrollably, all caught on tape and broadcast on the

175

national news. Got to get the story I guess but I wasn't about to deal with shit like that. I was going to say goodbye to Teak in my own way…. by myself at the bluffs, asking Michele and DK to show my friend around.

The Prongers got some grief for letting us drink at their house before and after graduation. We didn't actually drink that much there. We did our serious partying that afternoon at Donny's and Scraps and a couple other places. I just think the Prongers knew we were going to drink and they thought we might as well have a safe place to do it…

A few days later I was sitting on the their couch watching TV with his family when a news article on 20/20 came on about all the kids in the Palisades that were dying alcohol related deaths. The last photograph they showed was of Michele. At this point in time my mother hadn't told me that the kid driving had been drinking. Not that it would have made any real difference to me. But at that time in my mind, 20/20 was using my sister to sensationalize a story.

I'm glad Prongers parents were watching TV with us. They saw the look in my eyes when I got up off the couch and they called ahead to my house. I walked in, walked up to my room and grabbed a baseball bat…. That's the good thing about living in a city like LA. If a national news report pisses you off enough, you can grab a baseball bat, go down to the studio and see how many people you can kill or cripple before the cops shoot you dead. My mom stopped me before I got to the front door. She said "The boy who was driving had been drinking." I was a little upset with my mom for not telling me. But after saying as much I told her it was ok and that I wasn't going to do anything stupid.

I have no idea how much the kid who was driving Michele had to drink. I do know that the car they were in drifted towards the hillside on the right for a couple hundred feet before over correcting and driving off the road into the ocean. This could be a place where some would say something about how evil alcohol is. It was involved in Michele's death and it probably was involved with Teaks death. But that didn't have that much affect on me. DK was sober when he crashed. He was dead just like Michele and Teak. I am just telling my story. I am not trying to defend drugs and alcohol or demonize them. This is just what happened and how I was affected.

We also had some coverage from the LA times back when newspapers were relevant. Tuesday November 8 1988 one year and one day since DK's death, *Los Angeles Times* writer John Mitchel wrote a front page article entitled "Palisades High counts its dead and wonders why?" See, a few days earlier, another 3 Pali students were killed in a fiery crash on San Vicente Blvd in Santa Monica, just down the street from Teaks house. The same street we used to race down in Pats car. Cal Hoftizer, Lisa Goldberg, and Russell Kantor (son of Clinton staffer Micky Kantor). I knew Cal a little bit. We met on a Boy Scout trip to Canada some years earlier. He and his older brother who was a year older than me were on swim team together. I didn't know the other kids at all.

The deaths in the Palisades actually started with a very nice, super quiet kid who was younger than me named Clinton Hieleman. He was friends with the younger brother of the Boscoe brothers. They had a pretty bad reputation. They looked like Neanderthal OG punk rockers twins that you couldn't tell apart. One of the spots we used to party was at the back of the Malibu Getty Museum. There was a long empty road that had no buildings on it and a church at the top. You could see cars coming from a long way away so it was a perfect place to get loose. This is what I remember of this story. I might not have it all right but the end result can't be disputed. A vagrant was asleep in his van up there and came out and told the Boscoe's to turn the music down. They promptly told him to fuck off and may or may not have thrown him a beating. He went back to his van pulled out an assault rifle, shot into the Boscoe's car and blew a hole in Clinton's chest.

That was July 3 1987 4 months before DK and Michele. The scandalous part of that one is that my Boy Scout master, who was also a deputy DA for the city of Los Angeles, would hire this man to do odd jobs for him around his house. There were rumors that he had tried to do something to favor the killer and against the Boscoes. He definitely tried to play up their bad boy reputation. He should have been more worried about his own kid.

His kid was my childhood friend CK that had come over after I stole the weed out of that car on my paper route when I was 11. We were friends with this other kid named Eric (who OD'd and died when we were in high school) who gave CK a blue belly lizard he had caught. CK came back the next day with it looking like a little reptile Jesus lizard; dead, nailed to a board, belly cut open, screaming that he gave him a lizard with cancer. We were probably 10 years old. That's how you begin a career as a serial killer right? Anyway that's all I really remember about what happened to that nice kid Clinton.

A month after Teak was murdered my old punk rocker friend from Paul Revere John Liberty (Birdy) died in a car accident on sunset. We were still friendly but didn't hang out with each other anymore. He actually started hanging out with the Boscoe's and their crew. John was racing his mustang on sunset. That thing had a beast of a motor but shitty suspension. He accelerated into a corner and just lost it. They fishtailed back and forth then came to a safe stop in the opposite lanes of traffic. If that Mercedes had been able to slow down, all would have been fine. Birdy took the full brunt of that finely crafted German engineered motorcar right to his driver side door. He was killed instantly. I guess that's better than spinning out and ending up the other way and killing our friend Mike. I saw

Mike a couple of weeks ago. His back is still fucked from that accident 25 years ago.

So it was Clinton, then DK, then Michele, then Teak, then Birdy... then Lisa Russell and Cal. There were a couple others who were bused in that died that year but they weren't in the Palisades. One kid was shot and killed by his grandmother in a domestic dispute, and another kid was killed in a drive by. The main emphasis of the *LA Times* story was how so many more kids were killed from the supposedly safer school. The school in the nice neighborhood that parents in other neighborhoods wanted their kids to go to. All the schools "in the hood" Locke, Compton, Jordan and a couple others experienced no more than one death in the time it took Pali to burry 10.

The last holiday before Teak was murdered was Mother's day 1987. We celebrated, if you can call it that, at grandmas house. Jesus Christ! My poor mom. We were going through the motions when we heard tires skidding. I was up and walking out the door by the time we heard the impacts. Grammas house being just off Sunset, it was a quick six house walk to the boulevard. I must have gotten there within 30 seconds of the accident. There were 5 people in a car just south of the traffic light. 5 people, none moving. One person was smashed half way between the front and back seat in between the car door and the front seat. There was about a 3 inch space that her body was stuffed through. She had to be crushed, she had to be dead.

I walked on through the other cars in the accident as if I was window shopping for flip flops for my next beach day. I felt nothing. Literally nothing. There was no soul crushing sadness that I had been carrying with me for months, I wasn't worried about my mother trying to make it through her first mothers day since the accident, I didn't feel anything about the possibly dead body I just walked past...I felt nothing. I just sort of floated through the carnage like a ghost.

My favorite smell has always been the smell of a spring rain on hot asphalt. It's a super distinct smell that always brings back memories of my childhood. That mothers day, along with the smell of water on the asphalt, you could also smell gas, oil, antifreeze and blood all mixing together. I did not know it at the time but freshly bent metal actually has a smell to it as well. Once I placed all those scents in my mind, I realized that for the first time in months I actually felt at peace.

There was another smashed car off to my right that had people moving slowly around in it, trying to open their doors. I could tell they were probably going to be ok. They ended up in the driveway of a girl that used to baby-sit me. What was her name?? I think it was Jane?? Or Janet??...something like that. Up the hill a little was a car flipped upside down. I heard screaming so I walked around the car and saw a kid maybe a year younger than me lying half way out of the car with blood gushing out of his head onto the pavement. His head was pointing up the hill so the blood had to pass his face as it made a little river pouring back under the car. I didn't know him.

The yelling was coming from the young driver of the car who was still strapped in his seat upside down trying to get someone to help him out of the car. He was obviously scared the car was going to blow up but the only other person besides me that could have helped him was this Indian guy that must have seen the accident because he was leaning down and yelling at the kid for driving like an idiot. I actually laughed a little because he had such a thick accent and it sounded sort of funny to me at the time.

As I stood up I noticed people arriving to check out the carnage. I just walked past them back to grandmas. A part of me knew that whoever was going to live was going to live no matter what I did. Most of me was just tripping on the fact that I felt peaceful for the first time since that day earlier in my senior year of high school that changed everything.

Later on I heard that only one person died in that accident. Was it the no seatbelt wearing head wound kid hanging out the window? Was it the lady crushed into a space that she couldn't fit in? Did I miss somebody?? My money was on the squished chick. Truthfully when I heard it was only one… I don't know why, but… it made me a little bit mad.

Michele dying pretty much scattered everybody. All of her friends, and all of my family pretty much disappeared after that. All Michele's friends accept a couple never kept in contact with my mom. I'm not sure if they were supposed to. I don't know what the etiquette is. I just know as close as Michele was to some of those people, I think it would have been nice for more of them to reach out to her over the years. Maybe it was just too painful. Maybe it made death a little too real.

My extended family stopped meeting up every week after about a year. Everybody pretty much just went on with their lives. It was time for them to put that tragedy behind them. Those were the only people older or Michele's age that I looked up to that might have been able to help me out. I don't even know if any of them should have. I just knew I didn't have a dad to help give me some guidance and help me deal with my pain. My Mom was understandably broken. I knew she had to keep herself together. I knew she needed to be there as much as she was capable for Jessica. I was 18 years old, deeply hurt and in many ways, all alone.

Chapter 11

PLB

Most of the people I knew in my grade ended up going away to college. A few people with my academic prowess continued their education at Santa Monica City College or just bailed out of the whole school thing all together. Brendo went to Santa Cruz without DK. Besides that, most of the boys from my neighborhood were still around... and besides Takeo, they were my closest friends.

I had lost the only family that I knew, so the kids I was hanging out around became very important to me. I think it was right after the DK/Michele dying, someone said in a moment of reflection that us Palisades local boys need to stick together. That might or might not be the origin of that name. As far as it being a "gang", I always thought that was silly. People at Pali talked about PLB like it was a gang and pretty much made it one in the eyes of some. To me it was a bunch of kids from the same neighborhood who went through some shit and looked out for each other.

Gangs from West LA and South Santa Monica would come to the Palisades looking to fuck with us, which was just silly to me. It was mostly other people talking about us; a gang that didn't exist in the traditional sense of a gang- to people who actually were in gangs- that wanted to go test their metal against a supposed gang from the Palisades?

Funny part was that they only got the better of us on a couple occasions… and they way outnumbered us and usually had weapons. Marx got a screwdriver stuck all the way through his arm, pretty cool actually it went right between the bones and just hit meat. Zoyd and Fats got their jaws broken on separate occasions but there were never any real serious injuries. For the most part, kids from out of town rolled deep enough that you could see them coming from a mile away. If just a few came they would get their asses beat if they tried to pull anything so nothing would happen.

One fight I will tell you about. This one was a fucking free for all. For no reason at all, these kids started talking shit to us as we drove by. In Brentwood of all places. I pulled over and me and Duze walked up. This kid had his chest puffed out like 'what are you gonna do?' As I was walking up I realized he was smaller than me, about Duzes size. Duze was tuff as nails. I said "Man, I can't hit this guy, Duze, knock his ass out." Blip!!! We were on a hill and this kid almost flipped all the way over and he was out cold. As things developed, our cars stopped and it was apparent that these kids knew we were coming to this party and were ready to scrap. The only problem was that they weren't very good at it.

One guy with us was an older badass named Bryan; he had been in jail, knew martial arts and was a white boy that grew up on the islands (Hawaii-if you don't know that

183

means you fought a lot). Now there were probably 20 or 30 people fighting in the street, I grabbed one guy threw him on the ground, I got hit in the side of the head by someone who ran past me. I spun who I thought was the same guy around and cracked him with all I had in the jaw.... It was Bryan. I stopped and was like "holy shit dude I am so fucking sorry!" All the fighting and chaos became distant background noise. I just wanted to make sure he wasn't going to kill me. You could see him take a big long breath, then he just said, 'Dude, get the fuck away from me!' I was like.. "Later!" After the fighting was over and we were alone, victorious in the street, a couple of us were a little banged up and Bryan got hit only once... by me. I approached slowly and from a distance and yelled "Sorry Bryan!" He busted out laughing and it became the story of the night. 'I was knocking fools out left and right then some dude spins me around and cracks me in the jaw and its Fred.' (Yep the name stuck.)

Zoyd had a well deserved reputation for being something of a bad ass as well. Maybe it was his English soccer hooligan roots. I had known him just about as long as I knew Pronger. His balls were on full display when this kid named Milton Dent who used to live in the Palisades came to town one Moonlight Madness (night where the businesses stay open late). Milton moved to Santa Monica and befriended some locals who didn't like us and told them he could point out some of the Palisades Local Boys. Milton walked around the palisades till he found some of us. He was below the safe way parking lot and called up to us. Some of the guys laughed at him and told him to go back home and he shouted back "fuck you!" He was with a couple of guys so Zoyd and Trey ran down to see what the fuck had made him a tuff guy all of a sudden. When he got around the corner 3 vans with about 15 guys got out and surrounded him. They were all just standing around him saying stupid shit like "Whats up fool?!" Zoyd then sizes them all up picks a guy a little bigger than him and cracks him right in the nose. The guy dropped like a bag of bricks then all the fists started flying. He got hit in the lip with a ring but besides that he had slipped out and ran off before anyone could do any real damage. All he ended up needing was a couple stitches and a wheelbarrow to carry his balls around in.

In April of 1992 the LAPD officers that beat the shit out of Rodney King were exonerated by what was purported to be an older, mostly white jury from Simi Valley California. (9 of the 12 were white and none were black) You had to see that shit coming. I guess I really didn't until the day of the verdict.

They had moved the trial to an old, rich, white neighborhood. So you have a bunch of old white people, judging a giant black man who was admittedly on drugs and fleeing arrest. The older jurors were in there 20s when black people had to drink at separate drinking fountains in half the southern states. They were in there 30's when the Civil Rights Act of 1964 made it illegal to discriminate against blacks when it comes to voting. Now you think they are not going to have any prejudice at all when they look at his video taped beating? I mean he admitted that he put these nice officers in such a bad position himself.

I'm sure that there was at least one juror that thought to him or herself, "That nigger is lucky those nice officers didn't just pull him out of the car and shoot him." The beating was so brutal and it seemed so obvious they were guilty, I guess people just couldn't imagine them getting off… even if the trial was moved to such a Lilly white area.

So LA burned. Lots of cities rioted, and fires were set, but South Central Los Angeles burned. From the beautiful hilltops in the Pacific Palisades you could see what looked like a thick layer of low lying smog covering the whole city. It was actually smoke from hundreds of individual fires creating a blanket of haze over everything.

You could see plumes of smoke billowing up from the heart of each separate fire. The cops were nowhere. Some people said they were blocking all street access to places like Brentwood Beverly hills and Bel Air. What I do know is they set up perimeters around the ghettos and just let everyone go apeshit inside. I drove around the Palisades in Michele's swinger with my 44 Magnum and a cooler full of beer like a pistol packing Buttermaker from the Bad News Bears.

Amongst all the chaos of the riots and news anchor Brea Walkers jacked up hands, I had that same weird sense of peace I found when I was walking through that car accident by grandma's house on mothers day a couple years earlier. Once the riots kicked off you could watch it on the local TV news. You could see it live, people looting and burning down whole blocks of the city. Scenes seemingly one more devastating and tragic than the next…. and I felt great. It had been just short of 4 years since my senior year of high school and I didn't have many moments that I wasn't thinking about Michele's death in one way or another. All that chaos and madness took the place of the pain that I carried with me everyday. It made me feel sort of… I guess normal.

You are never supposed to see a news anchors hands. It was the unspoken rule of the 1980's, pre 24 hour news cycle, network news. Brea Walker was reporting the news and keeping it together until white people started getting dragged from their cars and beaten. Now it was apparently time to panic. So Brea Walker broke that cardinal rule and began waving her hands around during the broadcast. Brea Walker was born with ectrodactyly, a split hand syndrome. So with all the chaos of the riots, mass suffering and destruction, all I could think about was that I never knew her hands looked like that. I wasn't feeling bad about people being beaten and possibly killed. I wasn't scared for people I knew who lived in the places that were burning. All I could think about was her hands.

I kept carrying the handgun after the riots. The gangs coming into our town were getting a little more serious and I sure wasn't going to get jumped by 20 dudes or shot at again. As Dirty Harry famously said.. "This is a 44 magnum, the most powerful handgun known to man and can blow your head clean off...." (*Dirty Hairy*, Siegel 1971) Or something like that. Many a night we would be chilling at the top of Lachman or up by the church where Clinton was murdered and someone would ask if I had the gun on me. Before we left everyone would take a couple shots at a street sign or just off into the woods.

That thing was fun to shoot at night. It didn't have the 6 inch barrel like Callahan's but a much shorter 3 1/2 inch one. What that did was turn it into a fire-breathing dragon. You pull that trigger and smoke and flames shot out of that thing. If I took it to the Beverly Hills gun club, people would end up standing around me because of the flames and all the smoke. That thing is a diesel.

If there was a big party that I thought some gangsters from out of town were going to go to fuck with us, I would have that thing strapped to my chest. There was one party we went to where a group of other guys were getting beat down by what looked like a south side Mexican gang. I recognized a couple of the guys that were getting fucked up but I didn't really know them. I think they might have been a west LA gang that some people I knew also knew. Or they might have been two gangs that came to beat us down and ended up fighting each other. As was par for the coarse it was about 30 on 10. People were getting beat up and down the street. I decided to step off the curb, away from my few friends that were there and take a stroll through the battle. Again, chaos equaling calm, I

don't think anyone even looked at me. They straight ran
around me. One kid was waving around a .22 caliber hand
gun and all I could think is that you had to be pretty damn
accurate to kill someone with that little piece of shit. That is
if it doesn't blow up in your hand when you pull the
trigger. If I pulled out my shit and shot it in the opposite
direction I still might take out a chunk of your ass. I guess
that sense of calm I had was how Kwai Chang Caine made
it through 55 minutes on *Kung Fu* every week before he
had to beat someone's ass with his flute.

.

Chapter 12

Crazy Horse, Crazy H, Crazy

In times of tragedy, many people begin their search for God or some bigger meaning in their lives. My search began not long after my senior year and was a pretty short one. I couldn't see God anywhere around me and most of the religious people I had ever met seemed crazy to me. The only time I had ever felt remotely spiritual was when I was surrounded by nature.

I knew my mom's dad was a Native American so I decided to research his tribe and see if I could find some sort of spirituality that would help me out. What I found was something that I could grasp right then and there. I didn't have to sit around "keeping the faith," and finally when I die, then everything will be better. I could live it just by walking out into the woods.

My great grandfather was the product of a French fur trapper who married an Oglala Sioux woman. These unions were quite common during that time period with the trappers, the fur companies, and the Sioux, all supposedly getting something out of the relationship. So when I pull the cool guy card almost everyone does (regardless if its true or not) and say, "I am part Native American," I have to also say I am part French as well.

I don't know much about my Sioux heritage beyond the tribe because my great grandmother told my great grandfather he was white. I don't really blame her. After all, the battle of the Little Bighorn, more commonly known as Custer's last stand was about 20 years before they met and old whitey was still pretty sore about it. (The Slaughter that took place at Wounded Knee, where estimates reached as high as 90 Sioux men and approximately 200 Sioux women and children, were butchered by 500 US soldiers and left frozen to the ground, was a little more chronologically appropriate but nowhere near as funny.)

Great grandpa did keep part of his heritage alive by racing some of the first Indian Motorcycles. He lived in Wichita Kansa and was part of an Indian Motorcycle club that raced on the weekends. They would run their bikes full speed on dirt tracks with a "cider" prize for the winner. It must have been a pretty big deal back then because I have old photo's of dozens of bikes in front of the little Indian motorcycle shop on a dirt road in Wichita Kansas from 1914. The race day photos show hundreds of people cheering on the riders. I still have a couple of original patches and a silver Indian button that my grandfather gave me. Too bad he didn't hang onto one of those old bikes!

From here on out, I am going to refer to Native Americans as Indians. Some people find the term Indian offensive, but I have found most of those people to be white. It really depends on who you talk to. I got a chance to speak to a Hopi elder when I was at Santa Monica City College named Abbot Sekaquaptewa. He preferred the term Indian, he didn't like the term Native American. He said "That makes me feel too primitive... I drive a Chrysler."

I had read all the classic bullshit that the history books had to say in public school in the 70's and 80's. I am old enough that my history books at most credited Indians as being "noble savages." Thousands of lies, mass murder, and broken treaties were glossed over and explained by *Manifest Destiny*. It was white European right to take from these red monkeys the lands that they inhabited. I never bought into any of that shit. There was always something that spoke to me about these people. Not just because it was part of my own heritage, it was something more. There was something about these people that just seemed so..... oh fuck me.... noble.

Some stories tell of a wave of disease that took a pretty hefty toll on the indigenous population on the east coast right when the Pilgrims landed. Couple that with a welcoming attitude, when it was time for the locals to get rid of this bunch of pasty white frail pilgrims, there was just nobody left to throw them a beating. What can't be disputed was that the Indians were not ready for the number of people and diseases that the white people brought over. *Manifest Destiny* was really just white people killing lying cheating and stealing there way across the continent. If that 'first thanksgiving' story has any truth to it, Squanto should have let those fuckers freeze to death.

The first books I read were *Black Elk Speaks*, by Black Elk and John G Neinardt and *The Sacred Pipe,* Black

Elks telling of the 7 rights of the Oglala Sioux by Joseph Epes Brown. I also read books on Crazy Horse after learning about some of the spiritual aspects of the Sioux. Crazy Horse was a fucking bad ass. Not tall in stature but one of the most feared war chiefs in the entire Sioux nation. His name actually more accurately translates to prancing horse. Named for his presence when in battle and as a war chief. Arrows would be flying and braves would be warring and he would be…. Prancing through the battle field like… "What?" Then he would go to work.

The scene from Dances With Wolves where Kevin Costner doesn't want to live without his leg so he gets on his horse and tries to get himself shot was probably poached from a Crazy Horse story. Costner's character rode back and forth in front of the confederate troops trying to get shot. Nobody could hit him. So the union soldiers got all fired up and charged the confederates and won the battle. Crazy Horse was known to go out in front of the other Sioux warriors and war chiefs and prance on his horse wile arrows and bullets from the other warring tribe (or white people) flew all around him. That would fire everyone up and the battle would be on.

They would ride into the enemy screaming "Hoka hey!" Which translates to "It is a good day to die." This wasn't meant as a trivial thing. Like, "Today is as good as any,"… you were supposed to live your life to the fullest and that your causes be just, so that when you are ridding into a war, you have no regrets so that it truly is a good day to die.

I was so impressed with how a warrior tackled adversity and tragedy head on that I got a tattoo of a war chief offering the sacred pipe of the Oglala Sioux. The tattoo was taken from a bust from the Smithsonian that was supposed to be of Crazy Horse.

It was 1988 and I was 18. I went to get the tattoo with the only person I knew that had one already. My older boy scout buddy who turned me onto smoking weed Anthony Tittelli. Back then, tattoos still weren't clean and easy. Still just for the convicts, gang members, bikers and sailors. If you were by yourself and had a tattoo that someone could see they would either look down on you or try to fight you. Just like having Blue hair did years earlier.

I actually wrote a short story about the whole process of getting my first tattoo right after it happened. Here is some of my earliest writing that I still have.

Crazy H

He tricked me the first time. That's the excuse I used. I still sat and watched him pour the brown powder out of the balloon onto the spoon. I even gave him a lighter to cook it with. I asked him what the liquid was he was mixing it with. "Water" he said. I never thought water could look so evil. I guess it might have been the prescription pill case he had it in. So I drank my beer, smoked my pot and watched my Boy Scout buddy stick a needle into his arm and shoot heroine into his vein. I guess it wouldn't have been as bad but he had been clean for 32 days.

We got inside the tattoo shop and I could tell he was fucked up. He got some work done, then it was my turn. The guy started working on my back. I was thinking, new sensation... hey, this doesn't hurt that bad. Then Dusty, my tattoo artist, stopped and said.. "Hey are you breathing??" 'Yeah of course!' I said. And no, I wasn't. I was concentrating so hard on the pain that I forgot to breath. So after almost passing out and a couple snickers bars to get my blood sugar back up, he finished up that session.

A few days blurred by as they always do. Then it was a time again for more work on my tattoo. This time I knew we were heading for that same street corner. I was already buzzed from the 5 beers I had drunk. I told him I

193

wouldn't drive him down there again. He said, "Come on, you've got your buzz, let me get mine." I don't know, it seemed to make sense.... actually I don't know what it made. Walking back he said what's up to a couple of homeless looking guys on the street then jumped into my car. Now I needed to complete my buzz and he needed to start his. I would never do any needle drugs because it was too easy to OD and I couldn't hurt my mom like that.

I got a few more beers and found a good side street in a rundown part of Hollywood. He began the ritual again, pouring out the powder (this time from two balloons) and mixed it with the water. He had his own lighter this time. Usually you see people tie their arms off with surgical tubing or a belt. It was kind of neat the way he crossed his legs then stuck his arm between them to cut the circulation and expose the vein instead. He stuck in the needle, sucked some of his blood into the heroine and water solution and slammed it into his body. Last time he said the high was nothing. This time he must have gotten some better shit.

Right after he pulled the needle out, his head slumped lifelessly forward. I thought to myself, "damn, he is fucked up again." After a couple more sips of my beer I heard him trying to make a feeble attempt at a breath. When I put my head next to his I realized he was not breathing at all. I took his spoon and put it under his nose to make sure. (If it fogged up I would know he was ok) I was far too buzzed to panic so I kinda half laughed at the situation I had helped create.

His door was broken so I had to pull him across the center console out my door and into the street. I was a lifeguard at the YMCA pool at the time so I knew CPR. He had a weak pulse but wasn't breathing at all. Now what was it again??? 2 breaths every 5 seconds or 2 breaths every 7 seconds?? Oh yeah, First make sure the tongue isn't blocking the airway. When I swept his mouth I pulled out 8 more balloons of heroin. (They put it in balloons because if they have to swallow it to hide it from the cops, they can throw it up or sift through their shit later and still use it.)

I started to breath for him. 2 breaths every 5 seconds. It was beyond eerie to hear my breath coming out of his body. After almost 5 minutes and an on again off again thready pulse, he still couldn't breath on his own. Right then someone came up to help, thank god! They knelt down next to Anthony, grabbed the balloons of heroine and ran off. Thanks, thanks a lot. After another lifetime, which was really about another minute or two, I started slapping him again and got him to sorta come back around. Then I got to spend the next few hours just making sure he didn't die completely. He got me to take him to a Narcotics Anonymous meeting right next to the tattoo shop. He got up to the podium to speak and passed out. They threw us out because he wasn't supposed to be in there all fucked up so I dragged him back to my car. After a while I finally felt like he was in the clear enough and brought him back to his house.

The following Monday I saw him at the Y where he was a camp counselor and I was watching the pool. I was thinking that I had just saved this guys life and he was going to be forever in my debt. Maybe he will even kick heroine for good now. Anthony walked up to me and said, "Do you think you could help me out with some money for those balloons? They were for other people and they are pissed I lost them." 'No Anthony. I'm not going to give you any money for the balloons that were lost'.. Just fucking perfect.

End Scene.

I got my spiritual offering tattooed on my body. I guess that was the important part of the story. That and it solidified in my mind that it was way to easy to die fucking with needle drugs. I had already made the commitment to live for my mom so that shit was off the table.

All of the rights of the Sioux were finalized with the offering of the sacred pipe to the 4 winds and the sky and the earth. Everything in nature was sacred. That's what I had inked on my body. You could experience God, Buddha, Moses Krishna; whatever you called your spirituality in every tree animal or rock you see.... and there were no rules for me. I didn't have to do this or that in order to feel it. However I did believe in energy and its power. I didn't know it at the time but I also had an ingrained karmic belief that I wouldn't fully understand, and act on until later in my life.

What I could wrap my brain around was the fact that everything on this planet is made up of the same space dust. In my head that meant it truly was possible to be one with everything in the universe.

As for my understanding of energy and transference, I knew if I left a pot of water boiling on the stove, the water would evaporate. The water didn't disappear; it changed forms. That whole concept helped me deal with Michele's death. It made me feel like she was a part of me, and the universe. But there was so much more of me that missed her physical being. At the same time I knew that no earthly vessel could contain all of the energy and love that she had. Again comforting at times, but deep down the hurt of her being gone, even with my newfound spirituality, was absolute.

It was the ocean that took Michele from me, but it is that same ocean that has always made me feel grounded. Some people can get that feeling from mountains or wide-open plains (or Prozac). For me, I feel my place in the universe by standing on the shore, looking out over the vastness of the sea. It has been my playground, my best friend, my worst enemy, and it is where every one of us came from.

I had also tried to live my new spirituality outside of myself. I became way more concerned with the environment. When we were drinking beers at someplace like the top of Chautauqua I made sure to buy bottles and smash them before we left. Girls would wonder why I would yell at our friends for throwing cans into the bushes but I was fine tossing bottles at rocks. "Because I'm just turning them back into sand, not leaving a piece of junk that will be there in a hundred years!" I also went ape-shit when anyone threw a cigarette butt on the ground. "Those fuckers will wash into the sewer then run out into the ocean where we surf! Then a sea turtle or some shit will eat them because seaweed will grow on them. When they eat enough of them, they will die of starvation with a full stomach so throw that shit in a fucking trashcan!"

While I was starting to gain some spirituality to help me get by, Serena who I had been dating since half way through my senior year (about a year and a half) had decided she was going to school across the country and would no longer be seeing me. All that spiritual crap went right out the fucking window. I was devastated. I did really love her, but I knew that she needed to begin her adult life and if that takes her across the country she needed to embrace that fact. I knew that but it was buried under miles of self-pity and massive separation anxiety. She helped me live after Michele died! How can I let her go?? She knew how fragile I was and she handled me pretty well. Looking back on it I think she was and is an amazingly compassionate person. Having said that we now turn to my old friend Brandon Lee.

Brandon was the guy I brought with me to be in the Chili Pepper video. We had become good friends in 7th grade, when I was still not used to socializing in any meaningful way with anybody. He was an amazingly talented artist that could draw shit I couldn't even comprehend. Cartoon style for the most part but he could draw anything, and he thought I was the coolest. We became really good friends and he was one of the main kids I hung out with at school in Jr high.

A little known factoid for you if you don't already know; young boys going through puberty can get boners for absolutely no reason at all. Sometimes they show up at the same time every day. You could be cooking with your grandma, playing a game of chess, or as I had it, holding my math book in front of it because class had just let out. I needed to know if for the rest of my life I would be getting full wood at 9:45 am everyday…. for ever. "Hey Brandon,… for no good reason I get a hard on right after math and have to cover it up with my math book. Does that ever happen to you?" 'Yep, but I need a dictionary to cover mine.' We never had more than a couple seconds before one of us was cracking a joke. The best one was yet to come.

When I got out of high school, Brandon, my old glam rocker friend Pat, and Serena became much closer friends and hung out on holidays and whenever they could. At some point, Brandon decided it would be a good idea to completely fuck our friendship and profess his undying love to Serena. Ba-zing! I'm here all week, goodnight folks! Now that shits funny! No funny's not the word….it's another word that starts with F. Hmmm.. oh yeah.. FUCKED! This was supposed to be my first real childhood friend. We talked about being old fuckers still talking shit through our old toothless mouths. This dude watched me completely break into pieces not two years earlier when Michele died. He knew how much Serena meant to me and he did what???

If you go by any of the 'bro codes' (hate that term), he would have to at least run it by me….. and no, it wouldn't have been ok. FUCK YOU! To me what was even worse was why he did it. He felt super close to her because they were such good friends and he took advantage of that fact. I don't think it was because he was trying to be a dick, it was because he didn't have the self confidence to branch out on his own. So he threw away our friendship on a million to one… scratch that…. a 5 billion to one shot with Serena.

Crazy

Some time around then my mom got worried enough about me to have me psychologically evaluated. I had been to shrinks as a child but those trips were all based on a solid foundation of bullshit. They were all "what's the matter with Michael?" exercises. It should have been "Why is Dick such an asshole" but what are you gonna do.

A couple of shrinks I went to when I was a little older (before Michele died) were just picking up a paycheck from insurance and didn't give a shit about me. One shrink picked his feet the whole hour and pretty much said nothing to me. The other let me talk for a minute about my relationship with Dick, then stopped me and said "I see you turn 18 in 2 years…. So what's the problem?" My mom actually did some research after Michele died and got me in to see someone that was reputable. They are hard to find but they are out there if you need it…. and if you have gone through any tragedies like the ones that I experienced… you probably need it.

I do know that you should try to let your feelings out and not just bottle them up. I don't know if seeing a shrink still has a stigma attached to it but it shouldn't. Everyone is a little nuts. Don't let yourself feel like there is something wrong with you just because you need to talk some shit out. The sane people seek out someone to talk to in times of crisis. Why not talk to someone who is experienced with that kind of stuff? The crazy ones are the ones that try to go it alone. Having said this, after Michele died, I only went to shrinks long enough for them to diagnose me.

My scouting report was as follows; post traumatic stress disorder, manic depression, adjustment disorder, survivors guilt, separation anxiety and a couple other gems I don't really remember. I didn't know it at the time, but I was also addicted to tragedy. And not like it got me high, but how a heroin addict no longer uses the drug to get high, they just use it to feel normal. Tragic shit was the only thing that could get me out of my own head. That's why I would feel nothing or even crack a smile if something horrific happened.

The most fucked up part that became obvious to me was that it actually hurt me to be happy. If you ever saw *Con Air* (West, 1997) with Nicolas Cage (horrible southern accent--"Put the bunny down.") you saw Steve Buscemi describe the psychopath Cage kills in the belly of the plane. "Moments of levity cause him physical pain." I'm not that bad, but every time I get over the top excited or happy, I crash..... hard. I get overwhelmed with the feeling that I don't deserve to be happy. "Why am I here laughing? I'm the one that should be dead. I don't even deserve to be alive."

All of this would have made it difficult (to say the least) for me to attend a ceremony that was happening once a year on the day Michele died. The other kids that were in the car's parents wanted to get together on the 19th of November to remember our lost loved ones.... No thanks. If we would have attended, there's a good chance that I would have killed the kid that was driving's parents with my bare hands. I know it's not their fault, but I would have freaked the fuck out. My crazed thinking would have made me explode if I saw them hurting. "You don't get to hurt!! If it wasn't for you two fucks having that little piece of shit I would still have my big sister!!!" That would not have made Michele very happy.

Chapter 13

The University Of California At Santa Cruz

I barely graduated high school. No SAT, no foreign language, half the mandatory science and math. My two senior semesters of math were with Mr. Bones and Mr. Junit. Bones class I barely passed with a D UU. (The U's were for unsatisfactory.) I got that grade with 43 absences in one 20 week period.

The semester with Junit was pretty fun. You could tell this guy was a pimp back in his day but he played like he was stupid. He was just riding it out till he could retire. Everyone in the class was in 10th grade, a couple were in 11th and me the only senior. All the kids thought he was clueless, I knew better. I knew that he just thought nothing that bad was going on so why stress out about it.

When I had eaten shit skating and jacked up my ankle I walked with a cane for about a week. The first day I had it in his class he walked by, reading something from the math text. He picked up my cane with out missing a beat he twisted the handle and pulled out the 11 inch blade concealed in the cane, closed it up handed it back to me and said "don't bring it again" and kept on teaching. I was like, 'Holy shit!!' I looked around and the whole class was like, "Holy shit!!" He had to have one like it… or just knew me better than I knew myself. One of my yearly trips out to see my dad he bought it for me at a swap meet. Thanks Pop, that thing was cool as hell.

One class I took that helped me out a lot was called Work Experience. I had to have a job anyway to keep up with the Joneses so why not get some school credit while I'm at it. I had worked ever since I was 11 when I had the paper route, after that I would work at the Palisades Malibu YMCA. Summers at the day camp in Temescal Canyon. Camp complete with creek, quartz crystal mine, red Indian clay vein, and rock throwing range. The rest of the year at the office or at the pool that was also located in the canyon. Work experience enabled me to get two class periods off. That meant for my last semester I didn't even come to class until almost 11. If you counted my first class as a teachers assistant (who ended up getting fired for smoking weed with the kids) I really wasn't there till noon.

We would meet for Work Experience for 15 minutes a week to make sure we still had jobs. The program also had a link to Santa Monica City College. If we were going to go there we could take our placement tests and sign up for classes before the rest of the entire college. That might not sound like that big a deal, but knowing which classes to sign up for was key to surviving. Hard classes or teachers were easy to avoid. I knew lots of people that went there. Once you got the right classes you could get decent grades without trying that hard and then always be first to register for the right classes… and then repeat.

I still had to drop almost every math class I ever took because I was failing them all. I finally got through the easiest math class for non-math majors, statistics, which is too bad I guess because I love reading about physics. Not the actual formulae but as its applied to outer space. I saw astrophysicist Neil Degrasse Tyson *The Daily Show* with Jon Stewart and immediately went out and bought his book Death by Black Hole. Definitely not pen and paper working out equations interested in physics, more like a crazy- stars exploding- black holes- dark matter- outer space type of shit, interested in physics.

There was one class that was going to give me even more trouble then mathematics…and that was college level biology. First of all there were only 2 choices and they were both impossibly hard (if you didn't want to do all the work). They also assumed you completed high school biology and were starting from a place that was completely foreign to me.

The class had two lectures a week and one lab where we would work like mad scientists with beakers and fire and shit. The lab was basically pass/fail. If you were there and completed the work, you passed. I was really scared of the lecture part of the class because I knew a dick that loved failing people taught it.

Some how, some way, I was smiled upon. I showed up to class the first day and found out that the hippy lab teacher and the ball busting lecturer had switched roles for this one semester. At the end of the class she read my grade and said I got an 'A'. I was like excuse me? And she said it again, "you got an A." I said 'really?' She said "I can go back and verify it but that's what I have." 'NO NO NO!!

We're good we're good!' I still don't understand that one. I had done at best 'C' work.

After 4 years of a 2year college I had enough credits to transfer. That might sound pretty pathetic but in actuality most of the students that I knew never went anywhere after SMC.

I applied to a bunch of schools but only wanted to go to UC Santa Cruz to keep a promise I had made to an old friend. I applied to UC Irvine and a couple other places I knew I couldn't get into. With no SAT score and almost a B average I didn't know if I would make it in anywhere. Then the day came, I got rejected from every school I applied to.... except Santa Cruz. My mighty 2.9 grade point average must have done the trick! Either that or whoever read the essay on my application thought a promise I made to a dead friend, then having a sister and some other people die warranted a little bit of a break (I didn't know it at the time but Teak had been accepted and was going to go to UCSC before she was murdered).

Santa Cruz was exactly like DK described it. It was a fucking fantasyland. I lived 6 houses away from Natural Bridges State Park. A little cul de sac that you could look out over the Pacific Ocean and see the natural bridges that the ocean had carved out of the ancient cliff sides over millions of years. Off to the left was a blowhole that you could feel the water surging under your feet then spout sometimes 30 feet into the air.

Directly across the street from my house was another part of Natural Bridges State Park that was the Monarch Butterfly Estuary. In November the butterflies would come and land on the eucalyptus trees on their way down to Mexico. Every leaf of every branch would be completely covered with butterflies. The branches would look like giant marijuana buds, but were just thousands of butterflies on each branch of each tree in a grove of a hundred trees. You could just lie down and watch millions of butterflies flying around you.

You would also see imposters; Smaller butterflies that over time had developed the same coloring to keep birds from eating them. If you didn't know, monarch butterflies are poisonous. So if you add butterflies to your diet, you might want to start with some other species.

As if that wasn't good enough, when the wind blew off shore, the whole neighborhood smelled like juicy fruit. Wrigley's had a small factory just up the street. There was also the famous derby bowl right around the corner. This was 1992 and skate parks were nowhere. The litigious 80s destroyed them all. But I had this little famous snake run into a bowl practically in my back yard (the next year it would literally be in my back yard).

The UCSC campus was awesome. It was like 9 separate elfin villages. You drove up from the beach to a guard shack that would only let students up to the school. There were wide open fields at the bottom of the hill that gave way to a forested hillside complete with redwoods and mystical looking clearings. Some of the clearings were collapsing because the school in its infinite wisdom got rid of all the bobcats and coyotes that fed on the ground squirrels. There were so many underground tunnels that sections of the grounds the size of football fields were collapsing. They even gave instructions on how all school employees could run them down. I hitched a ride up to campus one day and this guy showed me where he had to line them up on his windshield to make sure he got them with his tires…. fricking morons.

The 9 campuses or "colleges" were basically broken down into majors and on campus living. Stevenson was mine. Named after Adlai Stevenson. Not really sure what he did. Almost ran for president? Governor of some state? Oh he helped ban atmospheric Nuclear testing. Not really sure what else the guy did. Anyway, as a student you would have classes scattered all over the schools. The knoll that sprang right out of Stevenson really reminded me of home because you came out of the woods and could see the Pacific Ocean and the Monterey peninsula out in the distance. Los Angeles and Santa Cruz look the same geographically because LA looks out onto the Pales Verdes peninsula in much the same way. There is just not the same hook off to the right.

Being a transfer student I didn't have the same college experience as Michele or most regular students. No on campus living and no undergrad classes. I moved straight into a house with 4 private school girls from Los Angeles. These were the girls that had there own cars by 16, pagers in junior high school, and car phones and cell phones in high school (no one had them in the mid to late 1980's). I had known all of them from parties and around town. Most of them went to Marlboro and I went to their prom with one of there friends.

I had every intention of going but I actually never even went to my own prom. Everyone got out of the limo to go inside but I was like, I've got a limo, a shit load of booze, a bunch of blow and the hottest girl in the world sitting right next to me. So Serena and I just partied and fucked in the back of the limo while driving through the Hollywood hills instead. Prom is a high school right of passage and a memory to cherish for a lifetime…. I stand by my decision.

Back in Santa Cruz, this was to be the first time since I was 11 that I didn't work. I had saved up some money working before I left to get settled. As far as tuition went my mom used the insurance money from Michele's accident. The kid who was driving's insurance paid us 100 grand. I guess that was the going rate for the person with the most potential in my family. My mother offered my daddy Marcus 10 grand of it and he freaked. He tried to sue her for half. That whole thing was way to painful so I don't even know how it worked out. All I know is I didn't have to work most of my time in Santa Cruz.

I had some interest in psychology but that major was impacted (impossible to get classes). So I whittled it down to the two majors that required the fewest classes. Politics or American studies. I sat down with a counselor and we figured out that Politics had fewer classes but American studies was probably easier because there are no orals. (Oral exams accompanied by a 30-40 page paper) American studies would have significantly more hippies as well. Then the counselor looked further and realized that orals were being phased out of Politics. So I became a Politics major.

Politics was by far the smallest major at our school. So everyone was in the same classes. For the most part they were an extremely intelligent but completely socially retarded bunch. A friend I lived with my second year was a politics major as well. We made study groups and tackled every thing together. Every test was open notes so we just copied everyone else's shit and took the tests that way.

There were no grades at UC Santa Cruz then because they are way to constrictive and don't allow a student to foster an environment of true and honest learning…. Or some stupid shit but for whatever reason there was pass/fail and evaluations. Which actually were much harsher than grades. A 'C' is just a 'C'. But a paragraph on how mediocre and uninvolved you are is much worse.

I would quickly learn that there was a price to pay for all the beauty I found in Santa Cruz. First you have to understand UC Santa Cruz in 1992. It made Berkley in the 60's look mainstream. Instead of the 60s Berkley, free love, social injustice anti established rule, no war hippies, 1990's

Santa Cruz was 90 % angry militant fuck you if you don't agree with me Nazi hippies.

When I got to Santa Cruz I was ready to take this country and give it back to the Indians. I had gay friends and family, black friends, Asian friends and was in small part a member of the group that whitey gave it to the worst. But it was quickly brought to my attention that I was what was wrong with our country. I was a white male so everything was my fault. This meant I had to hang my head sufficiently low for all to see, and wear my scarlet letter and beg for their forgiveness that I didn't deserve. In the 60's if a white male was down for the cause, he was embraced by the counter culture and seen as a powerful ally. Not in the 90's. Unless you had a high enough level of self-loathing long hair and bathed as infrequently as possible, you were out.

Santa Cruz in the early 1990's was also giving birth to the political correctness movement that we all know and love (sarcasm if you didn't get that). Like all young children we let them run riot for the first couple years because they are so precious. Then in time, rules are laid out and we expect them to become more in check. Then by the time they are 10 or 11 its time to make fun of them and talk about how they can be crazy and taken way too far.

Some kids that weren't in my major took some of our classes for their required course work. That would inevitably result in one of our Bi-monthly walkouts by the hippies and the politically correct. Some militant hairy bulldyke would interrupt the class, state her offence then walk out with a stink trail of hippies behind her.

One professor I had was Gwendolyn Mink. Her mother, a second generation Japanese American, had been a twelve term state representative in congress from the state of Hawaii. She assigned us Hunter S. Thompson's *Fear and Loathing on the Campaign Trail* to read for her class. Now you might think, Hunter Thompson, Rolling Stone magazine…. super liberal right??? WRONG!!! The only thing these idiots focused on is the fact that the book was vulgar, misogynistic and racist. They absolutely freaked that he called his best friend and cohort *in Fear and Loathing in Las Vegas* and on the campaign trail his 'spic' lawyer.

Graduate students led sections and they graded papers for the class. Mine happened to be a black lesbian. Both of which I think are just super. But when we began to discuss the Thompson book she took the side of the kids who were upset by its language and didn't think we should be reading it in class. I knew better, but couldn't stop myself.. "Don't you think there is a good reason she is having us read this account of the Democratic National Convention in 1972?" I got lots of hissing and lip smacking as if I had just said the dumbest thing you could possibly imagine. I had to let it go and turned in my next paper reflecting those same ideas I had voiced in class. I got a lecture in front of the group and what amounted to an unsatisfactory grade.

I was given an opportunity to make that paper up and I thought I would write the most sarcastic ass sucking paper that went lock stock with what this knucklehead believed. You couldn't help but know I was writing this to be sarcastic and the biggest dick I could possibly be……. she loved it. I didn't know to call it politically correct at the time, but I knew at that point some people were dead serious about this shit whatever it was.

I did get a little bit of love a couple weeks later when mid lecture something about the book came up and a bunch of morons started groaning. She stopped, cut them short and said "The only reason I assigned you that book is because it is relevant to the course work and is the ONLY accurate portrayal of what actually happened at that convention. I know… I was there" (continued) "Sometimes you might want to look past the verbiage of the day (which is what it was) to get the message of the work. Its better than being spoon fed what the mass media machine wants you to hear." I couldn't help myself. 'Yeah!' I shouted out looking right at my section leader, who was pretending she believed that all along.

I had one teacher make me sign up for this thing called an email account. I had no idea what the hell that was. It was 1993 and the only thing I knew about computers is that I didn't deserve one. I asked my mom for one before I left for college and she and Dick bought me an electric typewriter. "Its digital and can remember up to 4 lines at a time." Thaaanks, a giant paperweight. It was all right though, remember.. private school girls... There were 3 computers in my house.

The classes we took had a pho Internet of sorts, they were called readers. The professor would collect relevant articles, compile them into an inch or two think book and sell it for basically the cost of zeroxing, or mimeographing if you are even older than me. (Or like 20 bucks if it was a pain in the ass and they wanted the kids to pay for their time.) This great lands lawyers ended up coming after the teachers and saying they had to pay copyright fees on every article. That would make the readers cost about 500 to a thousand dollars a piece. Thanks a lot…. Dicks. I would have liked to see those same lawyers heads explode when the Internet kicked in a couple years later.

I had a blast in Santa Cruz. But that school experience was ripe for a rant. When I wrote a comedy set about it some years later it flowed pretty easy.

Santa Cruz

If you ever go to the UC campus at Santa Cruz, you will be overwhelmed by all the hippies. It will make you think twice about starting a college fund for your kid. Invest in something a little more reliable like some hookers and a pool table.

Not just 'free love, peace man,' hippies, but some kind of super hippies. A little heads up would have been nice. I went to school there and I didn't see any tree huggers hurling dung at people in the brochure. They were half stank, granola eating, grateful dead listening, Berkley hippies, and half hairy militant feminist bull dyke man haters. No free love hippies dancing around with flowers in their hair.. maybe a little peach fuzz under their arms. The only flowers in these chicks hair were growing out of the dirt imbedded in their scalps. And what's the deal with dreadlocks on a white chick?? You have the wrong hair. It looks like you followed your cat around and stapled a bunch of hairballs to your head. And not just hairy underarms but chicks that to look at them you'd think they were wearing a mohair sweater or a monkey suit! And how do you get so fat when all you eat is nuts and twigs? Ease up on the soy milkshakes and stop deep frying the granola. And you know there is only so much tofu wheat grass and hummus you can put into your body before you start to mulch.

Here was the breakdown when I went there; 2% Latino, 1% black, 97% hippy self hating white people, and me. I had to stick out 'cause I didn't hate myself and every time a dirt bag asked me to go to a protest I told them to go fuck themselves. "Reparations for the African American! Oppression can only go on so long!!!" OK, but riddle me this fucknut, what does a white kid with a trust fund that grew up in Sherman oaks know about oppression? The only oppression you've ever experienced is when your parents wouldn't buy you a Porsche for your 16th birthday and you had to settle for a Range Rover instead. Fight the system??? Why don't you start with your parents! Lets see how long this protest fest lasts with a lack of corporate sponsorship.

They were everywhere! Even at the market. "Do you realize how many crustaceans had to die so you could take home that carcass??" Lets see… 2 claws.. one shell… I'm guessing one?' If you want to get technical about it this entire country was founded on liquor slavery and tobacco so maybe you kids should go find another one. I on the other hand whole heartedly endorse 2 out of the 3, and had it been prostitution on as large a scale instead of slavery, it would have been a clean sweep.

And you have to stop with the all natural products. Toms of Maine was the biggest seller and was everywhere. I finally tried some of that shit out. Big mistake. Toothpaste that tastes like ass and not even one out of five dentists thinks its good for your teeth. Deodorant that actually found a way to make you smell worse. Look if you live in Maine and a blizzard has you snowed in, that deodorant might be all right, but here in California, you stink. And let's not forget the toilet paper that will actually disintegrate between the roll and your ass. You might as well just be wiping with your hand because that's all that's left when you get it back there.

"Fight the system", dumb ass you are the system. Guaranteed one year after you graduate you will be drinking your Starbucks double nonfat soy latte, working at daddy's corporate headquarters wondering "if Jesus drove an SUV would it be like mine?"

All that shit together didn't bother me as much as the smell of patchouli….and you can smell that shit everywhere up there. Don't you people know that it's the fragrance of vagrants? Look if you are homeless and stink so bad that flies are dying all around you, then by all means, a little dab'll do ya. But if you're pushing 30 and

you think its hip to get out of the shower then douse
yourself in an oil that clings to the nasal passage of every
unsuspecting person you go near, please, grab a fork and
jab it into a light socket. The only thing I want to smell
coming from you is burnt hair and smoke
    And don't get me wrong; I don't mind a little naive
idealism. I mean I once had wide starry eyes before the
weight of the world popped them out of my skull. I have
just gotten to the point where I can't believe that life is so
sacred. As far as I'm concerned a few million years ago if
one tree fell the wrong way and squished the wrong
monkey, there would be no one here to read this.

    Thank you thank you. The end of my Santa Cruz
rant.

    Full disclosure; I now use mostly natural products,
don't eat meat, drink mulchy smoothies and am pretty
much a hippy (who is not so fond of hippies) minus the hair
and the god awful smell of patchouli. Seriously people,
stop it.

    If you took away all the hippies or just blocked
them out, you were left with a slowed down pace and a
beautiful life in a beautiful place. The absolute best part
about Santa Cruz for me was that was wear I met Big Al.
Big Al would become my closest friend ever. Never talked
shit, always was there…all he wanted to do was be with me
and see me happy. Big Al was my dog.

    When I was a little kid there were two giant
Rottweiler's that lived next door to the Prongers. If a ball
went over that fence you could consider it gone forever.
Imagine the scariness of the dog from the sandlot, twice!
One barked at anything that moved and the other just paced
back and forth looking at you as if to say, "Go ahead… try

it!" Seeing those monsters every day made me want a Rot from a very young age.

Then pit bulls became popular again and I wanted a pit. Real quick for you anti pit bull people out there, they are the sweetest dogs ever. There is a reason they were considered the all American dog at the turn of two centuries ago. Tuff, fiercely loyal and sweet. The American pit bull was the dog in every advertisement that championed the American way of life. The RCA dog and Petey the Little Rascals dog were both pits. They symbolized strength and loyalty and... America. If you were to judge anything by what some idiots do with them then fast food, guns, cars... shit even children, would be outlawed. "The more you know.." (Star wipe)

I knew pretty early in Santa Cruz that I wanted a dog. I decided that I wanted a dog that was half Rottweiler half pit bull and was brindle head to toe. I always thought that tiger stripped shit looked crazy cool on a dog. About a week or two later my friend on the next block said his neighbor had a dog they were trying to give away.

The guy that owned the house was an ex motorcycle gang member that had suffered severe head and body trauma in a motorcycle accident. He was almost a quadriplegic but he could use his hands a little. He was always in an electric wheelchair brushing his teeth with an electric toothbrush and Capri Sun. It was something to do with brain damage and gum stimulation that he dug.

He could almost say whole words but the brain damage was pretty severe. Pretty fucked up but the pay off was a fat house next to the cliffs on the west side of Santa Cruz. He owned a giant Rottweiler named Brutus. This was not the tallest but was one of the thickest, best specimens of that breed I had ever seen. They had mated him with a 2 time best in show award winning red nose pit bull (that's a rarity in show dog circles... see the movie *Best in Show*

215

Guest, 2000 for reference). The pick of the litter was brindle from head to toe. He was given to a guy who lucky for me, got locked up on a murder charge for 25 to life.

When I met him he was about 5 months old and it was love at first sight… for me. He had to take a couple days to know me from Adam. I treated him like he had just joined my pack. I ate my meals with him on the ground. I wouldn't let him touch his food till I was done. Any time I had to discipline him I flipped him on his belly and grabbed his neck with my teeth (Sounds a little ruff but we had a great time doing it). As far as learning commands he had a German shepherd friend named Moose who helped him with those.

The crippled biker guy's brother brought Big Al to their house (he was actually named Aleister for Aleister Crowley then). He pulled me aside a few minutes after he got there. He was covered in prison tattoos, including the noose around the neck tat.. "You know what the color of that collar is for?" 'Why no sir….. no I do not.' "Its for the _____ (insert make believe white supremacist prison gang name that won't get me killed)" 'Well I can see why you guys are letting him go so easy. He has that shit all backwards.' Big Al was busy licking my friend Derek Brown who was black and had dreadlocks, nearly half to death…. Ok so I didn't say that last part but the scene was pretty fucking surreal.

That dog had some serious fun when we were in Santa Cruz. I would come home from class and he would almost never be there. Someone had taken him to derby to skate, or to the beach to run around, or just out for a walk. Big Al also loved to tow people on a skateboard. You had to be careful because he could get moving pretty fast for a good sized dog.

One time I had come home and Al wasn't' there. I sat down on the couch and started watching TV. Then I heard someone screaming Al's name yelling at him to stop.

I looked over at the open front door and saw Al run by..
Then attached to the other end of a rope was one of the
girls I lived with flying by on her skateboards. SLAM. She
came back bleeding and laughing hysterically saying "I
couldn't get him to stop!" Big Al would be my boy and be
by my side through thick and thin for the next 13 years of
my life.

The rest of my college experience was just lots of
beer lots of weed and lots of skating. A mushroom trip here
or there, dating a girl, not dating a girl. Pretty standard
stuff. My moms brother, uncle Mike (the one who sold
Brock the pills he killed himself with) came up for a while
because I told him my car (Michele's swinger) had broken
down and he said he would take a little vacation come up
and fix it for me. Cool. About two weeks later he had taken
a bunch of my money to get parts and never came back.
Thanks Unc

I spent much of my time there with Brendo who
was DK's best friend from the Palisades and his housemate
Derek Brown. The plan was for DK and Brendo to go up
there and live together. Its kind of funny to think back on.
Most nights I would be over at Brendo's and Derek's place
drinking 40's and playing dominoes, listening to gangster
rap. Monty would show up most days too at some point.
Monty's real name was Justin but one night we were
busting on each other and I told him he looked like Monty
Burns from the Simpsons and boy did it stick.

Derek had a shit crazy staff terrier (smaller pit) that
looked like a white lab rat and was Big Al's girlfriend. She
was small enough to play wildly with Big Al while he was
laying down just using his head. That dog was so white you
had to put sunscreen on it or it would get sunburnt. One day
we were barbequing and she came in looking like she had
done something wrong. Then I saw she had burns on her
forehead. We were using one of those little Webber
barbeques that was on ground level and she was licking the

grease trap while burning the shit out of her forehead. Frigging nut. So that was Big Al's bud. We all had our homies.

A typical day would start after class with a trip to skate derby or some other skate spot, then to get a burrito, then to the liquor store. A 40 oz of Mickey's Ice was about 2.09$. Regular Mickey's is gnarly malt liquor that is a high percentage of alcohol by volume. Mickey's Ice was a store leading 5.9% alcohol by volume. So that's what we bought. Oh and we smoked weed… lots of weed. It was Santa Cruz and that town had the best Indica bud, so you had to smoke it.

The first time I really got high from weed was on that camping trip with my boy scout buddy Anthony Tittelli. The one that keeled over on me when he OD'd on heroine when I was getting my first tattoo. I had thought about a memorial tattoo for Michele back then, but I didn't think it was the right time. When Damon Hughes (the guy that survived the crash with DK) moved up to Santa Cruz and told me he knew of a tattoo artist near the Flats, the right time seemed to be here.

I remember I almost passed out because I forgot to breath on my first tattoo. This time I was ready… more beer than last time!

We skated to the liquor store and got a few 40's then went down by the train tracks to do a little drinking. We stopped at a place down by the trestle and bridge near the creek. After a few minutes we saw some guys head pop up then back down real quick. I walked around above them and saw some guy in a dirty suit and a hobo shooting heroine they had just bought in the flats with the same needle. Yep, Venice isn't the only place where the ghetto meets the sea.

The flats were the Santa Cruz ghetto. It was more of a Mexican ghetto though, you couldn't find many black people there at all. Santa Cruz was a very dangerous place for anyone who wasn't white in its not too distant past. You didn't hear a lot about stuff like that, or the two serial killers that roamed the town in the 70's. I may or may not have found some bones from one of those guys that the police missed up in the hills.

I took my girlfriend up into the woods. We made love in a clearing with a beautiful secluded view of the canyon. When I was picking up the blanket getting ready to leave I picked up a spinal column and held it up to get a good look. "Must be a deer." I said to her and I dropped it and we left. It wasn't till I saw a backbone on one of those posters in the doctor's office a couple years later that I realized those bones were probably human.

If you were to venture just a little ways out of the town of Santa Cruz its like you go back in time a hundred years. Some friends and I made the mistake of going to a party up Trap Gulch, which is a place that is exactly what it sounds like. One way in, one way out, not many houses and definitely a place where no one would hear you scream. Not that I was counting, but I went to this party with 2 Jews 2 black people, an Asian and a couple assorted white people. The party was all white guys that looked like they just came from a rockabilly convention. I'll give them the fact that they were a little ahead of their time because this is 20 years ago. Before this hipster shit it seemed like everybody wanted to have tattoos and dress up like a greaser.

When we walked in, it was just like the scene in *Animal House* when Otter sees Otis Day and the Nights playing and they walk through the door and the music stops and everybody stares at them. Finally somebody broke the most uncomfortable silence. "Hey, who invited the niggers?" I jumped sides and said, 'Hey yeah, there's some heebs there too!' Ha, Not really. Can you imagine? 'We were just… leaving.' We went flying out of that canyon. We didn't know if we were going to come upon a roadblock of burning cars and more rockahillbillys trying to string us up. Lots of love in dem dar hills.

So back to getting my memorial tattoo. Damon Hughes and I had finished a six pack of 40s and bought a sixer of big mouths for the tattoo shop (that's about a hundred ounces of beer each before the big mouths). I wanted to get something classy in memory of Michele. I wanted old English writing down the back of my left arm and her birth and death dates in plain English. Now DK died 2 days after my 17th birthday, and Michele died 10 days after that. Or was it 12? But that party for Huey was 3 days after his actual birthday, which is 1 day after mine because he wanted it on a Friday to coincide with the weekend so I think that would make it the 9th, and Michele died 10 days later... Ok, so even as drunk as I was, I knew that one of two scenarios was right. I was 100% sure it was either the 17th or the 19 that she had been killed.

What to do, what to do....then Damon had a brilliant idea. "Just have them do the 17th because if you are wrong, its easy to make a 7 into a 9." You fucking genius! 'Slap it on me jack!' On the way home I was so hammered that I could push maybe two or three times on my skate before I would fall on my face. "You shouldn't drink before you get tattooed, it thins the blood and you bleed more." Try drinking a shit load of malt liquor, getting tattooed, then scraping most of the skin off your legs from the knees down with cobbly asphalt. That's gonna bleed a little too. (and I was wrong, it was the 19th)

I got my Tattoo for Michele right before summer break my second year at Santa Curz. I was home for about a week when my favorite aunt, Trudy, asked me to come by and hang out with her. She was cousin Andrews's mom and she was the coolest. Total counter culturist to the core. I even think she did the movie review for a local Venice communist magazine. She bought me the Bad Brains *I against I* album when I turned 16. She was the one who conspired with me to pass all the food to one end of the table that Thanksgiving, days after Michele died. She had been battling breast cancer and I had been away at school so I jumped at the chance to go hang out with her at her apartment that she had lived in for the last 30 years just off the circle in Venice.

We hung out and smoked some weed and just talked. We talked for hours. She was always one of the easiest people to talk to. She was the most real and down to earth person and was by far my favorite in my extended family.

Believe it or not, I had never had bagels and lox before. With Dicks last name Friedlander you'd think they'd have crossed my path at least once or twice. That all changed that night. I must have had 10 mini bagels while we were catching up and talking about everything and anything.

Getting the family together in any meaningful way just didn't happen once Michele was gone, so I was very excited by the time I was leaving and told her that I really wanted to do it again soon, like the next week. She smiled and began to laugh. I laughed along too at what a great idea I had, not realizing she was laughing at something completely different. I didn't realized how sick she actually was.

She had smiled and laughed at me because she was fully aware that she had only a little time left to live. I don't know if nobody told me because of my fragile state or what but it was a complete shock to me when she passed just days later.

What was left of the family got together and spread her ashes into the Venice Canals where she had spent most of her life. Andrew made sure to have the box her cremated remains came in cracked open before we got there. Not being able to open up your dead loved ones box of ashes was so 3 years ago. I am struggling with words here about her. I don't have them. All I can say is she meant so much to me and still does.

Chapter 14

"Its fun to play at the Y-MCA!"

(Village People 1978)

Limp Dick

I was working again at the YMCA day camp during the summers that I was off from school. I still remembered being a camper and getting a bunch of Dick's tools to try and flush out a rattlesnake after camp let out. We knew there was one in the rubble from an old outbuilding on a plateau in the canyon. We would throw rocks at it until we could get his rattle going. In a moment of sheer genius, one of us said, "Lets try and dig him out!" I was with a couple of older kids, one who would become my good friend and another that would be one of Michele's, who sang California dreaming at her service.. funeral… funeral service.. what do you call it? Funeral is when you have the body there right? Anyway a 7, an 8, and a 9 year old with hammers and chisels trying to dig out one pissed off rattlesnake. Thankfully there was enough room for him to retreat otherwise that would not have ended well for one of us.

Working at the camp was a good distraction from me missing Michele. It was a lot harder to deal with being back in the Palisades than it was up in Santa Cruz. I could take my mind off of it a little back home by taking my group on a hike up to the waterfall, which was just a couple miles up Temescal canyon. I could be in nature, the kids could run around and play in the water and try and catch pollywogs, it was good for everybody.

We had this set of twins in our group that couldn't have been more polar opposite. One was totally introverted and the other was an absolute freak. Funniest little shit I had ever seen. His name just happened to be Michael as well. We had sat down for lunch and Michael was just staring at me and eating his sandwich. Slowly. With an almost grin on his face he never looked away. Bite after bite, just staring. When he got down to his last couple of bites he took a big breath and bam! He blew all the snot he had in his nose all over his face and started laughing like a maniac. I was in the middle of trying to swallow a dry bagel I had brought for a snack and I couldn't help laughing too. Problem was the bagel got stuck and I was choking. I couldn't make a sound but I knew if I didn't moisten up that bagel I was going to choke to death. I snatched this other kids juice box and drank the whole thing in one shot just barley getting the bagel down, then continued laughing hysterically. All this poor kid had seen is his counselor steal his drink then start laughing at him. After many tears and explanation of how Michael's boogers tried to kill me and how he had saved my life by giving up his drink, we were off down the mountain back to camp.

To be good counselors, my friend Han and I had one of us (me), up front and the other keeping up the rear. I slowed down because I noticed a fat rat looking thing doing a commando crawl across the trail. I quickly realized there was a large rattlesnake following him, waiting for his venom to finish coursing through the rats veins. I thought quick and yelled "SNAKE!!!" Which is the worst thing you can yell to a bunch of kids you want to run the other way. If you yell bees, kids will high tail it in the other direction. If you yell snake…. they want to see it and even if it's a thousand pound anaconda they will run right towards it.

I threw up my arms and yelled "Get back!" To keep the kids from getting too close and getting bit. When my arms went up the same kid whose juice box I jacked took a shot to his eye.

Pickup was interesting that day. I watched as one of the children in my care, ran up to his mom with a black eye and started talking really excitedly about how I stole his drink, punched him in the face and showed him a rattlesnake. I didn't make things much better because once the kid opened his mouth my whole 'calm her down' speech went right out the window and I just started laughing out loud. Once I knew she completely understood the situation I made sure my favorite camper whose mom I just happened to be banging made it into her car.

She would drop her kid off at early care, come to my place, have sex, then drop me off to watch her kid for the day. Funny thing was her husband was doing the same thing with one of their daughter's tutors. Not my proudest moment. I think at the time I just wanted to have an affair with a married woman to see what it was like. Pretty shitty thing to do.

During the end of my college career I spent the summers in a tent in my moms back yard. A couple of years earlier, the company Dick had been working for, Corporate Events, got him to take out a second mortgage on our Palisades house and give it to them. When Dick told us of his brilliant investment I couldn't believe my ears. Even my mom was looking down and not excited or happy at all about the situation when they told me. I mean I knew nothing about business but I knew serious bullshit when I hear it.

Why would a company that was doing as well as he said need our piddly little 300 grand? Dicks response.. "If anything gets shady, I have it in our contract that I will own the company".... and Dick would own that company. The company was writing checks based on money they were going to get the whole time they were in business. Which can work if nothing goes wrong.... but at some point something inevitably will go wrong.

They had booked a country music festival at the same Paramount Ranch in Agoura Hills where Michele's ashes were spread. There were like 5 or 6 of the biggest names in country music at the time scheduled to play the event. They had hayrides, game booths, carnival rides, an old western town where they filmed Hollywood movies, pony rides and everything you could imagine. Radio sponsored, they were expecting close to 20 thousand people to show up. The event was on one of the last weekends of the summer and was supposed to be an end of summer blow out..... it rained. In Los Angeles, during the summer, it rained. And not just an LA freak rain shower, it dumped all day long, I think the grand total was 4 inches. Which equaled about 6 inches of mud across the entire fair grounds.

So Dick was now the proud owner of Corporate Events; A company that was in debt to the tune of a few million dollars. Up until that point Dick was just white noise after Michele had died. So that was when my mom had nothing left to lose. She told him she wanted a divorce.

Dick the monster… Dick the terrible… Dick the tyrant…. ran up into those same hills crying with a gun in his hand threatening to kill himself. Mom stayed strong, called his family and told them to go find him.

What a fucking piece of shit! What about your daughter Jessica?? How could you do that to this little kid that just lost her sister?? End result, he didn't….and probably the most fucked up part for me, he turned into Mr. Rogers. He became the nicest guy you have ever met. Changed on a dime. It infuriated me.

I can only guess what made him do that. Probably fear. Fear of dying alone…. fear of some kind of judgment day….fear of the unknown. Whatever it was something clicked inside him up in those hills that day. Maybe he was ready to kill the same person that he was to me…the asshole that treated my mother, my sister Michele and me like shit. Maybe in a moment of clarity he was on our side and despised the monster he was to us just as much as I did and he was ready to take that motherfucker out. Then when he didn't pull the trigger he convinced himself that he shouldn't kill himself because he was just misunderstood and really was a good guy.

I had always imagined the day that I would call that motherfucker out. As a small child I often daydreamed about getting big and beating the fucking shit out of him. I had become a man, despite him. Despite his lack of guidance, despite his abuse, despite his shitting on me, I had become a man. It was time. I told him that we needed to talk. I was going to tell him what a dick he was to me. How bad he had treated my sister and me. I was going to tell him it was too bad that the kid who would have forgiven him was dead and I was all that was left.

When we sat down across the street from Topanga State Beach at the Reel Inn, I looked across the table and realized that the vicious tyrant that had been so terrifying to me as a child had been replaced with an old broken down man. I had always envisioned him copping some attitude during our conversation and me kicking the shit out of him. I always imagined 20 years of hatred flowing through my body as I sat on top of him, fist raised ready to pound on him whenever I felt like it. Holding him in a vulnerable position like he had held that young kid that was me for all those years. I did none of it.

I looked across the table at that old man and just figured it was better for me to try and let go of my anger. He had no more hold on me, what was the point of standing up to him now? What I did do was tell him how things were for me growing up in that house.

This was a while after the suicide threat so he had been a "nice guy" for about a year now. He denied everything. He looked me right in the eye and claimed that he had always been there and cared about me in every way.

"What? Are you kidding me? Whose life are you thinking about?" There was no getting through to him. Every time I told him what a piece of shit he was to me he just smiled, slowly shook his head and told me how "neat" he always thought I was. Whatever. What was the point in arguing with him? I remember having that thought, then feeling the hate pretty much just leave me. I'm not sure how or why it happened. I know I wasn't emotionally mature enough to consciously release my hatred to the wind. Maybe it was a little bit of Michele that was left in me. Whatever it was, I felt like it was all ok. I didn't really need him to acknowledge my experience. All I needed was to be free of that pain. Besides, even if it was just sitting in his easy chair periodically getting up to yell at me because I was worthless, he was the one that was there. He was the one that put a roof over mine, and my sister's heads. In a very real way he did take care of us.

I kept a tacit relationship with Dick for a few years after but it didn't last long. He insisted on introducing me to the new people in his life as his son. Besides the fact that I have a father, Dick refused to call me his son for the entire life that I lived under his roof. Now all of a sudden I'm your son??

Dick had gotten remarried to a really cool lady. I would go with Jessica to their house for some holidays and things like that. But every time any member of that extended family said to me "So your dad tells me…" it made me want to punch them in the face. I finally had enough and I had another talk with Dick. I said it as gently as I could. I told him that I had a biological father and he was my dad. That he (Dick) had provided me food and shelter (I think I said he was 'there' for me to spare him) growing up and that I was very appreciative of that, but it made me uncomfortable when people referred to me as his son.

I asked him if he could tell them to call me his stepson. A fair compromise I thought. He did nothing. He pretended that I never asked him to do anything. It got so uncomfortable that I just started to ignore him. After a while he asked me why I wasn't coming around any more. I told him why (this time at a McDonald's) and he seemed to really listen, but again he did nothing. After about another year of me ignoring him, he sent me a letter. It basically said, 'I'm just trying to have some kind of a relationship with you but you wont let me.'

Again.. What? It was so simple! Change one little thing and I will basically overlook all the fucked up shit you ever did to me in my entire life! I didn't even respond. When my birthday came around again he sent me a super passive aggressive birthday card that basically said that he was trying to be cool and guesses I don't want anything to do with him and I had no good reason to feel that way. I responded. Without going into too much detail, I told him how it was his decision not mine. I thanked him for trying to guilt trip me on my birthday but it wasn't working. I took the opportunity to let him know how full of shit his new nice guy persona was and that he will always be a dick in my eyes. Great, you are a nice guy now. I'm glad you made the change. Only problem is the people that know who you used to be!!! So much for being all Zen and letting that hatred go.

A note to anyone who has changed for the better!!!

If you deny people their experience, they will not accept you. If you own it, they most likely will, no matter how drastic the change. I know there were a lot of things that were going on that led to his changing. One of the kids under his roof… a kid that he had to have known he was a dick to… was dead. There was no way to make up for that. She was never going to come back. She was never going to walk back through the door and say, "I forgive you for all the mean things you did to me when I was a child." That has to weigh heavy on any man. Now that I think about it, that has to be fucking terrible (maybe it was that alone).

I also actually believe that Dick did have those loving thoughts about me and Michele in his head at times. Maybe it was just the way his dad showed love and he had to keep tradition alive. His father was a nasty man from what my mother told me but every time I saw him he was the happiest old man you ever wanted to see. Maybe Dick was just waiting for the right time to be a nice guy. Maybe it was Friedlander tradition to be an asshole until the kids are out of the house, then it was time to be cool. The only problem was I had seen how he treated his own kid. It was too late. I was too fucked up. I was too hurt.

I know that the reality of the situation was most likely right in the middle of how Dick saw things and how I did. The difference is that I was the vulnerable one. I was the child. I was the one that needed guidance and a role model. He had an opportunity to be that role model and he chose not to take it. That is not my fault. But at the same time he really was there. Not in any magical, role model-y way but he was physically there. I will always be thankful for that. I haven't spoken to Dick in at least 15 years now. I can't believe I'm going to say this but I actually miss him.

Chapter 15

My Valentine, Crackomedy

Ok, I just found out Michele was hooking up with Flea when we made the Chili Peppers video. I guess there are some things you don't tell your little brother. Through the magic of Facebook, I posted the video and got in contact with her best friend who was in it too and he told me the whole story. Wow. So that means that maybe Flea was one of the people that called our number and asked if Michele was there. Maybe one of my, oh so callous, "No, she's not home, she's dead, thanks bye," remarks went to my all time hero.

I graduated college with the help of some classes I made up at Cal State Northridge. This was right after the big Northridge quake so my classes were in mobile units set in a big parking lot. They were still making sure what buildings were safe and which ones had to be repaired or torn down.

I must have had some earthquake luck. I missed the Santa Cruz earthquake of 1989, because I was in LA. I just missed the LA earthquake of 1994 because I was in Santa Cruz. Got to watch them both unfold on TV though. Got that good old feeling of adrenaline and nothing watching the people squished by the freeway in San Fran and crushed by their apartment buildings in Northridge.

Here is a handy little earthquake tip. Do not stand in the doorway in an earthquake. There is a triangle of life next to any sturdy object. When a house collapses the people who are found alive are almost always found right next to a couch a bed a countertop or some other object that can create that triangle. Curl up there and ride it out. If you are on the 20th floor of a building that collapses, sorry you are dead anyway.

I was done with college. To sum up my time in Santa Cruz, it was a time for me of selfish indulgence. I did exactly what I wanted to all the time. I made sure that I would get my degree, but besides that… all I did was play. It just seemed like it was necessary for me to do if I was going to keep pressing forward. Between skating and surfing and hanging out with my friends every available second, I was really able to mask the devastating hurt that I had lived constantly for the 4 years prior to my time at UCSC.

For most people, college is a time for experimentation and trying to figure things and yourself out. For me it was one big fun and awesome masking of the pain. I still didn't know how to deal with it so the next best thing was to cover it up. I was still very hurt but during that couple years of my life I lived like I was on an extended vacation, and I loved every minute of it.

When I came back home I started working at this café in Santa Monica to pay my bills after college. I had worked there for a while before so I remembered taking the day old bakery goods to this homeless shelter every Friday night. The only problem was that the shelter had been damaged by the Earthquake. I remembered a battered women's shelter that was on my route to work so I pulled up at the front after work one night and knocked on the door. No answer. So I went around to the back... No answer.

I started banging on the windows because I knew people were in there I could see them. Nothing. Then I started getting pissed. I finally went to the back gate and started yelling "I can see you!! Open the gate!!" Then I stopped and I looked at my car, which at the time was a two tone brown Pontiac grand prix (different model than DK's) with spoked rims and fuzzy dice hanging from the rear view. I at best looked like a wife beater looking for his beaten women. At worst....a violent pimp looking for one of his Ho's. I dropped the goods at the gate and bailed as fast as I could.

I was a fresh college grad, working part time, back home with no direction and not very happy. I think all I was really doing was molding my "fuck everything" attitude. I had genuinely tried to find a place within me that I felt comfortable. I had studied all that Lakota Sioux shit, brought it into my heart, used it to help deal with the loss of Michele and tried to work it into my life. I was able to keep a lot of those values but the comfort I was looking for I couldn't find. I probably should have just been looking for a career. I needed to prepare for what was next but I had no idea how to do it. As Niedermeyer famously said to Dee Snyder in that Twisted Sister video … "What are you gonna do with your life?" (Dee)…'I wanna rock!'

With no goals except surviving and a dead end job, I was looking for something but wasn't sure what it was. I went out with a couple of the boys and met one of the hottest girls I had seen in a long time. I met her at a bar after Matt said he was going to go talk to her. I said "Wait she's mine!!!" Her name was Gen. I babbled endlessly about LA even though she was from here. I told her how my grandfather started the Screenwriters Guild and my other grandfather built Pali High School and half the buildings downtown and my other grandfather was an Indian (ok the ones my step grandpa).

I ended up giving her my card at the end of the night. I said goodbye then off we went. To my absolute shock she showed up at the cafe the next day. We quickly became boyfriend and girlfriend and for the first year and a half everyone thought we were only together for 2 weeks. They thought that because of how infatuated we were with each other.

Our second valentines day together I bought her a dozen red roses and handed her only eight. I told her she had to find the other 4. Two were in my bed, and two were tattooed on my leg underneath her name. Our relationship was quickly heading for the next level. But I was not. Things began to deteriorate. Remember, I had a hard time being happy.

I finally realized that I needed to change my life completely. So I could do what I was supposed to do and go find a career… Or I could ride this misery thing and start a drug habit. I opted for the drug habit. Okay, it didn't happen exactly that way. I wasn't making enough money to get out of my moms house and I didn't know how to look for a career. I mean I had just graduated college isn't it supposed to be easy to get a job?? So being unhappy and partying with friends it just sort of happened.

Fats lived behind a guy who was in a Culver City and Venice Mexican gang and had crack all the time. We would go over there with our girlfriends, sneak off to the bathroom and take hits, then go back to partying and drinking. Then slowly the girlfriends were gone and we were spending the whole night smoking, then the friends were gone and I was smoking by myself.

It was actually a pretty slow progression. It wasn't like I saw some derelict tweaking in an alley and was like "you know if I play my cards right… someday, that could be me."

I tried to hang onto Gen but she left me. Before she did I was very unhappy and didn't know how to get out of the drug situation I had gotten myself into. I hadn't really gone over the edge and a push in the right direction might have changed my course (not that it was her job to give me that push). I reached out to her and she told me if I was smoking crack she was out. I then told her that I was smoking crack and needed some help to get out of it. I got a big "Nope", and she was gone.

She moved into an apartment in west LA that kind of gave her the creeps so she asked me if I would come stay with her for the night. I came over and she wasn't even trying to cover up the carpet burns on her knees. Classy. I always wondered if that was her way of telling me that there would never again be a chance, because she never said that with her words.

My pathetic ass actually tried to sleep with her that night. She doth protest. Or how do you say that in the past tense? Whatever, ole fuck me knees couldn't toss me a sympathy screw. Nope, I'm just the chump that's making sure you are ok in your new home in your new life without me.

In one of my very few moments of trying to figure out what to do with my life I had told her about how much I liked the idea of advertising. I thought it would be interesting to be on the creative side and come up with shit you could see everywhere. After she left me she went to school basically for advertising. She is now a high level executive at one of the worlds largest advertising firms. I've always wanted to run into her and ask her how my life is going.

Her leaving sent me over the edge. At the time I thought it was just her. Looking back I realized it was that feeling of being all alone again that completely fucked me up. Whatever it was, I started smoking crack more and more. In the moment, it gave me that lack of feeling that made the pain go away.

If you are going to go smoke crack, that is pretty much all you are thinking about. Buying crack wasn't like buying a bag of weed. When you are buying a bag of weed 9 times out of 10 you were meeting a good friend, smoking a bowl with him then going off for the rest of your day with a smile on your face. Getting crack was a fucking adventure into the tragic.

In order for your mission to be successful you had to wear the right uniform so you can blend into whatever ghetto you chose to go to. On any given night you might come across the homeless, the bloody and beaten, the prostitutes, the perverts the derelicts and the crazies. With all that chaos I again found that calm. In that insanity I had found my peace…. oh yeah and crack… Lots of crack.

I turned out to be a bad drug addict…. and not like "Oh my god look at him, he is twitching and yelling at that mailbox," bad drug addict… but like I wasn't very good at it- bad drug addict. Well I was plenty good at it but I was lazy about it. I was a lazy drug addict. Yeah, that's what I was. I knew people that would tweak for days and sell all of their shit for drugs. Rob their parents then end up in jail because they got in a fight with a hooker in a hotel room. Not me. I could tweak for only one night, going to ghost town (any spot you could buy hard drugs. For me it was the Oakwood section of Venice) sometimes 3 or 4 times a night. But after that… after maybe one daylight run, I had to stop. Sex or hookers??? Are you kidding me?? I could barely handle the fact that I had to do it with myself let alone someone else.

I was lucky to have something ingrained in me that would keep me out of too much trouble. It was probably fear. It had to be. I still didn't have that 'conscience' thing that everybody talks about so it had to be fear that kept me in line. It was obviously not anything that a positive male role model instilled in me when I was a child. At that point I think it was fear of going to jail or being a homeless drug addict on skid row. I even managed to keep the job at the café for a while. When you are young you can party all night and make it through the next day with out too much damage... even when tweaking.

I remember smoking rock till 5 am and having to be at work at 7. Driving to work I got to a 4 way stop and there was a cop on one side. I just gave him a look like 'Oh well.. What are you going to do??' I had convinced myself I had 4 flat tires and was driving like that to work. I didn't even get fired for anything having to do with drugs. I took a delivery to some lady on the north side of Santa Monica and was tired of getting stiffed on tips so I asked her how much change she wanted back. "Why??"She said. 'Because sometimes people tip.' She took offense to the insinuation that it wasn't good enough that she brought her food needs to us but that she should tip the lowly driver on top of that??? I was no longer in a position where I gave a shit so it wasn't hard for me after that to tell her to go fuck herself.

Venice ghost town: Oakwood

There was a black gang that had been around since the 70's and pretty much owned the Oakwood section of Venice. That's mostly who you got your drugs from down there. Their main rival was a Mexican gang from the same area that had been around a lot longer and had territory that was much larger than the Oakwood section of Venice. Therefore they concentrated their activities more on Culver City than Venice. Every few months the two would go to war over the drug trade in Oakwood.

So you knew when shit was really dangerous; When the Mexicans are out selling rock in ghost town. That meant that the black gang was regrouping and getting ready to hit back at the mexican drug dealers…. that meant gun battles. You would think that would keep me out of there…. Nope. It just added to the adventure. Plus you felt like you had on a cloak of invincibility because these gangsters were essentially fighting over you. I was the customer that they wanted.

Actually scoring the drugs when I was doing it on my own was almost more important than smoking the crack itself. Actually it was way more important. Once I had the drugs it was all shitsville. Is someone looking through my window at me?? Did I drop any on the ground?? You know, all the fun paranoid shit you have read about.

Prepare for battle! Once the thought entered my head I was single of focus. I put on my uniform. Black pants, flannel, something that lets me blend in to my surroundings. I could just drive through, but I might get ripped off…. Plus what's the fun in that?? I need to be in the trenches.

239

I had my back street route from my apartment down to the Venice ghost town, the area between Venice Blvd and Rose, and Electric Avenue and Lincoln. Oakwood. It was still pretty hood back then, as it is now. But I'm pretty sure the houses weren't going for 3 million dollars back then.

In the heyday you could get twenty young kids wearing bandanas over there faces like little black bank robbers in the old west, running up to your car to sell you rock. I would park a street over and walk up so I could haggle and get the best rock at the best price. If a bust went down on one street sometimes everyone was selling from another. Which would have been fine except on some nights if I had been drinking and down there for my second or third time I might forget where I parked my car. You are never more focused when you are wandering around ghost town with a mouthful of crack, car keys in hand wondering where the fuck your car is.

Sometimes searching for your car late night could be deadly, but that just added to the focus and determination. One time a bunch of Mexicans were running off from a bunch of pistol waving brothers. I was freaking out at this point. I yelled at one of the dudes in the back, "Have you seen a white dodge dart?" I was more concerned with getting home and smoking my rock than getting shot at that point.

The crack automatically goes into your mouth (I know, not very sanitary). One; you can usually tell that its real 'cause it makes your mouth numb and Two; you can swallow it (no thanks). If the cops stop you they are not supposed to be able to search you without probable cause. Sometimes the tricky fake dealers would take a hard piece of wax spray it with chloraceptic or some other numbing agent and sell it as crack. Once you got ripped off enough times you knew what to look out for.

One night I decided to go get some crack a little early. It was not even dark yet. I parked my car, walked up Broadway and scored a fat ass twenty rock. While I was walking back to my car the cops pulled up and started to question me. I was cool, answered all their questions. Then the cop asked me to open my mouth so he could check it. I did and he saw the crack, grabbed me by the throat and yelled at me to spit it out. I was arrested. The two cops brought me down to Pacific Division and gave me my very own jail cell. It was about 8 o'clock on Thursday night and they actually gave me a magazine to read. After reading every word in it I tried to get some sleep.

When morning rolled around I couldn't tell what time it was because there were no windows where I was. I didn't want to ask because I knew it would just make the time take longer till I got out. See, I didn't want to bail out. I wanted to punish myself for being such an idiot drug fiend. I wanted to wait for the next day to see the judge. Maybe that experience would help knock some sense into me. As if the gods were playing a cruel joke, I awoke to a marathon of Andy Griffith reruns on the guards TV. I paid special attention when Barney brought in Otis the town drunk to the little jail cell he occupied every night.

Pacific was just a holding area, not a full on jail facility, so the guards were kind of able to just chill and watch TV (much like in Mayberry). I couldn't help but think that the little cop that arrested me looked like he could grow up to be just like Barney Fife.

After what seemed like the 5th episode in a row I asked the guard when the bus was leaving for the courthouse? He said "It was full and already left. You're here till Monday... no wait... it's a three day weekend, you are here till Tuesday".…. 'PHONE!!! I WANT MY PHONE CALL NOW!!!' I needed to be taught a lesson but not that big a lesson.

I called my mom and she scraped up the money by getting cash out on a credit card. She needed a thousand dollars to pay the bail bondsmen. 1 tenth of the 10 thousand dollar bond that was required. I think I still owe her that money.

When I went to court I got my police report and couldn't believe what I read. The cops lied. They wrote down that from their car, they witnessed me throw something on the ground and walk off. That they then stopped me and held me while they went back and recovered the rock cocaine.

What they had really done was illegal. Stopping me and asking me to open my mouth when I had done nothing wrong was a violation of my 4th amendment rights and constituted an illegal search. They had to have probably cause. The only way they could secure a conviction was if the police report didn't reflect what actually happened. Fucking lying scumbag motherfuckers.

For those that don't know, there has always been a cop culture of illegal shit that was accepted by brass and commonplace throughout the ranks. This obviously wasn't the first time something like this had happened. There were two cops, one large black man, and the little white Barney Fife guy. They had to agree to falsify the report. They had to talk about it and say "So this is how we are going to say it went down." Either that, or one cop just signed off on the report without reading it, which is just as bad.

What I have heard from cops and former cops, is that the rational is that I was obviously breaking the law (which I was) so if they had to break the law too to secure a conviction, it was in the public interest. Some not so kind said that it padded their stats and made them look like more efficient officers.

I obviously couldn't afford a lawyer so I got a public defender. He sounded excited about my case. He said we could probably get me off if we got them on the stand. So he had my case continued. When I showed up again I was greeted by a new public defender. She was a chewer. She looked like a big ole cow chewing cud. She told me in her monotone voice that the other guy was gone for some reason and it was her now.

She looked at my case, listened to what I had told the other guy and she just told me that she was going to plead me guilty and ask for a diverted sentence. Now that is what we could have done if the court sided with the cops. This chick was less of an actual public defender than an expediter of court business. She had no interest in what was right. She just wanted to do the least amount of work possible. I was guilty of possessing rock cocaine. There was no question about it. I would admit that in court if the cops could have at least been questioned about their police report. So if they were to win, they would have to lie again in open court. That to me would have been ok. But to have a public defender that just did nothing was fucked. Justice was not something she was interested in. I can't imagine how many people that lazy pig screwed over.

Which leads me to the next tail of fuckery. The state of California, in a brief moment of sanity had just implemented a program where if you were a first time offender you could plead guilty and have your conviction set aside if you went to a court mandated outpatient drug treatment facility and stayed out of trouble. (Law still on the books today) See, before that, if it was your first drug offense, and it was powder cocaine, you had a chance for probation. If it was your first time drug offense and it was crack…. You were going to jail and you had a felony on your record forever.

The law seems like it is horribly racist. White guy with powder gets 1/100th the penalty a black guy gets with the same drug in rock form. The only problem is black community leaders were the ones that pushed for stiffer penalties for crack because of what it was doing to the inner city communities in the early 1980's. The white lawmakers just took those sentencing guidelines and ran with them.

I chose a drug program called Fresh Start. You had to go to two classes a week for three months and pass random drug tests. You could test dirty one or two times but more than that and they violated you. That mean you had to do an 8 month class that met 5 days a week and you only could test dirty one or two times. If you fucked that up they would recommend that you serve your sentence behind bars. They had a wife beating class in the same offices. Those classes were pretty intense. First offense you were in for 3-5 classes a week for 52 weeks, all because she wouldn't listen (sorry, that's not really funny).

There were some good things about Fresh Start, nothing that they as a rehab had anything to do with. Sitting in a room listening to all these tales of woe made me feel normal. Looking back, this is the first time I remember telling my story with absolutely no emotion whatsoever. It was like when I said it, I was completely checked out of my body. I didn't feel good, I didn't feel bad, I felt absolutely nothing. Like when I was watching tragic shit on the news. One guy told how his dad shot his mom in the face in front of everybody on Christmas. I was like, I hate Christmas too!! Right after Michele died and we are supposed to just jump back into life like nothing happed right? Fuck Christmas!!! I even learned some new drug terms. Some chick was like, "Yeah, my boyfriend beat the shit out of me and threw me out on the street. I forgot I had a dirty 'rig' on me and I got arrested." (Rig- hypodermic needle used for shooting heroine or cocaine…or anything else you want to mainline into your system.) Man! Hanging out with these people is going to be grrrrreat!

You could tell the state gave this place money and they didn't really give a shit who was running the show. We had two large lesbians running our group who were aggressively anti male. It would have been upsetting but it was so over the top that it was fucking funny. Everything negative any guy did was because of their aggressive male tendencies. Every woman had all this shit go wrong because of negative male role models. So every guy did it because he was a piece of shit. Every girl did it because of piece of shit guys. Good job state, good job.

I did learn something from Fresh Start. I learned that I needed to be much more careful scoring my drugs. The guilt about my habit was quickly replaced with the desire to do it again. I had a class on Tuesday so I could smoke rock Friday night and I would have enough time for it to get out of my system in case they tested me. I had already tested positive twice. They were giving me an extra one because I told them point blank, I smoked rock because the anniversary of my sister dying made me feel like I needed to.

For whatever reason they let me slide, but now I needed one more clean test before they could sign off on my court papers....but I was done with the class!! "Sorry we need one more clean test." 'Well can you test me on that extra class you are making me take?' They told me that then the drug test wouldn't be random. FUCK that made me so mad that I would show them. I smoked rock all night long the night before that class. I got in and they told me they were going to test me that day and sign off on my papers if it was clean.... again... FUCK !!!!

There was a kid that I had sort of befriended who had been arrested for having like a pound of weed and mushrooms and he had to stay totally clean. Marijuana lasts for 28 days in the blood where cocaine only lasts 3. How shitty is that? The drug that people are robbing, stealing, and killing over is out of your system right away and the drug that makes you happy and friendly might as well stay in your system forever. He overheard what was going down and caught my eye. He pointed to a trashcan then the bathroom, then his water bottle. FUCK YES!!! Kid peed in the bottle I went into the bathroom, poured it into my specimen container and completed rehab. I owe that hippy big time.

Some of my personally imposed therapy when I started stand up comedy was to write a set about my drug use. In some ways it sums up that period in my life pretty well.

Crackomedy

About 10 years ago I found crack cocaine... It's kind of like finding Jesus but when you talk to god... he talks back... He says "BUY MORE CRACK!" And cracks not one of those drugs you can socially get away with. Think about it.. Drinking, pot, pills. They all have some romantic or cool guy image attached to them. Even Heroine!! Heroine sheik... It's a fucking fashion term. What would crack sheik be? Tweaking half naked fighting an imaginary Oscar the grouch for a spot in his trashcan?

The first couple times you smoke it, it's just a huge rush. But immediately you get hooked and then you are fucked. I've seen grown men with families loose everything and end up on the street, sucking guys off for dope money. That is just wrong... So I refused to ever pay them.

Most crack heads are skinny, dirty, sunken eyes. The only reason my eyes were sunken in was because I gained like 30 pounds and half of it went to my face. I had this big, bloated, Rosie O'Donnell melon head thing going on. Yeah I guess standing motionless staring out the blinds for 5 hours straight doesn't burn a whole lot of calories. Great, fat and addicted to crack.. what a catch. No weight loss but I did manage to loose a couple jobs, my apartment and my self esteem. But its nothing a little rehab Prozac and about 20 years of therapy cant handle.

I was a bad drug addict. Scratch that I was a great drug addict. Phenomenal. In fact if they gave out awards for being a drug addict, I would have had the tallest nicest ones in the pawnshop. Why do people say that?? "He is a bad drug addict. He is a bad alcoholic." If you are talking about it, it seems like he is doing a pretty good job to me. A bad alcoholic would get pulled over drinking and driving, pass the field sobriety test, blow like a .06 and be like "come on dude, you've got to take me in. If I can actually get a DUI my friends will stop telling me what a bad alcoholic I am."

That's what jacked up the whole 'will power' speech for me. "If I only had the will power to stay sober." Bull shit. Will power isn't sitting on your couch twiddling your thumbs, 'not getting high'.. Will power to me was walking through ghost town at 2'oclock in the morning, getting robbed at gun point, then still having the 'will' to go back to the supermarket write another bad check, go back to ghost town, score rock while keeping an eye on the guys that robbed you in the first place, making sure you get something that is real that will get you high and making it back to your apartment so you can smoke. That is will power. Determination. Fortitude. I wonder if I can put that kind of shit on my resume?

Have you heard the term carpet farming before? That is the practice of crawling around on your floor for hours looking for pieces of rock you might have dropped. In the middle of farming my living room floor one night I was hit with a moment of clarity. "What happened to me? Did I snap all at once?? Or did it happen little by little." Then I sat and looked around my half empty apartment and thought to myself, "Do I have a problem??" YES...I have a problem... Lack of corporate sponsorship! Nike or Gillette has got to want a piece of this.

When I wasn't tweaking and made it out of my apartment I would always end up bumping into someone from my childhood who turned out to be super successful with a wife and kids and shit. They would say "So what have you been up to??" 'Apparently everything you haven't been up to.'

Crack is the quickest way to see how low you can get. When I hit bottom…..well it actually wasn't much of a fall. Lets face it when you start out unhappy in a shitty studio in Venice, the gutter isn't much worse. That's like falling off the curb. Or jumping down off a cheerio. I got to the point where I even contemplated suicide; which can be more difficult than you think if you are a crack head. I got all upset, "I can't live like this anymore I'm taking myself out right now.. Where's my gun????"…..… Pawn shop! Next time….. "This shit is for real!" (Blow the pilot light out and stick my head in the oven.) Would have worked but how many crack heads do you know that pay a gas bill? Riffling through the medicine cabinet… "That's it I'm going to swallow this whole bottle of…. Vicodin?!?! Hell yeah I'm going to swallow this whole bottle of Vicodin.. 6 pills and a 12 pack at a time!"

I was so tweaked I went to this out patient rehab. First thing they said to me is I need to be in an inpatient facility with more structure and boundaries….. and they said they would tell me of a good one if I put on some clothes and got out from behind the plants. The place I went was called Phoenix…. rising from the ashes. A lot of fucking celebrities at that place. In LA, fuck maps of the stars homes, they should just have maps of rehab centers. Screw driving around all day just knock that shit out all in one shot!

When I got out of rehab they said I was 10x more likely to relapse on crack if I kept drinking….. Now I'm a gambling man….and apparently not a very good one. But eventually I stopped drinking. And everything changes when you don't drink. You know that awkward few minutes when you first get to a party?? That's what the whole night is like now. Before it was fun... You're having a couple of drinks, things start to get exciting, hot girls start showing up. Hot girls don't show up. You throw back 5 shots when the ugly ones are in the bathroom they come out looking like lingerie models! Back then I would just hope to find some really beautiful girl that's liquored up enough to look at me the way I looked at the pigs I banged when I was drinking.

I knew I was fucked without a little more support so I started going to those 12 step meetings. I went for the sobriety, I stayed for the tragedy. Where else can you go and for 1 dollar you get all the watered down coffee you can drink, see just about every bar slut fresh off the circuit, and not feel out of place laughing at the sickest human antics you could possibly imagine. Who would have thought that the pretty rich lady who pulled up in a brand new Mercedes was going to open houses in Beverly hills for the sole purpose of raiding the medicine cabinets? Took her a half an hour to rattle off (pun intended) all the pills she was addicted to. "Klonopin Xanax Codeine Oxycodone Dilated Percocet Percodan Norco."

Or the dude that was cutting out pieces of his flesh that were getting gangrenous because he was shooting so much dope into his veins that pieces of his body were rotting. He was like, "I was thinking of getting tattoos to cover up my track marks"... Ok.. Now what about the pock marks?? You should be wearing a t shirt that says 'please replace divots' It would have taken 10 gallons of putty to spackle that guy back together.

Its all supposed to be anonymous.... They need anonymity. Which is funny because that word is impossible to say when you are fucked up. It was kinda weird because you would see famous people in there and want to tell your friends. Some people, they were worried, would go blab to the enquirer about famous celebrities being fucked up alcoholics. It's actually more of a story if they aren't! "Christopher Walken doesn't drink, loves his kids and never beat his wife, the unbelievable true story on the next Extra." I'm just kidding, I have no idea; he probably beats the shit out of his wife.

So after kind of settling into my sobriety I bumped into a friend I used to tweak with and he was like "Dude you're sober?? No rock?? No beer?? No bud?? Nothing?? Wow.. that's too bad." He said it like I just died. 'Yeah, I've got a job, an apartment, I can actually talk to girls and I own a 60 inch television. Sucks to be me. How's your grandmas basement working out for you?'

Nowadays I just want to live my life...get married, have a family... settle down, buy a house. Then when I retire, leave my wife and get a rock the size of a soccer ball... and marry a stripper. This time I want the trip down to be worth it. Spend my last days freebasing Viagra and doinking a girl my granddaughters' age. Gotta keep the dream alive.

So apart from the suicide thing, that shit pretty much all went down.

When you smoke rock cocaine, even if you are off it for a bit things are always fucked up. Case in point; I was actually taking care of my shit and hadn't smoked for two weeks. My dog Big Al was still rolling around and just fine being in an apartment because he was old and just liked to sleep. He would sit in between the couch and the coffee table, maybe nuzzling my feet a little before he drifted off to la la land where he was once again a squirrel chasing machine. He was nuzzling my foot a little more than usual, when all of a sudden I saw him walk out of my room and into the kitchen where his water dish was. After a second of sheer terror I looked down and instead of my dog nuzzling me, there was a rat eating my foot.

I'll give you a second to process that image.

Do you have it?? Can you see the series of two tooth scrapes with the little line from the gap in those hooked front rat choppers in my callouses? I have high arches and pretty constant beach feet. The only reason I knew I had stepped on a broken tack once was because of the clicking sound it made when I walked. So no I didn't feel it when that rodent began eating the dead skin on my foott.

Around this time the director of the day camps I had worked at just turned down a job as PE coach at Palisades Elementary and told them that I would be perfect for the job. Are you kidding me?? A job, in the Palisades?? Playing kickball?? There has to be a catch.. How much an hour... 20 bucks. WOOOHOOOOOOOOOO!!!!

That was a great reason to get shit a little more under control. I kept most of my drug use away from the kids, only doing it on Friday and Saturday night. That would have been too fucked up. I mean these kids were just pure balls of light. Untainted by all the bullshit that we go through everyday. I had a couple weekday slips, but one of the bussed in kids sat next to me on a bench and said "you smell like my uncle." Well your uncles a drunk kid. Couldn't handle that.

.

Chapter 16

Coach Mike, My Bank, A Suicide Success Story

     I knew the shape I was in wasn't very good but I was doing my best to make it work. The school was practically next door to the building that Teak was murdered in. A longtime friend named Jeff Cox worked at the bank in that same building. Jeff was one of those Palisades Park rats growing up that was down to play hoops every chance he could. He had gotten a job there so he was able to play with us more often than not. He never had a bad word to say about anybody unless he was playfully talking shit about your ball handling skills…and not in a way like you see in normal pickup basketball games either. Most times you play basketball there are two or three jock dicks that run their mouths while crying 'foul' the whole game and need a good ass whipping. You would still want to kill Jeff but it was because you missed your shot because he made you start laughing when you threw it up.

He was a manager at the bank and had his own desk. This was before all banks became run like a McDonalds. Gone are the days of the bank manager and actually caring about people. Now they just care about how much money they can suck out of you.

I had an hour or so to kill before I had to get back to the school for the kids lunch period every weekday. Jeff became my confidant. I didn't really have any friends I hung out with so I had no one to talk to. I would walk into the bank sit down at his desk and we would just talk for an hour. I would eat my lunch while watching the kids eat theirs so I had pretty much the full hour just to hang out with him and chill.

I told him everything that was going on in my life. Which was basically that I was a weekend crack addict and totally fucked in the head. I would tell him how I knew my sister would be fucking pissed if she knew I was using any part of her memory as a reason to fuck myself up.

He would talk to me about his life and about how much he loved and was excited about his little baby girl. He had a way of making me feel like there was a light at the end of the tunnel. Jeff did something that was very important to me at that time. He dismissed the most dominating thing in my life. Whenever I talked about doing drugs he would quickly dismiss it by saying, "yeah you know you're being an idiot" and then talk to ME. Not to the drug addict, not to the guy who felt like his life was in ruins, he would talk to the guy he knew, Michael. It might sound strange but it was a profound thing for me. He knew

253

that guy was still in there even though I didn't really feel like he was. He could see him. He was talking to him!

We would constantly tell each other stories to make each other laugh. He told me a story about going gambling in Tijuana. (Even he couldn't say that without laughing). There is no way that a story that starts out…. "So I won a bunch of money in Tijuana gambling," is going to end well. He was followed and mugged at gunpoint before he made it back across the border. I was laughing so hard at him I couldn't get 'what the fuck were you thinking' out of my mouth.

I went in the next week after he told me that story and Jeff wasn't at his desk. I walked up to the line and asked some new guy where Jeff was. He looked at me and said "He's not here, he's dead." (with a pretty familiar dead pan now that I think about it) I was totally horrified. The spot Teaks body was found was less than 20 feet away from where I was standing.

I wanted to yank this motherfucker over the counter and beat the shit out of him while telling him I wasn't a customer I was his fucking friend. But he didn't know what he was doing. Also I was in a bank and that security footage at my trial for bank robbery would probably look pretty bad.

I went back later in the day and talked to a woman who was very nice that worked there. She told me he had died while out with another guy from the bank that I had also played ball with at the park a few times. They had been out partying at a couple bars and were going to get something to eat. Jeff wanted to go to one place and his friend wanted to go to another. Jeff opened the car door while it was still moving and the seat belt hooked his arm and he fell under the suburban they were driving. His body got pulled through the wheel well.

After the familiar high from this tragic event, I was hurt pretty bad. I also didn't know it at the time, but his easy dismissal of this huge negative thing (drugs) that was dominating my life was to be very important to me later in my life.

That summer I found out some stock broker guys I knew growing up (Josh and his friends) were smoking cocaine after there long days at the office (There isn't a lot of difference between crack and cooking powdered cocaine on a spoon with baking soda except for the fact that it felt a little classier).

I would meet up at my friends house, they would get an 8 ball and we would take turns cooking it up on a spoon and smoking it. If we ever ran out one of the guys renting a room in the house was selling it so that wasn't really a problem.

My old high school soccer and Catalina buddy David Strickland started showing up to smoke rock as well. He had been pursuing acting and was getting some pretty big breaks. He had a significant role in a major Hollywood movie that had just come out and was also on a primetime sitcom.

Meeting up with Strickland again when we were older, I found out that he did something I did not know how to do. He would be sober for long periods of time. He would be going about his life as an actor like a normal person for sometimes 3 or 4 months at a time. Then he would get the urge to drink again and smoke crack. When we got together we talked about it and he told me he went to Alcoholics Anonymous meetings to help him get by. He said that it wasn't just for alcoholics and it helped him focus on something besides getting fucked up. I didn't want to be a drug addict. I had been doing this for 3 years and I was tired of it. He eventually brought me to my first AA meeting. I felt like a fucking alien in there. I didn't want to go back.

About 3 months after that first AA meeting, he came over to my apartment and we began smoking crack. A girl I had been dating didn't believe I was a crack head so I invited her to come over and bare witness. It was a pretty weird night. We ended up driving to ghost town in Venice about 3 or 4 times. We were well into the morning on the next day (usually the time I gave up) and he said he wanted to go get some really good shit at Macarthur Park then get a hotel room. My girl had come this far so she figured she would ride it out with us. We packed up and headed for the bank in Strickland's brand new Porsche.

In true Strickland form, even after being up all night smoking rock he was still on. We pulled up to his bank to get money and there was a middle-aged man wearing some super short shorts that would have been embarrassing even in the 70's. I was still tweaking pretty good but that kind of thing was hard not to notice. Strickland actually hung his head out the window and said "Hey man, I really like your shorts, where can I get some like that?" He was such a good actor the guy actually told him where he could purchase said shorts. Strickland turned to us all tweaked out and started laughing. Unbelievable.

We get to Macarthur Park and Strickland jumps out of the car. I was smashed into the back area because the car was a two seater and I was a gentleman so I offered the front seat to my girl. I offered the front seat of my friends Porsche on our way to the crack party to my girl... Jesus.

So she was giving me the play by play from that coveted spot in the front seat. "Ok he's walking over to some guys... looks like he got something. Ok he's coming back.. Now the cops just pulled up.. Now they are putting him in handcuffs.. aaaaaaaaaand he's gone." I thought she was kidding. She finally got me to look her in the eye (best to avoid eye contact when you are tweaking) and she said "Michael! He's gone!!" So we were stuck in Macarthur Park, next to downtown LA in another brand new Porsche, this one didn't even have the tags on it yet. Thank god he left the keys in the ignition.

She said "You have to get us out of here!" I said 'You are probably right. I've been up all night drinking and smoking crack, give me the keys I'll drive.' I broke it down for her like this.... If a pretty blond haired, blue eyed girl is grinding the gears and stalling out in an 80 thousand dollar car, the cops will give you a smile and a slight shake of the head.... 'Women drivers.' If a crack head with a goatee and a Pendleton flannel on is doing the same thing his ass will get shot and then they will see if the car was stolen.

So my girl drove us home and our little adventure was over. The next day I drove his car back to his apartment and he wasn't there. I just left the keys under the mat. I tried over the next few weeks to get a hold of him but I always seemed to miss him.

A few weeks later I was watching the news and saw a report on how a promising young actor was found hanging from a bed sheet in a Las Vegas hotel room. It was Strickland. He had a court date from that arrest on a Monday. On the Friday before, he went to party in Vegas with some people. He never made his court date.

I knew he was a pretty well functioning bi-polar guy. I also knew he suffered from some pretty bad depression and being inside his own head really got to him sometimes. He would go through black depression even though his life and career seemed so bright. So I don't know how much his impending court date from the day we were smoking was weighing on him or how much it was just the whole picture of his life. But what I do know is he took himself out with true Strickland style.

This summary is taken from a local tabloid but by all accounts was pretty much accurate: He had gotten a six-pack and a hotel room. After finishing up the beer he lined up the empty bottles on the table, folded the 7-11 bag facing the door then threw a bed sheet around one of the rafters and hanged himself. The placement of the bag meant that the cleaning lady would open the door and see him hanging there with a bag underneath him that says "have a nice day." True Strickland form. Fucking hilarious till the end. I love you Dave.

Chapter 17

Sobriety, Julie, & 9-11

At this point in my life I ready to do something about my drug habit. I no longer wanted to use Michele's death as an excuse to fuck up my life.

The Friday before I heard about Strickland's suicide, I actually went to an outpatient rehab that was really called Phoenix. A friend of mine told me they had a study going on where they took addicts and used them for research and gave them free rehabilitation services. I went down to the office and listened to the speech the guy gave about their goals and what I could expect and I was like "Great lets go!" The next thing the guy did was hand me a piece of paper and asked me to make a sober schedule for the weekend. I looked at the paper for a few minutes and shot it back across the desk. "Yeah this isn't for me."

That following Monday I found out about Strickland. On Tuesday I was back in the Phoenix offices ready to rise out of the ashes. Something one of Michele's friends Jim said to me a long time ago was ringing in my head. He knew I was smoking crack. He asked why and I told him because I couldn't handle all the shit that went down, like Michele dying. His response?... "So?" Two little letters, so fucking profound. People felt bad for me and couldn't say something like that when I went on about how bad I had it. Or if they did I didn't listen, or I tried to beat the shit out of them. Jim said it at the right time. I was truly able to hear it. After all, deep down I knew there were many people much worse off than me. Shit a hundred and fifty years ago the amount of loss I experienced would have been totally normal. Maybe that was the answer. I needed to be alive in the time of polio, scarlet fever, or the plague.

With the word "So" ringing in my ears and Strickland's suicide not even 48 hours old, I was ready to give up doing drugs. I showed up again that Tuesday at Phoenix and the same guy behind the desk said to me, "Yeah the study is over so you are fucked." Or something to that effect. That's what I heard anyway. "There are groups on going right now, you can pay, or if you have insurance it might be covered..."

I had no fucking insurance or money... and I couldn't do this shit alone. I started to become completely unglued right in front of the counselors eyes. 'I'm ready to quit! You have to help me! What am I going to do now???' He told me to hang on for a minute and he walked out of the room. He came back in with the head counselor. He took me back to his office, asked me a couple questions and I answered them through tears. I told him he had to help me. He took his sweet time before he told me that there was a very small group that just started that was short on members that needed more bodies to have the full 'group' experience. There is only one thing that he said he needed from me. He needed me to be completely silent about not paying for this outpatient treatment. Fuck yes!!! Thank you Phoenix!!!!

Phoenix was totally different from Fresh Start, they had there shit together, they were at the forefront of their field. I wasn't in an experimental treatment group like I was trying to get into days before. I was in the tried and true outpatient rehab that had made them famous. What was the experimental treatment anyway? "Ok you can keep using your drug of choice, but every time you use, you need to shock your balls with this car battery." Maybe they water boarded you with booze if you were an alcoholic. Here smoke this room full of joints to cure your weed habit. The only thing that cured me of my weed smoking was a nice crack habit.

I was going to this outpatient program 3 days a week and going to AA meetings everyday. I was done smoking crack and being a piece of shit because of the poor me syndrome. That was my thought process. I thought that if I loved Michele I needed to do something besides wallow. I needed to find a place where I was comfortable with myself.

I didn't fuck around. I made a decision to quit doing drugs and I did it. No falling off the wagon or drinking occasionally I quit everything the day I went in to phoenix that second time.

Josh called me up to smoke rock the day after he told me that Strickland had called him and left him a message right before he killed himself. He told me that if I ever felt that bad to call him. I told him I did feel that bad and that I wasn't going to do drugs anymore. He told me I had to let him come use at my apartment because he couldn't do it at his house because his girlfriend was there. I told him there was no way. So he convinced me that he wouldn't, that he just wanted to bang a hooker at my place. It seemed like the only way to get him to leave me alone so

I told him no drugs in my house. He came over and immediately started smoking rock. I asked him what the fuck he was doing and what about the shit he told me…. about how if I needed him he would be there. After I threw him out I made sure he would never be back. I called his girlfriend and told her I wanted to get clean and he was doing drugs and bringing hookers to my place and that not all of them were women. Haven't heard from him since.

When I started going to AA everyday it was amazing. More than half of the meetings was sharing, sharing the most fucked up stories you could imagine. Sometimes it was a one up fest. "My mother beat me with a wooden spoon on my birthday." 'I sold my baby for crack' "My dad blew his brains out at the table on thanksgiving and half of his head landed in my lap and the other half landed on the turkey. I have nightmares about turkey sandwiches all the time." We have a winner!!!

I went from not ever wanting to go to a meeting again to totally addicted to the tragic stories in Alcoholics Anonymous. Just like in fight club, the twelve step meetings helped him sleep (or so he thought). The twelve step classes helped me live my life. The 12 step classes made me feel normal, they made me feel comfortable.

Not to scare the shit out of anyone but my favorite meeting was in the Phoenix offices when they were closed on the weekend. It was all junkie and alchy doctors, a couple of famous musicians, a Goth ex-cop and me. Some of these guys were nuts. One doctor set up a hospice for cancer and AIDS patients at an apartment building he owned.

The state came to check on the place and they busted him with one question… "Where are all the patients?" He was having boxes of morphine and other opiates sent to his 'hospice' and using it all himself. There was Dr. Quack.. That was literally his name, who ran from helicopters that he thought were chasing him and crashed into a city bus, also the nurse who passed out on the job with a needle sticking out of her arm just to name a few.

The ex-cop was one of my favorites. He had just become a lawyer and was about 40 years old. He and his wife dressed as if they were cast in a Hollywood movie about Goths by someone who didn't really know what Goths looked like. All black, dog collar, silver jewelry, the works. They had all the right pieces there but they just didn't look believable. He would always start his stories with something like... "What I'm about to tell you will shock and amaze you..." Then he would launch into some totally benign story about his mother chasing him around with a broom when he was a kid. I kept waiting for him to finish with a story where he was a dirty cop on the take from the mob, killing with impunity.... beating off in front of young girls he pulled over.... Total rouge cop nightmare... What a fucking let down that guy was.

I had my share of stories too. Not just the death ones, I had accumulated one or two drug related ones as well. I met this pregnant lady a few months before I quit drugs. I told her I was smoking rock and she said that she used to as well. I saw her again after she had given birth and she asked me if I wanted to smoke. I went over to her apartment and we began to smoke crack in front of her newborn baby girl. After each hit she started twitching and farting and queefing and making the most fucked up noises you have ever heard. Nice job Michael.. Its nice to see you rose to your full potential. I wonder how that kid is doing right now. Probably about 15 or 16 years old. Hopefully that chick sold the little fucker so she at least had a small shot at a life... No, I can't say that....'cause she's most likely dead (too far??)

I tried going to a Narcotics Anonymous meeting one time at the suggestion of my group leader at Phoenix. I was sitting at a table with a bunch of tattooed convicts and criminal junkies on the south side of Santa Monica. I made the mistake of calling their book the same thing as the AA book. Everybody groaned and made noise and someone called out the right name of the book. I got up, flipped the table I was sitting at over told everyone to 'fuck off' and walked out of the room. I guess getting the book name wrong was grounds for making a newcomer feel like a piece of shit in NA. Fuck those guys. The leader of the meeting was some motorcycle gang member who came after me and tried to make it right but I never went to another one again. Besides, Strickland was right, most of the alchy's in AA are junkies anyway.

I couldn't have been more at home than I was at Phoenix. More tragedy than you could shake a stick at. Stop at the 7-11 next door, say hi to my favorite bum stink wrinkles, get a cup of coffee and on to my meeting. Stink wrinkles had more wrinkles than anyone I had ever seen in my whole life... and he stank. He has been dead for some time now but no matter what they do there is still a grease mark on the cement where he sat in front of that place for what must have been at least 20 years.

The other perfectly tragic part of that space was the fact that there was an abortion clinic in the back of the building. That address was one stop shopping for the unwanted and unloved. Not to get too political but I am all for a woman's right to choose. I mean who am I to tell some chick what she can and can't do with her own body? I'm not sure what was more depressing, seeing the group of junkies smoking a million cigarettes drinking coffee hoping to hang in there for another day.... or dudes helping their girlfriends on the slow, doped up, post scraping walk down to the car.

I was still working at the elementary school which probably was the only thing keeping me grounded. My life was half the black hole and constant tragedy fix of

Alcoholics Anonymous and half 400 little balls of light running around an elementary school playground.

Julie

I had been sober for about a year and a half when I met this girl that worked at the elementary school named Julie. She was about 5' 11" blond hair blue eyes and gorgeous. I had dated some pretty hot girls in my day but his one I had to work at more than just a little. We were very different. She was a very straight laced, by the rules kind of gal. I obviously was not.

Things started in a pretty weird way for us. When I finally broke her down and she went out with me, we fell hard for each other quick. We spent just about every hour of every day with each other for 11 days, then she went to Mississippi for the summer. It was the year 2000. I got an email address and a cheap computer from this guy at work and began a steamy email romance for the next 3 months. We planned on living together when she came back.

The only problem was we had filled in all the blanks that we had, just corresponding through email, by ourselves. Not that they were not right in a bad way they were just...... different. It was really sad because it threw off the entire relationship. A shaky groundwork that might have become a strong one had it been able to grow naturally was built and always made us feel a little off.

I loved Julie.... Although I didn't tell her so until after we had been apart for some time. We had normal ups and downs like any couple. One of the ups we had was on my 30th birthday and I took her to her first strip club. It was my birthday present. I told her I just wanted to see her get a lap dance from a girl. She had told me before she was curious about it so we went to a club just across the highway from where I lived.

I was looking at all these chicks with giant titties figuring out which one would be best for her and she said "That one!" She picked a petite small breasted girl that didn't even look like a stripper. Ah ha! I see said the blind man.. as he picked up his hammer and saw.... I told the stripper that my girlfriend wanted her first lap dance. She walked up to Julie and said, "Hi my names Candy what's yours?" 'Julie.' She was super cute and grabbed her hand and squealed with delight. "I would love to be your first!!" she said. I started walking back with her and she said I couldn't come back unless I got a dance as well. I said ok, but she had to focus on Julie.

"No problem!" She walked us back to the champagne room. I could not have been more turned on. Watching Julie tense, then relaxed, then ready to drool as Candy started grinding into her and ran her lips along the base of her neck. Julie's eyes were wider than I had ever seen and she looked like she was going to eat Candy. Just then she got up and got on top of me. I could see why. Candy smelled just like cotton candy and she knew how to move. I got her to go back to Julie as quick as I could because that was the turn on for me.

When the lap dance was over we made our way outside and I told Julie that was the hottest thing I had ever seen in my life. There was a pause where neither of us said anything for a minute. She looked at me and said "Do we have enough money for another lap dance??" Now I squealed with delight. We almost had to throw down change to get another dance from Candy. We tried to apologize but she was just excited to see Julie so turned on. I'm sure she was also happy to have the business. She was extremely cute but I think most guys go in to see big boobs at strip clubs and she probably missed out on a lot of dances because of her smaller than average stripper titties.

We got back to my apartment and had some of the best sex I had ever had in my life. She was so turned on that I had to do very little work the first couple times. After that I took control and was able to keep going thinking about Julie and Candy together. Every time I slowed down I got a huge whiff of Candy off of Julie's body and back at it we went.

We did have a very good physical connection that could not be denied. Sometime after the strip club incident, in passing I had mentioned seeing some girl getting choked on some Internet porn site. She looked at me funny and asked what that was all about. I explained autoerotic asphyxiation and how Michael Hutchins from INXS had strangled himself a little too much when whacking off and it killed him. "It is probably the same thing; it enhances your orgasm but someone else is doing it to you." She didn't say no.

The next time we were having sex and I was on top of her I put my hand gently on her throat. I continued to thrust in and out of her for a couple minutes not realizing that my grip had gotten much tighter. I suddenly realized what I was doing and quickly pulled my hand away. She immediately grabbed my hand and jammed it back onto her throat, squeezing even harder until she climaxed and almost passed out.

Julie is married now with kids. To this day she still says that cotton candy smelling lip smackers make her wet. I have to say I also have to think about grandma in a bathing suit when I smell that shit so that I don't get a boner. I wonder if her husband has ever choked her??? I am going to guess no.

We were driving one night from her place to mine and watched a girl run out in front of a speeding car and get absolutely obliterated right in front of us. It was weird because she looked up at the light and it was red. The light the other way was going from green to yellow and a car was trying to speed up to make it through the intersection.

She just ran out in front of it anyway. Skirt over her head flipping 20 feet into the air, legal documents flying in every direction. She obviously had been working late and wanted to get home.

I pulled over and grabbed the furniture blanket out of my truck. When I got up to her she was foaming at the mouth and panting, kind of like you'd think a dog would sound in the same situation. I pulled down her skirt to give her a little dignity. (If I had been destroyed by a car and my dick popped out, I would hope someone would do me the same solid.) I put the blanket on her to help with the shock as Julie called 911.

I noticed a silver dollar size hole in her head and what looked like her brain leaking out. Instead of feeling bad for this person that probably wasn't going to make it, my first thought was that there was no way I would ever see that furniture blanket again. Then I wondered if I was a bad person if I was always so calm and comfortable every time something horrible like this happened.

The ambulance came, we gave our statements to the police and went on our way. After driving silently for a minute, Julie looked over at me and said "Did you see that girls vagina flying through the air?" (I had been trying not to say anything about it.) I said 'I know it looked like a flying squirrel!' Remember the old axiom kids…. Always wear clean underwear in case you are in an accident. She had decided to go with no underwear at all.

This was the beginning of the creatively shaven era in American history; landing strips, hearts, close quartered…. Maybe a unicorn if you had skills…but this chick decided to go with no maintenance whatsoever. It was shocking to see a woman hit by a car and flipped through the air. It was also shocking to see a bush circa 1977 anywhere in the United States in 2001. Put them together and it's not something you can pretend you didn't see.

9-11

A couple months later I was still at home when Julie was at the elementary school. I went in later on Tuesdays and Thursdays and was still asleep when she called me. It was Tuesday, September 11 2001. She told me to turn on the news. I turned on the TV just in time to see video of flight 175 crashing into the south face of the south tower at about 590 miles per hour. My head started spinning. Drunk? Suicide pilot? Terrorists? Are we at war?? In all the craziness of the next couple of hours I realized that I felt great! Now I knew I had to be a bad person. It became the first time I was actually conscious of the fact that I was a tragedy junkie. I knew I was getting high from the adrenaline dump of seeing it on such a massive scale. The feeling was comforting. I justified it by saying to myself, if other people are going to feel what I feel on a regular basis how could it not make me feel good?

I knew more shit was going to happen but the entire building coming down? Mama mia! It was incredible… and once one building went down you knew the other couldn't survive for long. Conspiracy theories aside, that was a day that I felt like there was a whole city of American people out there that I could relate to. RIP to the people who died and my condolences to those they left behind.

I watched most of the coverage that day. I watched people jumping to their deaths live on the news. I thought back to grade school when someone told me that if you jumped off a building you would die from a heart attack before you hit the ground. Nope, not true. I just watched a man and a woman jump from around the 85th floor holding hands. They held hands all the way to the ground where there bodies became one.

One younger guy being interviewed talked about it raining bodies on the pedestrian mall. He said they were told not to look and just keep walking. He said there was no way he could. The sound the bodies made when they hit the ground was something you couldn't ignore. He turned one time to see a pregnant lady hit the ground and her unborn child go shooting out of her body as it popped on the ground. Most of those interviews and video's I have never seen again…only that day..

All in all the horror of the crashes and nonstop coverage for days on end gave me a break from my pain. Eventually they stopped showing the people taking control of their fate and jumping to their deaths rather than being burned alive. But the images were burned into my brain. When I thought about what I would have done, I would like to think that I would have done the most graceful swan dive ever. Gotten some photographer the Pulitzer while my entry was the inevitable cannonball.

I felt terrible for the people who lost loved ones for sure. I wanted someone to pay for what happened. But I couldn't escape the fact that this horrific event gave me a feeling of being centered and that everything was right in the universe.

Chapter 18

Children Are Our Future, The Death Of Personal Responsibility

       Back at the Elementary school, I knew becoming sober while working with those kids was a godsend. First of all I was in charge of everything fun. So I was only getting positive energy from these little guys. All I did every day was run recess lunch and Physical Education. It was probably one of the most Zen periods of my life. It was like I had 400 little homies that talked, laughed and played with me, pretty much forcing me to truly live in the moment. When you are running around the bases because you just kicked the ball almost into the parking lot and all the kids are looking at you like you are a super hero, you aren't thinking about much else.

My PE classes were serious but they were also easy for me to teach. I had been coaching every sport at the YMCA for years. I knew how to coach everything and even had some yoga training to help with the stretching. If anyone was fucking around in class I would make them run a lap..... problem solved. They got a little extra exercise and the class got some quiet for a minute. Some of the parents would argue with me about such a 'punishment.' I always finessed my way out of that one. I only had them fore about 45 minutes a week. If I spent all my time one on one with the kids that have a hard time listening I wouldn't have time to teach anything.

I would play basketball with the 4th and 5th graders during recess and hang out and talk with a group of younger kids at lunch. These kids were amazing. We had a Down syndrome kid named Timmy that loved to play basketball. The 4th and 5th graders would play all out until he got the ball. They would stop and all pretend to be on his team or on the other team. They would fake play until he shot the ball. On the rebound the game was live again. I had nothing to do with it. They made up the rules without Timmy knowing all by themselves. Timmy ended up needing to have Knee surgery and I almost lost it when he showed up in a wheelchair. This was right when *South Park* had introduced a character in a wheelchair named Timmy. 'TIMMY!' Sorry. Love you Tim Tim.

I actually really enjoyed writing a comedy set on the kids. It was partially inspired by the ringworm I got and the money I had to pay out of pocket to treat it.

Kids

I think the only time growing up that I had no worries was during recess in elementary school. Playing handball… butts up…tetherball… Hey what was the point of that game?? For me it was trying to read the word VOIT written backwards on another kids forehead. But my favorite game was dodge ball. Especially when the yard guy went in and deflated the balls just a little to give 'em that extra POP! Most schools don't let you play dodge ball any more. I guess kids have a hard enough time trying to figure shit out without the several concussions a day. Yard guys out there… "Hey, no headshots.. Billy you're still in…. Billy…….. Oh thank goodness. Hey…. why are you crying?? Those were baby teeth." That was the only game the cross-eyed kid in your class was good at. Nobody ever knew where he was aiming. And what better way to get that little girl with the pigtails and Battlestar Galactica glasses attention then stapling her braces to her cheek with that dodge ball. Other kids diving out of the way of the head gear and rubber bands shooting out of her face. I mean it had to be hard to get out of the way with those leg braces on. "Run Forest run!!" (Jokes a little dated. Be thankful I took out the matrix references)

I actually worked for a few years as that yard guy on the playground at Pacific Palisades Elementary. What a fucked up job that was. I got paid a lot less than the teachers and had no health insurance. What the hell is that?? Would you take a job working with a bunch of outbreak monkeys with no health insurance?? That's what I did. Here's me on the yard… "Hey Miss Plant, why does Jimmy have puss and scabs all over his face?? A fungus he won't stop picking?? Tell you what Jimbo, you can keep that ball." I mean what happens if I get sick. After a while I didn't see children coming out on the yard I saw a bunch of pint sized infections. I'm ok with kids names but I am much better with a child's last known illness. "Pink eye, influenza, how are you girls doing? Hey hepatitis, mono, you boys stop picking on scabies! Why don't you run around on the grass and try to catch chicken pox!" (badump bump)

I was constantly bombarded with disease. This one kid came up to me and said, "I don't want to eat this...." and put a tinny turd in my hand. What the fuck!!! How long was he holding onto that thing?? What did he do, squeeze it out in the middle of class then sit there...... "Should I eat this??" Or was it somebody else's and he just got tired of carrying it around?

Even if they don't give a shit about me, what about the kids? Didn't the parents understand that I needed to be healthy and on that yard every single day? Otherwise little Aric who's parents dressed him up like Peter Pan everyday since he was in kindergarten was going to get beaten out of his tights and stuffed into a trash can....and that nut bag Tommy would finally figure out how to un-childproof those little scissors with the green rubber handles.

I was convinced this kid Tom was tweaked because he was a Jehovah Witness, which was the worst religion for a kid to get sucked into because they don't celebrate any holidays. That's like saying, "Ok kids, lets get ready for the greatest day of the year!!!... except for you. According to your parents you will burn in hell if you make this turkey out of Popsicle sticks and a paper bag." Spent every holiday in the library. I felt so bad for that little fucker walking down there on Valentines Day that I took a valentine out of my pocket scribbled on it and gave it to him.... "Happy Valentines Day... Love Jesus!" This kid was fucked. Silent, loner, devoutly religious parents.... Serial killer!! I didn't want to run into him in like 10 years and be like "Tom!! What are you doing?? .... In my house... That's a nice ice pick. Huh, I see you've carved your name in my dog... Do you mind if I use my phone??

If kids are our greatest resource, the people watching them should have some goddamn benefits. Otherwise you will get people watching your kids like... Me

When they hired me I couldn't keep any other job because I was drinking heavily and in and out of rehab. Who'd they pass up?? A guy who showed up driving a windowless van? I was so fucked up I was 12 stepping the kids one day, then sharing with them my crippling depression the next. "Why are you crying Johnny?? Maybe no one will play with you because you can't admit to yourself that you have a problem." Yeah and catch me on a bad week it would be "What Johnny?!?... the girls are teasing you?? Maaahh! You are better off without them. Look at me! My girlfriend left me... just because I got genital warts from a hooker. Johnny how do you get genital warts inside of your ass? Its not even really apart of your.... Oh wait... now I remember."

I was fuuuucked up. Dope sick on the kindergarten yard..... Funny thing about kids, if you vomit on a small child right after they've eaten lunch 9x out of 10 they'll yak right back atcha. On a good day you can get like 5 or 6 of 'em going. Blah, Blah, Blah. It's like a tinny bulimia support group.

You get what you pay for. No benefits and a non livable wage??? You'll get people who take the job for other reasons. Like .... access to children! This is 400 sweaty little kids and a janitor's closet. It's like a little kiddy smorgasbord.

The guy before me got fired for letting the kids sit in his lap. That's horrible! Would you want your kids pawing around in some strange guys lap? Makes you think twice about those mall Santas. You know they don't really background check those guys. "Beard.....smell like gin... your good." I hope they at least check those Santa pants for holes in the crotch. Can you imagine the cops actually

busting one of those guys? "Freeze Kringle!! Drop the boy.. Ok on your feet.... Whoa sit down sit down. Some one want to get those kids out of here?? Yeah, cuff 'em Lenny... and put a muzzle on Rudolph there will ya."
---End

I took some liberties in that set as well. Most of the drug and kid together stuff obviously (and hooker) didn't happen. But there were things that were horribly creepy that I didn't put in as well. During the height of the catholic priest scandal we had one teacher's aid that was trying to get classroom hours for his teaching credential. He was a little weird. You couldn't quite place it but he just seemed... off. They were thinking about asking him to leave when Halloween came around and he came dressed as a catholic priest. Awesome move my man, just awesome.

Most of the kids were pure raw unjaded energy. There were also some great parents that I will never forget. The negative to that positive was a lot of their parents were idiot motherfucking over entitled scumbags. It was sad when you could see the older kids with asshole parents start to act like little assholes themselves.

When I was a kid and I got into trouble, I would find myself cowering next to my mother in the principal's office with my mom sternly asking me "What did you do?!?!" Now a kid gets in trouble, ends up in the principals office and his parents are screaming at the principal, "What are you not doing for my child!"
Sometime between when I went to elementary school and when I started working at one, personal responsibility died. These same parents were coming out of the politically correct madness that spawned no score keeping in sports and an everybody wins mentality. I was

on a soccer team as a kid that probably lost every game we played. So fucking what!!! It taught me that you can't always win, a great thing for a child to learn. I would go so far as to say it is abusive to keep a child from learning that kind of lesson at a young age.

What happens when that child grows up, works 15 years in a cubicle and loses a promotion because someone's nephew just got hired and is on the fast track to corporate management? Much less likely to go ballistic with AR 15 assault riffle splattering the brains of his coworkers across the office if he learned a lesson or two about losing when he was a kid.

I'll take it a step further and say all of these campaigns against bullying aren't the greatest things either. More than half the reason a kid goes to school is to learn social interaction. There are assholes out there that will pick on you. There are politicians priests and cops that will lie to you. There are thieves and gang members that might try and jack you for your shit or try and just outright take your life. A kid who has had to learn how to avoid the neighborhood bully is going to be much better off than a kid who has been so sheltered that they have no idea they are about to walk into a bad situation. (I might be a little dated on this concept. Cyber bullying is not something I take into account here. When I was young and got bullied, there was an escape. You get away from your tormentor and you were safe. The way kids are so hooked into social media and the Internet now, they might feel like there is no escape.)

A kid who has lost at something, then goes and practices and tries to come back and win will become a better person for it and that is a fact. The kid might keep losing and then find out that they are better at something else and that's great too.

A lot of the parents that were so concerned about bullying or everyone winning at everything were fucking huge bullies themselves! At the PTA meetings, there were parents unwilling to listen to anyone with an opinion other than their own. Talking over each other, forcing minority opinions to be quashed before they could even be heard. Threatening other parents teachers and staff with the fact that they could use the schools charter status against them (Palisades Elementary was a charter school which meant the parents raised funds and paid for programs, like my PE classes.)

I mentioned before, a Hopi elder (Abbot Sekaquaptewa) had come to a class I was taking at Santa Monica City College on Native American studies. One exercise he had us do was organizing a tribal meeting. We picked a topic, chose sides, discussed our points, then prepared for a debate. Right before the debate started he gave us the guidelines of the meeting, which were based on the rules set out for Hopi tribal meetings. You could not look into the eyes of anyone else. You could not speak for 30 seconds after anyone else had spoken. You had to have the talking stick in your hand before you could speak.

It was truly an amazing experience. So often you aren't even listening to what anyone else says because you have your argument all loaded and ready to fire. If you are forced to listen to what someone else says it can change the way your response will be. You could really understand what someone else you are supposed to be arguing against had to say during that silence. Compared to that room full of college students debating the pro's and con's of having a bar on campus, the parents at the PTA meetings at Palisades Elementary Charter school looked and sounded like a bunch of shit flinging monkeys.

When I was in elementary school, even in the Palisades, lunchtime and show and tell was a bologna sandwich and a yo-yo. These kids in 2003 were eating sushi and bringing in Golden Globes. When the Red Hot Chili Peppers released *Californication*, one of the kids brought me a CD signed by the band. His parents were somehow involved with their label. How funny is that shit?

One kid named Arnold's mother had a very condescending way of talking to everyone. Arnold seemed fine, maybe a little too quiet but fine. She was helping out in his classroom when instead of going out to PE, the local wildlife way station gave an assembly. If you don't know, wildlife way stations take possession of illegal live animals, furs, pelts, and bones confiscated by customs officials and use some of it for educational purposes. Towards the end of the assembly, the ranger from the station held up an illegal snow leopard skin complete with head, and started to talk about how tragic it was that this species was endangered and being poached at an alarming rate.

Arnolds mom leaned over to me and asked, "Do you know how to clean this??" I said, 'Excuse me??' "I have this exact same fur at home and don't know how to clean this without ruining it." She wasn't listening to a word of what this guy was saying. My reply was a simple one.. 'Why don't you ask the ranger, I'm sure he could help you out with that one.' The look on his face after she asked him that gem was fucking priceless. The Palisades sure has changed since I was a kid.

I recently saw a news report that called some lady at an elementary school the hero of the week. Saved a kid from choking. Made me remember the Superman baseball I have on my shelf. On the yard a little quick thinking girl named Andrea ran up to me and screamed "Sandra is choking!!!" I ran full speed with her and found Sandra, who was the thinnest 3rd grader you have ever seen in your life, standing motionless shaking and turning blue. I told her as I got behind her that she had to make some noise for me so that I could tell if she was choking or not. Nothing. You use both hands to go up under the sternum to dislodge something from a full grown mans throat. What kind of force do you use for a 30 pound child. As I saw the lawsuit for breaking all of Sandra's ribs flash before my eyes, I bent my thumb out and started to jam it into her gut. On the third time this sour ball that fit perfectly into her throat popped out and broke on the ground.

She immediately got her color back and started crying. I walked her down to the office and left her to get checked out. I went back and told Andrea that she had just saved Sandra's life. The next day Sandra brought me a Superman Baseball that she had signed, "To Coach, You are my hero." It's one of the most valuable things I own.

The last 3 years I was at that school were some of the most fun I had. I made 3 very good friends. Lila Annie and Eddy. Lila was the little sister of Elton one of my first favorite kids at that school. I knew Lila from before she was in kindergarten all the way through 5th grade. She was like one of my little homies...and Eddy was her gay best friend.

Lila was genuinely the nicest, most caring, funniest kid ever. We would sit and talk everyday at lunch and recess. She definitely ran around and played with her friends, but she was more interested in hanging with me and her best friend Eddy. He was much like Robert Arquette (now Alexis) who I went to CES with, a very good argument for being born gay. Eddy was as gay as the day is long from the day I met him, 1st day of kindergarten.

Now Eddy, like Lila, was a very smart, very compassionate little fruit loop (I think that's ok if it's said with love). You couldn't help paying attention to him because he was more feminine than almost all of the girls. Some girls are still tomboys up until they hit Jr. high school, Eddy was all woman. Put that together with a recent sexual harassment lawsuit and you get the automatic suspension of any student who calls another student gay, let alone a fag…and it happened to Eddy. He would walk like he was on the cat walk turn with his hands on his hips and some kid would make a comment on how gay that was.

They would get suspended for calling Eddy gay, as they should. But far more often the word just popped out followed by an immediate apology. Those times Eddy would tell me he might have heard something but he wasn't sure. I would tell him that if anything happened that made him uncomfortable I would handle it immediately.

He knew the power he had…and he did not abuse it. More often than not he would follow it up with nah they said sorry or I didn't really hear them anyway. Fucking great kid. The offender would then be treated to a hypothetical on how lucky they are that Eddy told me he wasn't sure what he heard. That this kid they might or might not have called gay just saved their ass and they had better be thankful….and they always were. Besides, all the kids loved Eddy.

Those last two years there was also Annie, she was a celebrity child. There were a few of them at the school but this one became part of Lila's crew the day she showed up for 4th grade. She was one of those super energetic, spastic kids….always all over the place. She loved Eddy and Lila and they loved hanging out with me. This meant that she had to be over the top with me. She was also one of those super handsy kids that always wanted to hold hands or try to crawl up and sit in your lap. There is nothing worse than a kid that tries that shit (unless you own a windowless van and a clown suit as we have previously discussed).

Those last two years you would frequently find me, Lila and Eddy sitting on top of the lunch benches with my foot extended into Annie's chest keeping her away from me. It became a game for her. If I was walking I would keep my arm extended on her head, keeping her away from me. If we were sitting, it was the foot to the chest.

My favorite Lila story started about a week before Christmas break when she was in 5th grade. 3 weeks of no kids…no work…vacation for all! Everyday that last week, every time I saw her, she said to me, "I'm going to Puerto Rico for Christmas! I'm going to Puerto Rico for Christmas! I'm going to Puerto Rico for Christmas!" Every fucking day every fucking time.. "I'm going to Puerto Rico for Christmas! I'm going to Puerto Rico for Christmas!" "I'm going to Puerto Rico for Christmas!" End of the day that last Friday I said 'Have a good break Lila.' She said, "I'm going to Puerto Rico for Christmas! I'm going to Puerto Rico for Christmas! I'm going to Puerto Rico for Christmas!"

3 weeks later, back at school, she runs right up to me first thing on Monday morning and says.. "I got robbed in Puerto Rico on Christmas!" I burst out laughing hysterically, which kind of sucked because it was pretty traumatizing for her and she started to cry. I tried to explain it to her and after a few minutes I knew she got it. She started to turn away from me so I wouldn't see her smiling through her tears. I told her how much she annoyed me that last week by saying to her, "I'm going to Puerto Rico for Christmas!" like 8 times in a row then finished it up with "I got robbed in Puerto Rico on Christmas!" and she actually laughed out loud.

She recently reached out to me on Facebook and I told her that she was in the book I am writing. The first thing she asked me was if that story was in it so I'm pretty sure I didn't traumatize her too bad.

One other kid that I liked a bunch who was older than Lila and a little younger than her brother Elton was a kid named Dakota. He was way smarter than most of the kids at the school. Or maybe not as much smarter, but he was always paying attention so you couldn't slip anything past him. All teachers talk to each other in ways that kids can't understand to keep sane and release some of the daily frustrations. You could never do that with Dakota around. He always got it... all of it. He was always on it and funny... and you have to be really smart to be funny on the level that he was funny. Another Christmas break story.. Wait, was he Jewish???.. What's the PC term now?? Holiday break?? Winter break?? Whatever. I've now decided that I am not a theist, or an atheist. I am a nonsectarian spiritual wanderer.

Over break, his dad took him to see his brother... the kids' uncle, who was in a nut house. He wasn't on lockdown so they all went out to lunch. They didn't know it but his uncle was having a paranoid episode. He took a steak knife from the restaurant and hid it inside of his sleeve. While they were driving, he stabbed Dakota's dad in the heart.

His dad bled out in probably under a minute. But 5 minutes later he was pulling into a gas station after fighting off his brother, throwing him out of the car and driving off with Dakota to a safe spot, all on adrenaline. He was already dead but his body wouldn't quit until he got his kid to safety.

Back at the school it was a trip to see how these kids handled it. I couldn't help remembering how I handled Michele's death and how people around me acted. These kids were so much younger. Dakota came and sat next to me during that first recess back at school. I told him that I was sorry he had to go through this. The other kids came up at different times and just said that they were sorry about his dad. He never cried or freaked out. If he wasn't handling it too well he would just look down instead of in the eyes of the child that just apologized to him.

What was truly amazing to me was that none of the kids said anything stupid. Not one kid tried to relate to him

on some level that they never could. They just said they
were sorry. They were feeling sad for Dakota losing his
father and instead of overthinking it they just expressed that
emotion the easiest way they could... a simple apology. It
was quite a sight. That reinforced in me the idea that we are
born knowing everything we need to know. Everyday we
are alive we loose a little bit of that knowledge. The older
we get the more sure we are that we have it all figured out.
That's when we come up with one of those gems like the
oh so sincere "I know exactly how you feel".. that I got
when Michele died. We think we know just what to say to
make that person feel better. We don't. But every single
one of those 9 and 10 year old kids did it just right.

Fear....Fear like you have never experienced
before. Scared half to death... then scared some more. I
have had a gun held against my head, stood on the ledge of
a tall building, stood on stage with 500 people who didn't
have any idea who I was and tried to make them laugh. But
the most scared I have ever been in my life was at a Special
Olympics training center. One of the women I worked at
the school with named Miss Sally, volunteered there a few
days a week. She helped coach the power lifters. She had
told another kid with Down syndrome named Bobby that I
might be coming by. Bobby could bench press over 400lbs.
Now those kids are stronger than average people to
begin with....and this kid was a power lifter?? We are
talking super hero strength. And not like Batman, I know
some cool karate moves strength.... but like Superman,
bending steel n shit strength. Over the past few months she
had told all the kids about the coach that she worked with at
her school. This kid was like most people with Down
syndrome, they are balls of love and light when it comes to
the things they love.... and they love hugs. I saw Miss
Sally and she said to Bobby, "There's coach Mike!!!"
Bobby said 'coach Mike??.... COACH MIKE!!!!' And

started running towards me. He picked me up off the ground and started to squeeze. I now know how a boa constrictor kills its prey. As I exhaled, he compressed my chest and I could not breath in. Each time air escaped from my lungs, things grew a little darker. This was going to be the end. All I had been through in my life and I was going to be killed by this giant Down syndrome kid. Killed with love. Just as I began to see the light at the end of the tunnel, I got a huge breath of air and started to come to. Apparently Miss Sally had been beating on Bobby yelling at him to let go and Bobby finally noticed her. Formal introductions were finished as I was still gulping in air and literally seeing stars.

I worked for a total of 9 years at Palisades Elementary. In the years since, I have seen quite a few of those same kids I taught receive an award that my family gives out to honor my sister. We started giving out the Michele Friedlander Misetich Memorial Award for Theater the year she died. I didn't make it to very many of the awards in the first five or 10 years we gave it out. I was way too fucked up and couldn't handle any part of it. Thankfully Jessica, and Michele's friends Josh and Lindsey helped my mom give out the award.

For the last 10 years I have been there handing it out and saying a couple words about it and who Michele was. We wanted to give it to a senior that lived, ate and breathed drama. We also tried to get these kids to tell us a story about themselves that was just totally outrageous to try and get a sense of their personality. We always want someone that in some way embodied Michele's spirit. It's kind of impossible to do based on a couple questions. So all of this would be why I know about good and shitty high school plays. I've seen some ones that I couldn't get out of fast enough, and I've seen some that I never wanted to end.

At this point, I was more open to the possibility of living a life that was not defined by my own personal tragedies. I felt like I was dealing with the death of my sister in a better way and trying to live a life that she would be proud of. I wanted to try to find myself and not live my life like I was a victim of my stepfather. I didn't want to live like I was a victim of Michele's death. So I decided to start a business with my old boy scout, saving him from dying from a heroine overdose on me buddy, Anthony Tittelli. (I did say *trying* to make her proud right??)

Chapter 19

Businessman, AA Kidnapping Of A Hollywood Mogul, Internet Dating; Rape Me, & A Gothic Hoedown

    The comedy career was still going, but I wasn't exactly selling out shows at the Improv. In fact I wasn't even a comic on their roster. I was feeling a little antsy and wanted to start something else. I had a friend (my ex that went on the ill fated crack run with me and Strickland) that was selling t-shirts and custom made furniture on her own online store. At the time my housemate Helen was a super driven semi failed writer. She made a very successful Indi film with the outcast grandson of a robber baron.

This kid was so nuts he was banned from the Scientology Center. He was trying to get Tom Cruise to star in the movie he already made staring himself. He did have a decent independent movie but it pretty much had run its course. It had won a bunch of film festivals but nobody wanted to distribute it. It was a good story of triumph over adversity and it had a good message but he had re-edited this thing so many times he actually began cutting himself into the film to explain what you the viewer were watching. It was totally surreal.

Partially using my ex's business model, I would then get my old buddy, Anthony Titelli, to take a quick break from making BDSM (Bondage Discipline Sado Masochism) porn videos and design an online women's clothing store that would appeal to a woman's sensibilities. Helen used to work in fashion, more on the men's side but she and I could do all the buying and shipping and run the place day to day, and we could have Anthony build the website and upload the photographs.

I remember sitting in his parent's garage.... the same room he slit his throat in (I didn't want to tell his whole suicide story but I figure he wouldn't have been alive to attempt it if it wasn't for me saving his life after he OD'd when we were young....so lets just say it involved him cutting his throat then having to take a shit and slipping in his own blood and the noise waking up his dad.)

While we were talking about the layout of the website, I noticed he had a bunch of thumbnails up on his computer that I couldn't really make out. Then, knowing his June Cleaver-esq mother was involved in the local orchid society, I asked him, "Is that a tomato plant?" He replied rather matter of fact-ly, 'You've never seen a guys ball sack filled up with saline and a flashlight behind it?' So there it was. Something perverted that I couldn't even imagine. Then he proceeded to show me pictures of the mistress he worked for shoving shit the size of my thumb up this guys pee hole. *Fifty Shades of Grey*?? (book by EL James 2011) Try 50 shades of What the fuck?!?!?!

The pornographer lasted about 3 months before we had to pay him to get rid of him. Believe it or not it was because he thought of himself as an artist that couldn't be rushed and got a stick up his ass when we recruited someone to help him to post more than 3 new items a day. I told him in the beginning that if things got weird I would pay him for all the work he did. I did my homework and priced his work out with several reputable sources.

I offered him the highest estimate I was able to obtain and he told me he would settle for 15 thousand dollars more than I had offered. I thought fuck it! We are making money why not give him a little severance package. Once he cashed the check he sent a letter from his lawyer saying we couldn't use any of the shit that we had just paid him for. After freaking out for a few seconds we were told the jumbled pile of shit he made for us was worthless and for 300 bucks our new guy could make us a brand new one that would actually make it cost less to post everything going forward. Awesome.

He didn't even have the balls to look me in the eyes and say "No. I do not think this is fair." I didn't have a father growing up but I still know how to be a man. I never should have brought him back to life. I should have left him dead on the side of the road in Hollywood. Ok maybe that's a little harsh. But with all the stories he told me about him doing similar shit like that to other people, (and taking any of their shit of value) that might have settled his debt.

We did quite well for the first few years. Times were good. People had money and they were spending it on shit that we had. Our basic plan was to buy shit you saw the celebrities wearing in 'Us' and 'People' magazines that was all coming out of LA. We were Ed Hardy's first online account, well before it was bedazzled and on every New Jersey shore reject in the country. We were also given free shirts from a new company around the same time but we thought it was a little bit much so we passed on it. The company was called Affliction.

The first year we did better than I ever thought we would. We had to expand our space almost immediately and went from my apartment, to a loft, to a loft and a 4000 square foot warehouse space in downtown LA.

Downtown LA sucks! We were on the backside next to the greyhound station. You could actually see teenage girls get off a bus, not realizing that their ticket from bum fuck Iowa to the city of Angles would drop them off in hell. They would come with dreams of making it big in Hollywood, then they would get talked into walking off with one of the pimps that hung out there. You could watch their faces melt over the next couple months. First they hook them on drugs, then they get them street walking to keep doing the drugs, then you can see their souls die right in front of you. But I was on the 6th floor of the old toy factory so it was kind of like watching it on television.

We only had one parking spot so sometimes I had to park my truck with a camper shell on it on the street. I figured it might get broken into so I never left anything too valuable in it. What I didn't figure on was that my favorite hobo who pushed around a shopping cart full of lampshades screaming about how he had found the shroud of urine (that's a shroud of Turin joke if anyone's paying attention) would turn up living in the back of my truck.

There is also nothing green downtown either. No trees, no grass, nothing. They have been 'gentrifying' downtown Los Angeles for the last 30 years. I think it might actually work now because of the new breed of cool guy…the hipsters. By definition, hipsters can't care about that kind of thing. If there are no trees, its dirty and smells like piss; its got character and is cool. Not for me, I had to get the fuck out of there.

Then came 2008; the ass fell out of the stock market and our sales dried up. We tried to keep the store open but it was a loosing battle. Every small 'boutique' store like ours was gone within 2 years, but not before we changed the way department stores across the country did their buying. It was just a matter of how quick you bailed and how much money you burned trying in vain to save it.

If there ever was a good side to the addiction to tragedy, for me, I wasn't devastated when the business shriveled up and died. However it was a pretty shitty thing to have happen nonetheless. It was my baby that we built all by ourselves and we had to put 'er down. Bullet in the back of the head…"You get to tend to the rabbits Lenny…." BAM!!!!!!!! (*Of Mice and Men*-Steinbeck, 1937) No more company. I think having it in me to be expecting something devastating to happen made it not really that big of a deal. Plus I had no wife or children relying on me for money.

I was talking with my real dad recently and told him about my bankruptcy from the business going under and he told me how he couldn't believe I had my credit all paid up and good and I blew it like I did. Thank god my mom stepped up and acted like my father should have and she said to me that I had more strength then her brother Brock or her dad. She said her dad would have never had the balls to try and start a company all on his own. It was an important thing to hear. It was like she was telling me that they would have been proud of me. That she was proud of me. If my step dad was ever proud of me like he said he was when we had our talk, he never let me know about it.

291

I have a really good relationship with my real father now. I told him how that had made me feel and he said that I missed the point. He was proud of me. But I didn't need to use my credit. Dammit. He was right.

I am also proud that I am writing down my story. I'm mostly doing it for myself but I was thinking it might be able to help someone who has experienced loss or had similar drug or recovery issues. Or help someone who thought they had a sick mind because they felt addicted to tragedy, feel not so alone.

I was still regularly attending AA meetings and had met up with one of Helen's friends, who happened to be a big time Hollywood agent, manager and producer. A guy named Jim Pollack. Jim and I had some things in common, like an affinity for drugs and he had also lost his sister after she Supermanned off of a horse.

He had a similar story to mine. His big sister was the one who was going to make it big. She pretty much raised him just like my big sister raised me. He was also into the punk rock scene way back in the beginning of things. The only difference was that his sister lived for about another 5 or 6 years more than mine. Long enough that she was able to set out the coat tails that he would get to ride. I also liked him a lot because this guy was pretty fucking nuts.

First of all he was the most politically conservative guy in Hollywood. Besides having a 4 story house in the Hollywood Hills complete with its own elevator, he also drove a gold Hummer that said 'MERICA' on the license plate. I actually dug it. I mean most Hollywood types have a giant home that sucks up more energy than a small community, then they drive around in their hybrids and give everybody shit for the size of the carbon foot print they are leaving. You want to really live that ethos people of Hollywood?? Kill yourself.

Helen, Jim and I spent some time trying to develop a show we came up with called the Carl Lewis show. We came up with the idea after Helen saw Carl Lewis on the studio lot. The idea I had was that it would be a behind the scenes type of show about a show that never would have worked. Let me see if I can explain it better. Carl Lewis is known as a runner and nothing else. If you had him as an actor, to be believable, it pretty much has to be one note. Every show ends up with him running to escape some craziness. Every show. Every time. So that would be the humor. Showing a 'behind the scenes' of writers and producers constantly trying to find new dumb reasons for his character to take off running again.

The only problem with the idea for the show???... He didn't get it. Carl Lewis actually thinks he is an actor now. So he didn't see how that could be funny. "I'm not a runner anymore I'm an actor." 'Yeah but all of America only knows you as a runner.' "Yes but I'm an actor now." 'But nobody knows you as…. Is this guy serious or is he fucking with me??' I don't know if its that he is really that deluded or just a fucking moron, but needless to say, despite writing a whole season by herself in one weekend, Helen's project went nowhere because Carl Lewis is not a runner any more. Carl Lewis is an actor!

Jim, Helen and I found ourselves at an AA meeting with a particularly charismatic speaker named Steven. Steven was the only son of a world famous professional athlete and had an equally intriguing and tragic story. We talked with Steven at length after the meeting and left with each other's numbers and a promise to go for lunch in the next couple of days.

Steven turned out to be a person who turned his ability to score his drug of choice no matter what the odds against him, into an ability to manipulate and get whatever he wanted from you. After Steven found out who Jim was, he basically moved himself into his house. He was Jims 24 hour a day sobriety coach. I didn't like the way all of that went down but I had been sober for 5 years and had zero desire to do drugs, while Jim was hanging onto an ever decreasingly skinny thread and was one bad day away from a bender. So I tried to stay positive and left it alone, until I got a call from Jims ex-wife.

She told me that Steven and a bunch of people from one of their AA groups had kidnapped Jim and taken him to get drugs and hookers and he had been on a bender for the past 3 days. What had apparently happened was that Jim had said something that all people in recovery say.... "I'm sick of this shit! I want to get high.." Steve who had been at Jim's side everyday since we had met him, took the opportunity to use that as an excuse to take him away under the guise of 'getting it all out of his system.' It was a perversion of the idea that if you aren't ready to be sober than you should go out and do your drug of choice until you are ready. Sweet idea! (I hope you are reading the sarcasm)

I started to call Jim and after about two hours and a couple hundred phone calls he finally picked up. He told me that he had been kidnaped and taken to palm springs. He said he thought they were now in Monterey and was at some fat hotel on the beach.. Now I knew Steve well enough to know that the best case scenario was that they were getting a free vacation from Jim. He had a couple of ex-wives and a kid to take care of so Steve blowing a bunch of his money was not something I was going to let happen. I figured out what hotel they were in, I called his ex and jumped in my car for Monterey.

5 ½ hours later, I finally got to the hotel, it was mid afternoon and the concierge told me they were in the presidential sweet. Figures. I knocked on the door and was greeted by Steve and 8 other guys. The main room was gigantic and covered with room service carts and a bunch

of guys staring quietly at each other. I said where the fuck is Jim? A second later I heard him call out from behind a locked door that he was almost done with the blow.

I sat down and waited for him to come out. After a few minutes the guys in the room started to get back to what they were doing. I watched as Steve started doing business in Jims name. Then I watched him call up a charter yacht company and set up boat for the next day. I walked over saw Jim's credit card on the table grabbed it and said "What the fuck are you doing?" He said 'We are flying an investor out to see if he'd be interested in a project and we need a place to talk business.'

After pointing out the fact that a real investor doesn't need to be flown anywhere and no project that he had anything to do with would ever amount to anything, I pocketed the credit card and told him that his little run was over. His response? "Jim okay'd all of this!"

I said "You helped him get a quarter ounce of blow and 8 guys from your AA group fucking kidnapped him! He has been up for 3 days because of you and he wants to go home!" I yelled through the door… "Do you want to go home Jim?" 'I want to go home Mike!' He called back. "He wants to go home!" I told Steven that I was taking Jim home and if he wanted to try and stop me he could but it wouldn't end well for him.

Jim called through the door and said he was out of drugs, thanked me profusely for coming to get him. He told me to pay for the room with his card then have his wife cancel it and they would go home in the evening. He called out to Steve. "You are taking me home tonight right?" Steve agreed. I told him that if I didn't hear from Jim's ex-wife that he was back in LA by 11 pm I would call the cops with her and have him arrested for kidnapping. I left that room full of scumbags and I did as Jim asked, and drove back to LA.

I couldn't baby sit anyone at that point so I pretty much lost contact with Jim. He stayed sober on and off, then he used the connections he had and got himself imbedded in an army unit in Iraq. He abandoned his home, his car, and his family for a video camera and a chance to make a documentary. The raw footage he showed me when he got back was pretty crazy. I haven't seen the documentary since then but over the last few years he has become a pretty big conservative blogger. He thankfully abandoned his first website name, deadjihadi.com for a URL using his own name instead.

Because of who he was about a year later there was interest in his life story (there is talk of making his life into a movie as I write this). His ex-wife gave a freelance writer for Vanity Fair my number. He arranged to meet Helen and me to interview us about those times we had with Jim. Later when the article came out he had attributed all of our quotes to famous Hollywood people. I actually didn't blame him. I mean it's way cooler to hear a story like that from someone like George Clooney than from me.

Up until this time (about 35 years old) I hadn't been in a really serious relationship since Jen 10 years earlier. I spent many years pining over her and she was the gold standard that other girls could not meet. The reality was that she was my first real girlfriend after my high school sweetheart Serena. I felt really strongly for Jen and she left me when I was already in severe pain. It mimicked the separation anxiety I experienced with Michele being taken away enough that it totally devastated me.

The only important people in my life were women. Michele raised me and she was gone, now another important woman was leaving me. At least that's how it played out in my head. In hindsight, yes she was very pretty and very cool, but the truth was we had issues before I started to smoke crack. She was not extra ordinary. She was a girl who I dated when I was young and fucked up. That was it. She was not some incarnate of my sister. She was just one of the plain and average people that died before their time (so to speak).

I really did feel strongly about Julie but we didn't work out. It must have been hard for her because I had gone through all the loss, gotten on drugs, gotten off drugs and was trying to sort out all of my issues through sobriety when we met. I had a sponsor in AA so I was taking direction at the time from my old heroin addicted future business partner friend Anthony. That couldn't have been a tiptoe through the tulips for her. The bumpy start we had when she bailed for 3 months right off the bat didn't help things much either.

Most of my life I have joked that I never got married because my real dad had been married so many times. (Somewhere in the neighborhood of 5 or 6 says he. Tis more than that says I.) It's obviously a lot more complicated than that.

I had been single for a while but it was hard to meet people when I was always hanging around Helen. She was a former model, a huge personality, and pretty intimidating. Most people I met assumed we were a couple and didn't believe me when I said we weren't. I got the feeling that they would think we were swingers and I was trying to bring someone home for the both of us.

Nothing could have been further from the truth, but that always killed any chance I had at a date. It was because of that I decided to give Internet dating a try. Maybe if I could meet somebody, it would add to my attempt to become more of a whole person that my sister would be proud of.

At first, women I wouldn't have thought to be so picky were turning me down. I guess having three inches of forehead on one side of your face and 6 on the other doesn't shake your confidence when 9 million dudes with 10 year old photo shopped pictures of themselves are constantly hitting you up. Even if I did manage to make it out on a date with someone it became obvious to me very quickly that most people write there profile based on who they want to be, not who they actually are.... and while we are on the subject... why take pictures that don't show what you really look like? Do you think the person you are meeting for a date is going to somehow not see you?? It doesn't matter what you look like! You are the perfect person for someone. Own who you are!

     The first girl I actually dated for a little while was a pretty little blonde girl from Huntington Beach. I found out pretty quickly that she had a fetish that was slightly unusual. Right after Michele died, I dated one of her older friends... much older. I was 17 still and she was 26. She had a strange fetish as well (besides banging young boys). She had to burry her nose in my armpit and take deep breaths. Nowadays, I'm kinda into the whole pheromone thing but way more on the down low. Like taking in the way someone smells and becoming more aroused (or totally repulsed as the case may be). This girl smelled my armpits like she was huffing paint. Being that young and having something so extreme was a little unsettling. This girl in Huntington had a fetish that was one better. She couldn't have regular sex... She had to be raped.

     It wasn't like I had to knock her teeth out and hold a knife to her throat, but the only way she could do it was by stiff arming me, pushing me away and yelling "NO!" We would start making out then she would say "No!" She would wait for me to go back in and we would make out some more than she would start hitting me to get me away and again yell "NO!!!" The first time we did it, it was around this time that I backed off and she said, "No its ok, that's how I like it!" I had to push forward, lean into her and get her into a place where she couldn't use her arms against me. I had to hold her arms down, rip off her panties, then force myself inside of her before she would give in. That was a little too weird and wouldn't have lasted for me past the first couple of times... buuuut... she was something of a bitch.

Every conversation we had I couldn't help thinking what an asshole she was. At a restaurant she would berate the wait staff at the smallest thing and then say something fucked up or mildly racist. By the time we got home it seemed like I was doing the world a favor by tossing her around a little. This chick needed her ass kicked. If I could help even the score for a couple people she was abusive towards and get laid at the same time that's a win win right? There was no way it was going to last and after dating for a few weeks, one night she turned that nastiness at me and I never talked to her again.

I gave up on the whole internet dating idea pretty fast, but in my searches for dating sites I got a free membership to a gothic dating site. I checked it every once in a while because chicks with dark hair and pale skin are pretty hot. I actually started writing this girl who looked too young for me but was really cute. Every week or two we would write each other and be a little flirty. After a couple weeks of no contact I wrote her and told her again that we should hook up. She wrote back with a different response than usual.. "How big is your cock?" Ehhh excuse me?? I wrote her back that in the hands of a midget it looked like a can of Pringles. She agreed to meet up.

She worked a job in law enforcement near downtown LA. She wanted to meet me after a shift at like 4 am in a hotel room. We started writing back and forth what we were going to do to each other. In one exchange I wrote how I was going to take her from behind and pull her onto me by her hair. She wrote back that I couldn't pull her hair.

Then she told me that there was something I needed to know about her. When I asked what, she told me that she had Systemic lupus erythematosus (lupus), a disease most people can manage. Then she said she had other complications and that it was killing her and there was nothing she could do about it.

Turned out if I pulled her hair it would come out in clumps. Her immune system had been attacking her kidnies and other organs for years. When most people with the disease just had flares at her age. This shit was killing her, she knew she was going to die. This beautiful 25 year old girl knew she was going to die. So what did she care about a body that had turned on her years before.

When she got to the door of the hotel room she looked beautiful. The only way you could tell she was sick was that she was a little bit jaundiced. I grabbed her, pulled her through the door and we had mad crazy sex on every surface in that hotel room. She was screaming as I was pounding her up against each of the four walls. We must have had sex for hours. I was jabbing myself in the thigh with the corner of the dresser so that the pain would help me hold out as long as possible the first time….. and did something similar the second time… and the third time.. and the fourth time.

By the time we fell asleep we were both drenched in sweat and thouroughly exhausted. Before we left each other that next day we had the one night stand version of love making. It was soft, it was slow, it was sweet. We looked deep into each others eyes and just became the moment. We climaxed at the same time. While still inside of her and a little bit dizzy, I swear I could see her energy trailing away from her body. We kissed for a while, then we got up and got dressed. She thanked me and told me that she knew it sounded crazy but that what we had just experienced was very important to her and that she would never forget it. I told her that she was an amazingly strong person and I wanted to know her. She smiled, touched my cheek and said "good bye." I never saw her again.

Throughout my life, I was never a "player" and actually had a hard time meeting women. Once I was introduced to someone I had no problem. It was the walking up and saying "Hello," to a total stranger that I wasn't very good at. I know some of my lack of confidence came from being beaten down by Dick. I'm not sure where the rest of it came from. I really wasn't expecting to find tragedy so fast when I was trying to find love, or some version of that word that I could make work. Sometimes things you are not expecting to happen just happen. I guess that's a good part of what I am trying to say with all of these words I have written. Shit happens.

Chapter 20

(Insert meaningful last chapter title here..)

By the time I was 36 I was beginning to have a hard time with Alcoholics Anonymous. I will however say that without it, I don't think I would have made it sober that first year. As a matter of fact, I know I wouldn't have. I knew it was a vital tool to keep some people out of the gutter, the morgue, or jail but it was time for me to move on. I wanted to get in touch with who I am….the old me. The kid that Michele helped come out of his shell and be whatever he wanted to be. I liked that kid. That kid was fucking happy. I wasn't seeing the good in AA anymore. All I was seeing was people that were manipulators, schemers, tragedy junkies like myself and the hipsters (2005 pre hipster hipsters. These were the people who thought because they were in AA that they were way cooler than everyone else on the planet.).

What probably tipped the scale for me was the organized AA drug run/kidnapping. It was nice to see people with 20 plus years of sobriety, who would otherwise be dead, being happy with their existence but I myself had to get out. I don't need to constantly focus on not doing drugs or on other people's tragedy as well as my own to feel like a whole person. I no longer wanted to try to relate to all the fucked up things that I never even did. I had also started to become that person that Jeff Cox was talking to on my lunch breaks from Palisades Elementary before he died. According to what they teach you in AA, that kid was dead forever. I was now this new person who was powerless and needed some kind of god or higher power to be anything at all. That no longer felt right. I could tell that I was coming back.

In AA, the person who you were dies the day you walk through that door. That is why you have your biological birthday and then your AA birthday. That is the day you turned your life over to god, (they say a higher power is all that's necessary then use the term god every time you turn around) admitted you were powerless over drugs and alcohol and were ready to accept direction (from other people who may or may not be way more fucked up than you are)

I got sober at the end of March 1999, which you will remember was right after my friend David Strickland hanged himself in a Las Vegas motel room. I stayed totally sober for more than 6 years after that day. Today, (ironically) I am bartending and I do drink occasionally. I have been for about the last 8 years and the desire to do drugs is no longer in my system and I feel as though they are truly a part of my past.

I never really had major problems with alcohol (except for a couple of bumps in the road) and it doesn't act as a triggering mechanism for me anymore. I do find comfort knowing that a program like AA exists in case my life somehow spun out of control again, at the same time I didn't want to be completely focused on this one aspect of my life (drugs) that I have no real desire for anymore anyway.

I'm not going to write much about bartending, but I will say that I am fascinated by the fact that it is one of the only arts that the United States has given to the entire world. That's right, the cocktail was born right here in the good ole US of A. I will say one thing about the new hipster version of the bartender.. the Mixologist (stupid, new word for the actual drink making part of the job). A bartender has to be a great mixologist, a great mixologist doesn't have to be a great bartender. That speaks to the service aspect of the craft. In fact, some places seem like they actually want you to be a slow arrogant dick.

Anyway, working in a bar is a great way to open up your days for things like writing. A pretty crazy twist of fate is that the bar where I have been working is half owned by a guy who's first endeavor out of USC business school was a roving night club called Power Tools. Yep, the same club I went to with my big sister Michele to see the Chili Peppers. Trip.

My life has become much more normal now. I still deal with the loss I have experienced but no longer through the veil of hopelessness that I felt by myself, or powerless that I felt in AA. I try to pay homage to those I have lost and not use them to consume me. After all, we all have to die sometime right?

I am battling with myself on how to end this story. It would be pretty powerful if a truck hit me tomorrow, but I'm not that lucky. I have never really worried about dying myself. In my darker times I have said that I am cursed with life. Dying would be easy, its living that is hard. I guess writing about how sometimes I survived, sometimes I lived, and sometimes I flourished, despite and because of the lack of a father figure and untimely deaths around me is enough.

I also try not to dwell on the 'if onlys.' They can drive you mad. I know far too many people who consume their lives with questions like "If I only did this, then so and so would still be here." You can't do that to yourself. Your loved one would not want you to. Even if you drove a car into a tree, killed your best friend and you came out fine. There is no point in ending your life out of guilt. Use it to do something positive. Start a foundation, talk to kids… Shit even just trying to be a positive person in that loved ones honor is enough. Just don't waste their life and memory and yours on the things that did, or might or might not have happened.

What you have is a miracle to begin with. After all, we are on a rock hurdling 67,000 mph around another rock through outer space. Life is such an amazing thing that it's pretty shitty to fuck it up.

I look back on the life I have lived so far…. Beaten down little boy with no friends that nobody liked. Then with my sisters help, I was a popular kid at that most awkward part of adolescence and by her example a pretty nice kid as well. Then my world collapsed on itself when she and others died and I spent the better part of the next 15 years completely fucked in the head.

My mother showed me that it is never too late to try to get yourself into a better place. She was in her late 50's when she found a great psychologist to talk to and really deal with her issues. She was finally able to step out of the shadow of her abuse, fear, and loss and truly live.

She is an inspiration to me. She just acted in the musical *Oliver* with her church. She didn't have more than a line or two and a bunch of singing numbers with other people but she was amazing. I always knew she could play guitar and was musically talented but seeing her onstage made me think about Michele. It made me think that Michele was probably going to be who my mom could have been had she not been so abused as a child. With that thought I don't know how she survived Michele's death.

Be it Dick or anybody else, I think it is important for you and those around you to own who you are, and who you have been. I have figured out for myself how that is a part of what it means to be a man. I recently made a comment to an older kid who didn't really pick on me too bad but yanked my ear really hard on the bus one day when I was a kid. I saw it again as a badge of honor. One of the older punks is fucking with me… more right of passage shit.

I jokingly said something on Facebook and his response was "I hope you can learn to forgive that young troubled child." What??? Dude, that was you!!! You might have turned into an adult but that was fucking you. Accept who you were, that has made you who you are! You are really going to try and turn that shit back on me and be all serious about it?? Seriously?? Be a fucking man!

Everybody has their own way of coping with things they have done in the past. Dick pretended they never happened. It seems to have worked for him. By all accounts I think he is a happy guy now…. and nice! He just denies all that I lived and that's how he copes. I don't have to do that. The only things I really regret that I have done in my life have been to myself. But if someone were to come up to me tomorrow and tell me that I was mean to them when I was young, I would simply say that I was sorry. I wouldn't try to put any bullshit on them or deny what they feel. Even if I never meant to be a dick, their feelings and how they remember shit is real, period.

Death is a normal part of life. The older you get, the more you come to understand it and its place in the human condition. The challenge comes when you are faced with death at an earlier stage of development. This is compounded if you don't have a guiding force in your life or if it is that guiding force that dies. Life progressively gets harder. You have more and more responsibilities. You have to get out of your parents house, you have to get a job, you have to find direction in the world; all of these things prepare you for life and inevitable death. Death becomes a concept you can accept. Weather or not it has directly affected you, you still can start to understand it.

For most people, by the time they are in their late teens to early 20's, death hits people around them. It slowly becomes something they can accept and understand. Having no cushion like a grandparent or family friend or acquaintance passing can make it extremely difficult for a young person to deal with.

Most things people gave me to read right after Michele died were along the lines of *When Bad Things Happen To Good People* (book by Harold S. Kushnner- Random House, 1978) or "Its all in gods plan" or "That which doesn't kill me only makes me stronger." (Nietzsche) None of those meant shit to me. I just ended up doing my best to find my own way. If you are young and going through something tragic, I think that is the most important thing. However you do it, you just have to find your way. That is much easier to do when you know that you are not alone.

Everybody handles tragic shit differently. Having said that, I still think it is a good thing for anybody who has experienced loss to talk to someone who has experience with these kind of things. It doesn't have to be a shrink. As a matter of fact it is probably better to seek out someone who has experienced tragedy and ask them how they cope. I wish I had done that when I was younger because I might not have felt so alone. Although part of me didn't want to feel any better because that would mean accepting the fact that Michele was gone.

Left to my own devises I had to survive the only way I could. That meant sometimes blinding my true feelings with my own personal tragedies. The robotic way in which I tell people how the most important person in the world to me, my sister Michele was killed in a horrific way. I watch the look of sadness on their face and in that moment, I don't feel bad, I don't feel good…. I feel nothing.

I wish I had a "Stay gold Ponyboy" (*The Outsiders*, book by S.E Hinton Viking press Dell publishing) type of ending. That would make this much easier. I guess I would want more of a *Count of Monte Christo* ending. The Dumas ending not that Hollywood bullshit that they had in the movie where everything gets wrapped up in a nice little bow. I once heard someone say that a happy ending is a story that hasn't finished yet. The Dumas version ends with two words. Spoiler alert!!! "Until the day when God shall deign to reveal the future to man, all human wisdom is summed up in these two words,-- 'Wait and hope.'" (Alexandre Dumas *The Count of Monte Cristo*) That would be cool tattooed across the knuckles WAIT HOPE.

When it comes to dealing with loss for me on a daily basis, I have found it necessary to have a balance between staying busy doing things I enjoy, and making sure I don't forget the people who have gone. Some people find a need to escape the pain by burying themselves in work or drugs or go to some other extreme. If I don't take time to reflect on those I've lost I get upset for no reason. If I'm always reflecting I stay depressed for weeks.

I have also found some comfort in the laws of physics that cannot be denied. I spoke before about the pot of water boiling on the stove evaporating and the energy transference. It is comforting to know that Michele's energy is still here, it just sucks I can't wrap my arms around her.

I hate to end with the old cliché but if you have people in your life you care about, let them know... and let them know why they are important to you. If you don't and something happens to them, you are going to waste parts of your life wishing you had. As for consciously seeing Michele again, some people find comfort in believing that they will on the other side. For someone like me that doesn't really believe that's how it works, all I can do is wait and hope.

Chapter 21

Last One I Swear

I changed all the names of the people in this story except for the ones who have died. Just before finishing this I had to go back and change all the Darren Hodges's to the name Damon Hughes. He died about two weeks ago. I have cried about it and talked to him and told him I miss him. But when I first heard what happened, I closed my eyes, opened them up…and felt nothing

Damon Hughes Memorial

We all met up down at the beach, first jetty, our old stomping grounds. The place most of us learned how to surf. Life long surfer and waterman, drowned in a swimming pool. What the Fuck! It was good to see a lot of the boys all in one place again. Some had wives and kids, some got fat, some got bald, some had successes some had failures, some had been through divorce, and some didn't look any different than they did when we were kids.

We did the traditional Hawaiian funeral. We paddled out into the water with his ashes and leis. Said a few words about him then each one of us grabbed a fistful of Damon and threw him up in the air. The wind was blowing off shore so most of him was blowing right back into my face like in *The Big Lebowski* (Cohen bros. 1998) I had him stuck in my eye for the rest of the day. It was too bad that it took someone dying to get us all back together again. But I guess that's just how it goes.

As you know from this story, Damon was the last one to see DK alive 25 years ago. DK had gotten out of my car then drove to pick up Damon, then was killed. Now there were two people I was supposed to talk to about my last moments with DK. His sister, and his first love who spoke at his funeral, Linda. They were first loves and stayed together for most of junior high and high school.

Standing on the sand before we paddled out I saw a girl I remembered from my past. She was beautiful in a way that I cannot put into words. As I walked up to her to say hello, I realized it was Linda. We had actually carpooled to kindergarten when we were tiny kids. I told her that I would love to tell her what I knew about the night that DK died. Damon could obviously no longer tell her what he remembered about the actual moment of his death so I was all that was left. I asked her if she was going to go back up to Craig's house for the rest of the memorial and told her we could talk about it then.

Time sort of slipped away and we never got to speak. We mostly just told stories about Damon and how balls out he always was. At the service, Tano said that

Donny had told him that while you were standing on a rooftop trying to figure out if you could make it to the pool or would just splat on the concrete, that Damon would just run past you and do a back flip. That was actually me that said that… the day before at lunch. I almost said "Hey, that was me!" But I caught myself right away. It really was ok. Donny was much closer to him over the last few years and probably needed it more than I did.

At one point I wondered out loud which one of us was going to die next. Craig immediately said "Me." It was kinda funny but doesn't seem that far fetched either. He has been partying pretty hard and you can see it on his face. But then there's Donny who has been drinking like a fish for the better part of the last 25 years. He's become like my uncle Mike, having seizures and shit. When he quits drinking for a while he has to go to the hospital so the detox doesn't kill him. I can remember when I was deep in my crack habit thinking that this dude is going to die if he keeps living this way. If I were to make a death pool it would be one of those two for sure. But I can tell you from experience, you never really know.

I got Linda's number before I left and told her we would meet up in the next couple days to talk. We met near the Palisades at some benches over looking the water. Even though I had seen her a couple of days before I still could not believe how unbelievably beautiful she looked. I almost couldn't speak to her. But then I remembered why we were there and I told her about how excited DK was to go to UC Santa Cruz and everything else I remembered about the night he died. Besides the solemn stuff we had a very good time and I asked her if she wanted to get together sometime. She said "Sure, why not."

We made plans for the next Monday, but by the time Thursday came around I realized I couldn't wait to see her. I asked her if she wanted to get together earlier and we ended up meeting down by the beach in Venice that

Saturday. After walking on the boardwalk we went out and sat on the sand and talked for a couple hours.

She reminded me that we were actually in pre-school together as well. She told me stuff about myself that I couldn't remember and had to guess at. She said I was a little monster. She told me I used to spit water at her, throw things at her and generally torment her on a daily basis. "But that's what little boys do to girls they like right???" (Ok maybe I shouldn't be so hard on ole Dick or Mrs. Kammin.) We grew up less than a hundred yards away from each other but were as different as two people could be. She was a good girl. A good Catholic schoolgirl ('s Rule!!!!). I was mommy's little monster (SD).

I walked her back to her car and gave her a hug. Then without even thinking about it we kissed. It just felt so right. There was none of my usual nervousness, should I shouldn't I, does she like me, will she slap me.. There was just nothing but the two of us… making out basically in the middle of Main Street.

That night my tradition of saluting all the people I know that have died hit something of a snag when I got to DK. I immediately started to cry. I asked him if it was ok if I fell in love with his girlfriend. It would have been funny if there was an earthquake or something fell off my bookcase but there was nothing. It was ok though. I know he would approve but I still had to ask.

I have fallen hard for Linda. We have a shared experience. She loves me too and it is all a little overwhelming. I have never been this happy before. Not since the day the whole shit show that has been my life started when her childhood sweetheart DK died. November 7 1987.… Our senior year. Its kind of a trip the way shit works out. The date today is November 7, 2012. 25 years to the day that he died.

If this were a made up story, this love connection that brings me back to the day that my life changed forever would not be believable. I talk shit about Hollywood endings but this one is too corny even for Hollywood. But there it is. I am with DK's first love. We went through some seriously tough times together, but apart. (I might have actually seen her only a handful of times since I saw her speak at DK's funeral) We both experienced loss of friends and family around the same time. Her father past away not long after DK. I obviously lost Michele. We both spoke to DK all the time over the last 25 years.

That connection to Michele and also DK is the hardest thing to explain to someone I am dating, and it is the most important thing to me. Its so easy for people to be somehow jealous or put off that you have this thing that they could never really know or be a part of. The strongest of people would just do their best to be understanding of it. That is something that we share together on many levels so an absolutely huge hurdle we don't have to get over.

To me, being happy is fucking terrifying. It is way more scary than all of the tragic stories I know put together. I know tragedy. I can do that. That's where I feel most comfortable…it's my fucking wheelhouse. But happy??? That just seems crazy.

I keep finding myself crying over Michele if I go out and have too much fun with Linda. I get so excited and happy, then when I am home alone I can snap my fingers and just start crying like a baby. I think its just left over survivor guilt. 25 years later I still find it hard to be happy. But now it somehow doesn't feel so hopeless. (It has already gotten much better in the months since I wrote this ending)

I have no idea what the time I am spending with Linda will become if anything. All I know is that I love her and she loves me.

314

I do know I will still have some tragic shit to look forward too, it's just part of being alive. As for living it everyday, I want to be done with that. I'm pretty sure there are a bunch of dead people that would smack me in the back of the head if they could for wallowing for so long. After 25 years I feel like I am actually ready to really live my life. I think its time for me to see what this happiness stuff is all about.

MICHELE FRIEDLANDER

Palisadian, 20, killed in accident

Car carrying four goes over cliff

Services were held Monday at Pacific Palisades Presbyterian Church for Michele Friedlander, 20, who died tragically last Thursday morning when the car in which she was riding with three friends went over a cliff into the ocean just south of Point Mugu on Pacific Coast Highway.

Friedlander was a sophomore at UC Santa Barbara majoring in Theater Arts. She grew up in Pacific Palisades, attending Marquez Elementary School, Paul Revere Junior High and Palisades High School.

Interested in acting since age 10, she had planned to be an actress.

The car was discovered offshore by fishermen about 8:30 a.m. Thursday with the bodies of Friedlander and 21-year-old Michael Plaskett, a college friend, inside. A two-day ocean search by Ventura County Sheriffs retrieved the body of Miguel Garza, 20. Another passenger presumed to be in the car, Wendy Finkel, 19, was still missing as of press time.

The four were returning to Santa Barbara from a Wednesday night outing in Los Angeles. Plaskett was reportedly driving when the car went out of control on a steep and winding stretch of road.

Friedlander is survived by her mother and stepfather, Sherry and Dick Friedlander, both of Pacific Palisades; father Mickey Misetich, of Huntington Beach; brother Michael, and sister, Brandy.

The family is suggesting that contributions be made to a special fund that has been set up in Michele's memory to benefit Theatre Palisades. Donations should be sent to Theatre Palisades, P.O. Box 881, Pacific Palisades. It should be indicated on the check that the gift is in memory of Michele.

To Michele, Who Died Young

What can we say when all is said,
The prayers done, the tears shed?
'You are not gone, you are not gone.'
You stayed a while, then went ahead
A different land, a timeless land.
In time to come we'll join you there
And breathe with you its different air.
'Yet you're not gone, you are not gone.'
Within our hearts we hold you yet,
Your love, your warmth, your zest for living,
Your special wondrous joy in giving,
Forever we shall feel you near,
Forever we shall hold you dear
Hand in hand. . . .
'You are not gone.'

Sheldon Stark
grandfather of Michele Friedlander

(November 26, 1987) Palisadian, 20, killed in accident, The Palisadian Post pg3

Garmanian arraigned in Teak Dyer killing

By CYNTHIA FRAZIER

Associate Editor

Security officer Rodney Darnell Garmanian, 31, charged with murder, rape, robbery and kidnapping in connection with the death of Brentwood teenager Teak Dyer, entered a plea of innocent Tuesday in West Los Angeles Municipal Court.

Prosecutors will seek the death penalty for Garmanian, a Reseda resident. He is charged with murder with special circumstances, committed while in the act of rape, robbery and kidnapping. The defendant is being held without bail pending the trial. A preliminary hearing in the case was set for July 11 by Judge Rosemary Shumsky.

Defense attorney Victor Sherman, whose request to delay the arraignment proceedings was denied, indicated he may utilize an insanity defense and change the plea at a future date. Deputy District Attorney Harvey Giss agreed not to oppose a future change of plea, after arguing that the proceedings should not be delayed because of the sensitive nature of the case.

Sherman then asked the judge to move his client away from other inmates in the West Los Angeles jail because of harrassment.

The partially clad body of the 18-year-old Dyer was found last Wednesday morning in the second-floor restroom at Palisades Plaza, a commercial building on Sunset Boulevard and La Cruz Drive in the center of the Palisades village. A Palisades High School senior, she was due to graduate last week. A tearful memorial service attended by about 150 friends was held for her Thursday at Stadium-by-the Sea following the commencement exercises.

She had been raped and also shot several times in the upper torso and in the head, according to police reports. Garmanian, an employee of Pacific Palisades-based MacGuard Security Systems, had himself reported finding the body at 6:40 a.m. last Wednesday morning.

Initially questioned as a witness, Garmanian was taken into custody late the same evening at MacGuard offices on Sunset Boulevard after police had conducted a thorough investigation of the murder scene.

Police reports state that a slug found under Dyer's body matches a .38 caliber handgun carried by Garmanian. In addition, Dyer's fingerprints were found on the passenger door of the company patrol car that Garmanian used.

Police also noticed scratches on Garmanian's nose and on one arm. The guard's uniform, the shirt of which was missing a top button, was taken from him during initial questioning.

The report also states that Dyer's left wrist sustained pronounced bruises that could have been caused by handcuffs.

Garmanian, who worked as an armed patrol officer on the night shift from midnight to 7 a.m., was responsible for unlocking the building during the course of his morning rounds, said Kirk McDowell, owner of MacGuard.

"I'm shocked and deeply upset, and our hearts go out to the parents and friends of this young girl," McDowell said. He said the police have asked him not to discuss the case, but stated that Garmanian posessed state and local permits to work as a security guard. "This guy's permit was clear, and his driver's record was clean. We did a background check when he was hired," he said.

Dyer and several of her friends had thrown a large party that night at the Santa Monica Pier carousel. The party was broken up by pier personnel at about 10:30 p.m., after alcoholic beverages were discovered, said Carousel employee Barbara McCoy.

The police report states that Dyer was last seen by her friends at about 12:30 a.m. Nicole Rabin, a classmate of Dyer's who had also hosted the party, told police that after the party broke up she drove with Dyer to a house on the 300 block of Swarthmore Avenue. Rabin said Dyer complained that she was not feeling well and wanted to remain in the car, which was parked on the street, while Rabin visited friends in the house.

(Continued on Page 6)

Excerpt from previous page

319

Community Beset by Tragedies

Palisades High Counts Its Dead and Wonders Why

By JOHN L. MITCHELL, *Times Staff Writer*

Some brought flowers and others scribbled notes saying "We love you" and placed them at the base of the battered coral tree on San Vicente Boulevard in Santa Monica. Billy, a 16-year-old Palisades High School student, brought a T-shirt from a concert of the Lynyrd Skynyrd band.

"It was Cal's favorite group," he said.

Days earlier, Calvin Hoftyzer, Lisa Goldberg, Russell Kantor and Reid Mangels, all 17, had been killed in a fiery crash when their 1985 Dodge Diplomat struck a light pole along the boulevard, veered across its park-like median and hit the coral tree at the intersection of 11th Street.

Three of the teen-age victims were seniors at Palisades High School. Since the accident Oct. 28, hundreds of their schoolmates, relatives and curiosity seekers have made a pilgrimage to the site of the crash.

For many in Pacific Palisades, an affluent community of rambling canyons and ocean-view estates that once was home to President Reagan, it is becoming an all-too-familiar ritual. In the last 16 months, 10 young residents of the community—seven of them students at "Pali High"—have suffered violent deaths, most involving alcohol or drugs.

Alarmed by the series of incidents, about 200 parents held a meeting earlier this year to discuss what was happening to their children. Students at the high school,

Please see TRAGEDY, Page 3

November 8, 1988, Los Angeles Times , Page 1

Los Angeles Times

TRAGEDY: The Toll Mounts in Palisades

Continued from Page 1

in turn, have established a chapter of Alcoholics Anonymous, the only such group anywhere on a high school campus, a spokesman for the organization said.

"People are surprised that this has happened again, but I'm not," said school psychologist Linda Levine. "These children are living in the fast lane."

The number of deaths is unusual not only for a school in an affluent area, but for those in inner-city neighborhoods plagued by gang violence. Officials of several such Los Angeles-area high schools—Locke, Jordan and Compton—said they knew of no more than one death among their students over the same period.

Earlier Losses

The toll in Pacific Palisades, meanwhile, had been mounting well before the San Vicente Boulevard crash:

• Clinton D. Heilemann, a 15-year-old sophomore, was shot to death by a drifter after midnight on July 3, 1987, as he was drinking beer with a group of friends in a church parking lot.

• David deKernion, 17, who lived in the Palisades but attended a private school, was killed Nov. 7, 1987, when his car collided with another on Sunset Boulevard. DeKernion had been drinking, authorities said.

• Twelve days later, Michele Friedlander, 20, a recent graduate of Palisades High, was killed along with three companions when their car plunged over a cliff and into the ocean along the Pacific Coast Highway near Point Mugu. Friedlander was returning to UC Santa Barbara, where she was a sophomore.

• Alvaro Velasquez, 15, who had just transferred to the high school, was killed in a drive-by shooting March 25 in a West Los Angeles park. Police attributed the incident to gang rivalry.

• John Liberti, 19, a former student at Pali High who had been transferred to a "continuation school" for students having problems, was killed about 2 a.m. July 21 when he drove his car on the wrong side of Sunset Boulevard and collided with an oncoming vehicle.

• Jose Williams, 19, a senior, was shot to death by his grandmother in a family dispute in Venice on May 29.

• And, in a highly publicized incident, Teak Dyer, an 18-year-old senior, was found beaten and shot to death in a Pacific Palisades office building June 22, the eve of her graduation. Security guard Rodney Darnell Garmanian has been charged with her murder and rape. According to a toxicology report, Dyer had a .15% alcohol level and traces of cocaine in her system.

Mitchell, John L (November 8, 1988) Palisades High Counts Its Dead and Wonders Why. Los Angeles Times, pg3

Simple

HAPPINESS..

On a sunny day
On any day
I can find happiness.
Today I made a daisy chain
Out of miniature daisies.
Simple happiness.
Flowers induce a smile.
Maybe tomorrow
I'll make another daisy chain
For You!

12-16   Michele

MICHELE WAS AN UNUSUAL GIRL WITH A FLAIR
FOR LIVING LIFE TO ITS FULLEST AND
BRINGING A PARTY WHEREVER SHE WENT.

MICHELE MARIE MISETICH FRIEDLANDER
DECEMBER 6, 1968 — NOVEMBER 19, 1987

322

David Jean de Kernion

February 22, 1970 - November 7, 1987

PALISADES HIGH SCHOOL
Commencement
June 23, 1988

325

Made in the USA
Middletown, DE
11 February 2016